VOCATIONAL TRAINING IN THE NETHERLANDS:
Reform and Innovation

ORGANISATION FOR ECONOMIC CO-OPERATION AND DEVELOPMENT

ORGANISATION FOR ECONOMIC CO-OPERATION AND DEVELOPMENT

Pursuant to Article 1 of the Convention signed in Paris on 14th December 1960, and which came into force on 30th September 1961, the Organisation for Economic Co-operation and Development (OECD) shall promote policies designed:

- to achieve the highest sustainable economic growth and employment and a rising standard of living in Member countries, while maintaining financial stability, and thus to contribute to the development of the world economy;
- to contribute to sound economic expansion in Member as well as non-member countries in the process of economic development; and
- to contribute to the expansion of world trade on a multilateral, non-discriminatory basis in accordance with international obligations.

The original Member countries of the OECD are Austria, Belgium, Canada, Denmark, France, Germany, Greece, Iceland, Ireland, Italy, Luxembourg, the Netherlands, Norway, Portugal, Spain, Sweden, Switzerland, Turkey, the United Kingdom and the United States. The following countries became Members subsequently through accession at the dates indicated hereafter: Japan (28th April 1964), Finland (28th January 1969), Australia (7th June 1971), New Zealand (29th May 1973) and Mexico (18th May 1994). The Commission of the European Communities takes part in the work of the OECD (Article 13 of the OECD Convention).

Publié en français sous le titre :
LA FORMATION PROFESSIONNELLE AUX PAYS-BAS :
réforme et innovation

Foreword

In 1990, the OECD launched a programme on the changing role of vocational and technical education and training (VOTEC). The activity included: country reports examining recent developments in national VOTEC systems and their responsiveness to changing jobs and needs of young people[1]; a cross-national study of educational pathways and participation in VOTEC[2]; a study on the integration of practical and theoretical learning[3]; and a series of international meetings providing lively information exchange and debates culminating in a high-level conference in November 1994: "Vocational and Technical Education and Training for the 21st Century – Opening Pathways and Strengthening Professionalism"[4].

Four policy seminars focused on the following themes of particular interest to OECD countries:

- linkages between various types and levels of general and vocational education and training[5];
- implications of technological innovation for VOTEC;
- assessment, certification and recognition of skills and qualifications in VOTEC[6]; and
- advantages and pitfalls of modern forms of apprenticeship[7].

This volume presents the "country report" on recent developments and current policy objectives in vocational education and training in the Netherlands. The study is based on a conceptual and analytical framework jointly elaborated by the OECD Secretariat and representatives of Member countries.

Prominent themes in this report are: the organisational conditions for shared responsibility and co-operation of government and industry in developing open and effective pathways for education and training; the successful expansion of high-quality vocational-technical education and training at the post-compulsory stage and in higher education; the consolidation of VOTEC institutions and the importance of organised industry involvement at the level of sectors and branches of economic activity.

This study was realised under the responsibility of the Dutch Ministry of Education and Science by a working group including researchers from the following institutes: Institute for Research on Education, Amsterdam University; Institute for Applied Social Sciences; Rotterdam Institute for Social and Policy Research, Erasmus University; Faculty of Applied Education Science, Technical University of Twente. Within the OECD Secretariat Mrs. Marianne Durand-Drouhin was in charge of the VOTEC activity.

This report is published on the responsibility of the Secretary-General of the OECD.

Notes

1. In addition to this book, a study of the German VOTEC system is available.
2. Forthcoming in 1995.
3. Forthcoming in 1995.
4. Conference report forthcoming in 1995.
5. *Vocational Education and Training for Youth: Towards Coherent Policy and Practice*, OECD, Paris, 1994.
6. *Assessment, Certification and Recognition of Skills and Qualifications in VOTEC*, forthcoming in 1995.
7. *Apprenticeship: Which Way Forward?*, OECD, Paris, 1994.

TABLE OF CONTENTS

Part I

THE CHANGING ROLE OF VOCATIONAL
AND TECHNICAL EDUCATION AND TRAINING

Part II

SECTORAL CASE STUDIES

5

Part I

THE CHANGING ROLE OF VOCATIONAL
AND TECHNICAL EDUCATION AND TRAINING

In the Netherlands there has been a growing emphasis recently to bridge the gap between general and vocational education: the vocational element in university programmes is being strengthened and the vocational sector is increasingly seen as delivering programmes and qualifications equal in value to those of the universities.

Part I of this report begins with a general overview of the Dutch system of vocational education and training, its historical context and the policy debates that have influenced its development over the past 20 years. Part II takes a closer look at developments in four areas of economic activity which have affected the needs and demands for knowledge and skills: tourism, the printing industry, installation technology and CNC machining and flexible production automation. As these sectoral case studies reveal, the shifts in vocational education and training run parallel to changes in industry structures. The national and sectoral qualification structure presently being elaborated will re-inforce the integration of school-based and firm-based pathways, thereby permitting a closer match between training provision and the needs of industry.

1. The Current System of Vocational and Technical Education and Training

Outline of the Dutch vocational education system

In the Netherlands, there are four types of vocational education: pre-vocational education (VBO), senior secondary vocational education (MBO), the apprenticeship system and higher vocational education. A brief introduction to these categories of education follows. In a sense, university education also trains people to exercise a profession, but it is not included in the scope of the present study. For an overview of the whole education system, the reader is referred to the Netherlands' report to the OECD, *Richness of the Uncompleted; Challenges facing Dutch Education* (July 1989). Figure 1 schematically represents the situation in 1993.

Figure 1. **The Dutch education system**

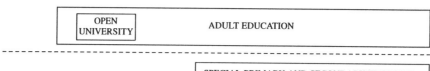

OPEN UNIVERSITY

ADULT EDUCATION

SPECIAL PRIMARY AND SECONDARY EDUCATION

Apprenticeship Training (LLW)
tert.   sec.   prim.
4 years 3 years 2 years

Pre-vocational Education (VBO) 4 years

Basic Education

Senior Secondary Vocational Education (MBO)
4 years 3 years 2 years

Junior General Secondary Education (MAVO) 4 years

Basic Education

Higher Vocational Education (HBO) 4 years

Senior General Secondary Education (HAVO) 5 years

Basic Education

POSTGRADUATE AND CONTINUING HIGHER EDUCATION

University Education (WO) 4 years

Pre-university Education (VWO) 6 years

Basic Education

PRIMARY EDUCATION (AGE 4-12 YEARS)
8 YEARS

→ main internal flow

18 17 16 15 14 13 12

12 11 10 9 8 7 6 5 4

COMPULSORY EDUCATION

PART-TIME

FULL TIME

8

Dutch secondary education is extremely hierarchical in structure. At the end of primary schooling, students are assigned to pre-vocational (VBO), junior general secondary (MAVO), senior general secondary (HAVO) and pre-university (VWO) education streams. Selection is based mainly on students' proven learning abilities in abstract/theoretical subjects. The first-year curriculum, known as the transition class, differs between AVO/VWO and LBO; for most students, assignment to AVO/VWO or LBO occurs immediately on entry into secondary education (a minority spend one or two years in joint AVO/LBO transition classes). The recent introduction of basic education will lead to a more homogeneous curriculum in classes 1 and 2.

Pre-vocational education (VBO) which replaced junior secondary vocational education (LBO) on 1 August 1992, lasts four school years. Years 1 and 2 are transition years, though pre-vocational subjects are introduced as early as the second year. Years 3 and 4 relate directly to a particular occupation. The examination includes six subjects, two to four of which are vocationally oriented. The content of the subjects remains relatively general as students are not intended to enter the labour market without further vocational training. However, a proportion of those successfully completing this sort of programme receive no further education (women 18 per cent, men 11 per cent). A considerable proportion pursue their education within the apprenticeship system, working three to four days a week, or in other forms of part-time education (women 22 per cent, men 44 per cent); for them VBO constitutes a vocational starting qualification. Another group continues in full-time education, mainly in senior secondary vocational education (women 59 per cent, men 45 per cent; 1990 figures).

VBO embraces a number of different types of programmes in the commercial, technical, home economics, agricultural fields and other trades. Within the technical, home economics and agricultural sectors, there is also an individualised stream directed at students with more limited learning abilities. Known as individualised pre-vocational education (IVBO), this includes fewer general subjects and the content of the programmes is more practical. There is more potential for tailoring methods and content to individual students' needs. The vocationally oriented subjects integrate relevant theory and practice. The examination is generally set at a lower level.

Senior secondary vocational education (MBO) comprises 2, 3 and 4-year programmes, preceded by at least 4 years of secondary education. The programmes are divided into four sectors: technical, commercial, agriculture and natural environment, and services and health care. The 3 and 4-year programmes are divided into "long" programmes that train students for jobs in middle management (European Union level IV) and lead to related programmes in higher vocational education, and "intermediate" programmes that train students to work as independent tradesmen (EU level III). Entry qualifications are VBO or MAVO certificates. The two-year programmes (the former "Short MBO", integrated into MBO in August 1991) train students for junior positions and concentrate mainly on practical work (EU level II). Admission is open to students leaving the first stage of secondary education without qualifications. For students as yet unable to make a choice or with inadequate admission qualifications, there are orientation and bridging programmes lasting at most one year.

The introduction of this structure in 1991 has led to a concentration of teaching in 145 schools, most of which cover two or more sectors. Regarding the organisation of teaching, the schools operate to a large extent independently of central government and thus are able, for example, to enter into contracts with private enterprise to provide specific types of training. The attainment targets for the mainstream programmes are set by the Minister on the recommendation of the social partners and representatives from the education field. The examination is organised into units of certification corresponding to concrete subject qualifications.

The *apprenticeship system* comprises on-the-job training combined with part-time programmes in related theory and general education for one or two days a week; it is therefore a dual system. Programmes generally span two years training students to a level which allows them to take junior positions (European Union level II). The qualifications obtained in the apprenticeship system are officially equivalent to those from two-year MBO programmes. In addition, there are follow-up programmes of a more specialised nature (EU level III). programmes in related theory and general education are largely concentrated in regional apprenticeship training institutes. The negotiation of work-study contracts between companies and apprentices is achieved with the help of the "national bodies". These are funded by central government but governed by boards comprised of the social partners and representatives from the education field. They submit curricula and examination syllabuses (attainment targets) for ministerial approval, organise the examinations and award the certificates. There are currently 31 such bodies, each roughly covering a single branch of industry. After August 1993, a concentration into a fewer number of bodies is expected.

In addition to the national bodies there are 14 regional ones, whose main task is to disseminate information on the system, assist in the negotiation of work-study contracts and maintain contact with parents, schools and employment agencies.

Higher vocational education (HBO) comprises three to four-year programmes at a highly specialised and professional level. It includes a large number of different programmes, roughly divisible into the same sectors as in MBO. HBO includes tertiary level theoretical education, combined with practical training and on-the-job experience through work placements. The knowledge level is frequently comparable to that of university programmes, but presentation is oriented towards practical application rather than research. The admission requirement is generally the HAVO or a three- or four-year MBO certificate, but some VWO graduates also enter HBO.

HBO is predominantly concentrated in large institutes of higher vocational education, some of which provide programmes in several different sectors. These institutes operate to a large extent independently of central government. In contrast with the situation in MBO, the attainment targets and units of certification are set not by government but by the colleges themselves. Similarly, central government has little responsibility for examinations. The colleges themselves are responsible for establishing links with trade and industry, and the business community is strongly represented on the governing boards of the institutions.

Public/private education and the Constitution

The Dutch education system is divided into public and private education. Public schools are set up and maintained mainly by the municipal authorities, private schools by independent foundations and associations. Private schools can be divided into denominational and non-denominational. Approximately two-thirds of the Dutch education system falls under the category of private education. In vocational education, the proportion is even greater (85 per cent).

The distinction between public and private education is entrenched in the Constitution and set out in various education statutes. The statutory provisions with regard to organisation and examinations are broadly the same for both public and private schools which are also funded according to the same norms. Within this broad framework, private schools are free to set their own curricula and teaching content, appoint teaching staff and choose their own teaching materials. Central government, however, monitors the quality of education.

The strong position of the private sector in vocational education stems from its historical evolution, and legislation in force prior to 1968 which assumed that establishments for vocational education would be founded by private initiative. Such initiatives were primarily taken by employers, which explains the high proportion of private non-denominational establishments in this type of education.

The development of vocational education prior to 1968

The first "trade school" was opened in Amsterdam in 1861 to provide full-time education for boys from working class backgrounds. By 1880, despite objections to the 3-year training period from industrial circles (where many people wished to retain on-the-job training of tradesmen), the number of such schools had increased to six. By 1921 there were already 83, with a total of around 10 000 students. In addition, there were 52 vocational schools with around 2 000 students.

Vocational education for girls also began at an early date. In 1865 the first Industrial School for Young Women was also set up in Amsterdam. The school's purpose was to broaden the education its students had received at primary school and to teach useful skills like needlework, lace-making, etc. By 1900 there were six such schools with a total of some 1 300 students. It proved impossible, however, for trade schools to survive in all parts of the country. From sheer necessity, therefore, vocational training had to be provided through some form of apprenticeship, through evening classes and in "winter schools". By 1900, a total of around 20 000 students were in some form of occupational education, 70 per cent of them attending evening classes. This period also saw the founding of the first "secondary technical schools", from which the higher technical education system evolved after the Second World War.

Statutory arrangements for vocational education were made in 1921 when the government passed the Occupational Education Act, whose aim was "to train students on the basis and with the continuance of general education for crafts, trades, the shipping industry, domestic work, rural home economics and domestic crafts". The Occupational Education Act made provision not only for full-time education but also for an apprenticeship system, then seen simply as a necessary stop-gap alternative to school-based education. The inclusion of the apprenticeship system in the Act was the first indication that it was now an accepted form of vocational education.

After the Second World War, secondary school attendance increased rapidly and the number of primary school leavers directly entering the work force dwindled. This period also saw the emergence of the earliest forms of senior secondary vocational education. The first of these was "advanced elementary technical education", initially a follow-up to junior technical education but later also provided in separate schools. Numbers in this type of education remained low, however, until the late 1960s. Most young people entered the labour market on leaving junior secondary vocational education, often combining work with training in the apprenticeship system. In commercial and administrative fields in particular, most people began work without any specific vocational training. However, in these very sectors adult education flourished, especially the evening classes given, for example, by commercial establishments.

Factors in the development of vocational education prior to 1968

a) Compulsory education and prohibition of child labour

A 6-year period of compulsory education was introduced in 1900. This was extended to 7 years in 1928, to 8 years in 1950, to 9 years in 1971, to 10 years in 1975 and to 11 years in 1985. The Compulsory Education Act is complemented by the Labour Acts, which with exceptions, prohibit child labour. A comparison of trends in secondary education attendance shows that the successive extensions of the period of compulsory education occurred only once the vast majority of the generation concerned were already attending education establishments full-time. On each occasion, the law simply confirmed a situation which already existed.

b) Changes in the employment structure

Modern capitalist society emerged in the Netherlands around 1870. From that date onwards the country experienced the development of large-scale industries, and the beginnings of an organised labour movement and social legislation. After the turn of the century, the Netherlands witnessed an economic boom accompanied by a substantial increase in the population from 5 500 000 in 1889 to 11 500 000 in 1966 and 15 000 000 in 1990.

The early years of the century saw an extensive process of industrialisation, including an increase in trade, navigation and harbour traffic, and an expansion in banking and agriculture. The workforce changed radically in both composition and size from 2 000 000 in 1899 to 4 000 000 in 1947. Between 1899 and 1947 industry's share of total employment rose from 33 to 37 per cent and the service sector's from 36 to 44 per cent, while that of the agricultural sector declined from 30 to 20 per cent. Between 1947 and 1974 this trend continued. By 1974, agriculture had fallen to 6.6 per cent of total employment while the service sector had risen to 57.9 per cent. The industrial sector rose initially from 37 per cent to peak at 40.9 per cent in 1965, but declined thereafter.

c) Trends in attendance

Education has been a key factor in this social, economic and cultural process of development. In modern capitalist society, the extent of an individual's education is one of the principal criteria for obtaining employment. Increased participation in education therefore plays an important part in promoting social mobility. Since 1900, there has been a steady increase in participation in different forms of full-time education. Between 1900 and 1958, the number of students in trade education increased from 21 000 to over 400 000, over half of them in full-time education. The share of the apprenticeship system expanded during the post-war period relatively sharply from 18 000 in 1950 to 72 000 in 1965. This rapid growth was due to industry reconstruction following the Second World War.

In 1930, 15 per cent of boys leaving primary education went on to trade schools, 20 per cent into advanced elementary education and 10 per cent into secondary or pre-higher education, while 15 per cent of girls went on to trade education, 15 per cent into advanced elementary education and 5 per cent into secondary and pre-higher education (in 1965 the corresponding figures were 45 per cent, 30 per cent and 20 per cent for boys; and 45 per cent, 35 per cent and 15 per cent for girls). In the mid 1960s, 95 per cent of all boys and girls were attending some form of secondary education institution and by around 1970 most young people were attending school until at least the age of 15. Attendance was lower in the older age groups however, a fact which led to specific government measures to promote lengthier participation in education. Between 1930 and 1965 the numbers entering vocationally oriented education increased three-fold. During the 1970s, however, there was a reversal in this trend, and a decline in the social status of junior secondary vocational education. It is noteworthy that the maximum figures of participation in the apprenticeship system coincide with a peak in industrial activity. After 1965, the share of industrial employment declined, as did participation in the apprenticeship system.

d) The apprenticeship system

During the post-war period, the apprenticeship system expanded considerably. The reconstruction of industry required large numbers of people to be trained in a short time. The apprenticeship system thus gradually developed into a form of training to be entered after junior secondary vocational education (which was itself gradually changing, becoming more introductory and general in character). However, trades and small business demand different skills than large-scale industry. Large-scale industry requires greater specialisation than in small enterprises, where all-round development of skilled workers is preferred. Large-scale industry therefore offered more opportunities for further training. During this period, many companies even had their own company training schools.

Deferring specific vocational training to a later age was encouraged by the belief that schools should not only develop the technical skills of students but also provide an all-round general education. This trend was reflected in various commission reports and ministerial memorandums. In 1949 a "Memorandum on the industrialisation of the Netherlands", followed by other policy documents laid the economic foundation for the development of the apprenticeship system into an organised form of vocational training.

The increasingly independent status of the system is also reflected in its structure. On the basis of recommendations made in 1947 and 1948, a nationwide structure of apprenticeship systems was created to serve the different branches of industry, which together with regional bodies were to be responsible for running the apprenticeship system.

Developments after 1968

Since 1951, successive ministers had been exploring ways to achieve greater harmony between the various forms of secondary education. Finally in 1963, the Secondary Education Act was passed with the aim of integrating the provision of education with the exception of primary and university education. This Act came into effect in 1968. The apprenticeship system was covered by a separate Apprenticeship Act of 1966, which also came into force in 1968. This represented a major step in the modernisation of the Dutch education system. Over the years the existing system had come under criticism concerning for example:
- inadequate interfacing between various school types, presenting serious obstacles to both vertical and horizontal transfers;
- the extremely early and therefore frequently mistaken choice of school;
- the very uniform and rigid school system which did not take sufficient account of differences in the pace, aptitude and interest of students.

The basic tenets of the Secondary Education Act are that:
- Every student leaving primary school should have the opportunity to receive both general education and vocational training;
- every vocational training programme should be preceded by a phase of general education;
- the time at which the vocational element comes to predominate should be linked to the students' ability; generally speaking, the greater the students' intellectual capacities, the later it will come;
- the structure of secondary education should guarantee opportunities for both horizontal and vertical transfer.

The Act emphasises that general and vocationally oriented education are to be regarded as complementary parts of a single coherent whole with a common purpose. An important new element in the Act was the concept of the first year of upper secondary education as a transition year, the aim of which was to give the student an insight into his/her talents and capacities, with an eye to a further school career. The transition-year curriculum comprises the same subjects for, on the one hand, MAVO, HAVO and VWO and on the other, the various forms of LBO. One difference between the AVO/VWO transition year and the LBO transition year is the number of foreign languages studied, two in the first case, one in the second.

Another major change was the introduction of combined schools. A combined school is one in which two or more types of secondary school are united under a single board of governors and one principal. These schools are allowed a good deal of freedom in the way they organise their teaching. This makes it possible, for example, to extend the transition period to two or three years. Since the Act came into force, the number of combined AVO/VWO schools and the number of schools combining LBO and AVO has been expanding rapidly.

In addition to schools for full-time education, virtually every sector of secondary education has schools providing evening classes, and daytime schools providing part-time education. The latter direct their programmes at adult students and are now considered part of adult education. The final examinations at these schools are equivalent to those of full-time educational institutions. Like junior and senior secondary vocational education, higher vocational education was originally covered by the Secondary Education Act. Since 1986, however, it has come under separate legislation and from August 1991 senior secondary vocational education is also governed by new statutory arrangements, which are however included within the Secondary Education Act.

Junior secondary vocational education (LBO)

The evolution of junior secondary vocational education since 1968, and its transformation into VBO in 1992, was determined principally by the discussion as to whether it should be general or specifically vocational in character. Broadly speaking, there is a trend towards more general education. The reasons for this relate to students' opportunities for personal development, and to developments in the business world, where versatility and the ability to continue learning throughout life are now seen as increasingly important. This trend has not, however, been without its critics and in the 1970s there were complaints regarding the direct employability of those leaving LBO. According to the current policy, VBO schools are not intended to be the end of the line, but rather are meant to be followed by further vocational training. A major step in this direction was the 1973 decree on junior secondary vocational and general education. This set the length of programmes in all types of LBO at 4 years and introduced a 2-year transition period.

There has also been a trend to reduce the gulf between junior secondary vocational and junior general secondary education which has resulted in particular in the harmonisation of the examination syllabuses for the general examination subjects. In 1989 regulations for the VWO, HAVO, MAVO and LBO examinations were laid down together in a single examination decree.

The percentage of students in LBO has declined steadily over the last 20 years. As selection at the end of primary education is based chiefly on academic performance and there is a strong tendency among parents to send their children into general secondary education, there is an increasing degree of "negative selection" in the intake of junior secondary vocational education. Since the late 1960s, large groups of immigrant workers have come to the Netherlands and their children mainly attend LBO schools. Particularly in the major cities, a large proportion of the students in these schools are now of foreign origin. These trends have contributed to the relative and absolute growth in individualised vocational education.

a) Basic education, pre-vocational education

Since the early 1970s, there has been an ongoing debate about the desirability of integration in the early years of secondary education. Various more or less radical plans for integration have failed to make it onto the statute books. Recently however, a bill has been passed to introduce "basic education" spanning the first three years of secondary schooling. This entails further harmonisation of the curriculum among existing types of schools. Basic education will be designed around the minimum attainment targets every student needs to achieve at school in order to gain a sound basis for further study and for participation in community life. These targets will be set for 14 different subjects (Dutch, English, French

15

or German, mathematics, physics and chemistry, biology, IT studies, technology, history and civics, geography, economics, visual arts, music and physical education). Lessons in these subjects are to take up at least 80 per cent of classroom time. Parallel to the basic education proposals, another bill has converted junior secondary vocational education (LBO) into "pre-vocational education" (VBO). The changes will affect only the senior classes (following basic education) and will mean that the various types of LBO will be replaced by a single LBO with different departments. The compulsory number of hours allocated to vocationally oriented subjects in the senior classes will be slightly increased and the choice of examination subjects better structured. In addition, there will be an introduction to business life through short work placements. The principal aim of this bill is to strengthen the role of VBO as a preparation for further specifically vocational education within senior secondary vocational education (MBO) and the apprenticeship system.

The Basic Education Bill became operational in 1993, while the Pre-vocational Education Bill has been in effect since August 1992.

Senior secondary vocational education (MBO)

The growing segmentation and specialisation in the labour market, the need for good vertical and horizontal communication and the expansion of the service sector have all increased the demand for middle management, leading to a rapid growth in senior secondary vocational education. Also there is increasing demand for further education from those leaving junior secondary vocational and junior general education. When the Secondary Education Act came into force in 1968, MBO comprised seven different types of schools: senior secondary technical, senior secondary nautical, senior secondary home economics, senior secondary agricultural, senior secondary tradespeople's, senior secondary commercial and senior secondary social work education. These categories were replaced in August 1991, by four sectors (technical, commercial, agriculture and natural environment, and services and health care) which can be combined in one school. MBO also used to include programmes for nursery school teachers, but these have now been absorbed into higher vocational education.

a) The short MBO programme

In 1979, the "Short" MBO programme was introduced by decree. It was designed to provide training for young people who cannot find a suitable programme in senior secondary vocational education or in the apprenticeship system. The Short MBO could also provide a safety net for dropouts from the first stage of secondary education and MBO. It consisted of two- and three-year programmes leading to qualifications comparable with those in the apprenticeship system. Part of the programme took the form of work placements. In August 1991, these separate programmes became part of regular MBO, as the lowest two-year level.

b) Senior secondary personal, social services and health care education (MDGO)

A second major structural change since 1968 has been the amalgamation in 1984 of the senior secondary home economics and social work programmes to form senior secondary personal, social services and health care education (MDGO). The change, which followed several years of extensive experimentation, was achieved through a statutory amendment to the Secondary Education Act.

One aim of the amendment was to broaden the educational aims and improve opportunities for training in the sectors of education involved. To achieve this, some 35 narrowly job-oriented programmes were restructured to form ten MDGO departments.

The organisational and examination regulations for this type of education, unlike the older types of MBO, were issued in a single decree. This allowed closer harmonisation of the arrangements for monitoring standards and a better definition of the freedom enjoyed by the schools. The decree included attainment targets (which replaced the previous examination syllabuses), a school work plan and programme of activities. Most of these innovations were transferred to the other kinds of MBO in the "SVM-operation" described below.

c) The SVM operation

The need for a different kind of MBO structure was also making itself felt in the other programmes. In March 1987, the State Secretary for Education and Science published a policy document on sector formation and innovation in senior secondary vocational education (the "SVM operation"). The aim of sector formation is to concentrate within a single institution training programmes of varying length directed at a specific labour market sector or occupational category. The goal of the innovation is to achieve a differentiated and high-quality range of training programmes able to respond flexibly to the needs of consumers of education and labour market demands. This SVM operation resulted in the SVM Act of 23 May 1990, which introduced amendments to the Secondary Education Act with regard to sector formation and innovation in MBO. The new structure came into effect in August 1991 and the Short MBO programme (see above) was then absorbed into mainstream MBO.

One aim of the SVM Act is to increase the autonomy enjoyed by MBO schools. This relates not only to the organisation of teaching within the school but also to financial expenditure and the staff policies of the associations of competent authorities. Regarding the organisation of teaching, the Act simply states that schools should provide education in accordance with a school work plan. The detailed regulations concerning the organisation of education lapsed. In their place, the school work plan constitutes an important means by which central government can assess the soundness of the education provided at the school and so control quality. The Education Inspectorate plays a major part in this: it can assess the school's work plans and enter into discussion with the school where it considers the plan of insufficient quality.

The central government, however, sets the attainment targets for the programmes, mainly on the basis of advice from the business world. The school refines these into teaching objectives, which are then included in the school work plan. At the same time, the Act provides for measures to strengthen management and the board of governors and establishes a central directorate. In addition it creates the possibility for the competent authority (i.e. municipal authority or private school board) to transfer powers and responsibilities to this central directorate.

It was felt that, in order to cope with their new responsibilities and be able to provide a sufficiently broad and differentiated range of education, the schools should meet minimum standards in terms of student numbers. The SVM Act. thus included higher norms to encourage the formation of larger units. The result is a much smaller number of schools (down from 438 to 145) of larger size. These often encompass several different sectors.

A major element of the legislation is the new relationship it establishes with the business world. Their wishes play a decisive role in shaping programmes (both with regard to new programmes and change in or cancellation of, existing programmes). The business world is responsible for establishing job profiles. Training profiles are then jointly established with the education field through bodies responsible for branch consultations between education and industry.

The consultative bodies generally adopt the job profiles and translate them into training profiles, including proposed (draft) attainment targets incorporated to (draft) units of certification. Draft attainment targets and draft units of certification are submitted as recommendations to the Minister who sets the final targets and units.

Under the new arrangements the examination syllabus will be set by the school itself, although the various components of the examination must coincide with the units of certification. In the examination syllabus, the school decides how it intends to measure performance against attainment targets. Central government can, however, designate particular components of the examination to be examined centrally, in which case it sets the examination syllabus.

Day-release programmes (BBO) and the apprenticeship system

Under the apprenticeship system, the student receives on-the-job training in the company for which he/she works, while at the same time attending day-release programmes at a regional apprenticeship training institute or a VBO school.

The structural relationship between on-the-job training and the supporting/additional education is laid down in the Apprenticeship Act (replaced by the vocational education act in August 1993). This outlines the dual structure of the scheme: on the one hand, on-the-job training in a particular occupation, and on the other, general and vocationally oriented education. In the Secondary Education Act the central focus is on the school, while in the Apprenticeship Act the stress is on the apprenticeship agreement between student and employer/trainer. In practice this means that students in the apprenticeship system are at the same time employees. They are covered, therefore, not only by the provisions of the apprenticeship agreement, but also by all the rights and duties in the employment contract. Since the statutory introduction of the youth minimum wage in 1974, this link between apprenticeship and employment contracts has been a controversial subject. The trade unions feel that the link must be preserved, while the employers' organisations consider the minimum wage too high in relation to the productivity level of apprentices.

Day-release education (BBO) was originally closely associated with LBO schools and took the form of follow-up programmes. Gradually, however, a need emerged for separate BBO institutions. A Committee was set up in 1961 and in 1967 issued a report arguing for the development of regional apprenticeship training institutes to provide day-release programmes. Following more detailed recommendations, 30 such institutes were set up for this type of education. A small proportion of such programmes still remained in the hands of LBO schools. BBO is structured into 8 to 10 teaching periods, divided between general and directly vocational subjects. There has been a growing tendency to teach directly vocational subjects in the form of workshops integrating theory and practice. The general subjects focus particularly on promoting students' social development.

Since 1979, the apprenticeship training institutes have been closely involved in the development of the Short MBO, which trains students to a comparable standard through full-time programmes (including work placements). The amalgamation of the Short MBO and the regular MBO through the SVM operation has led a proportion of the apprenticeship training institutes to be merged with MBO institutions, forming combined schools.

Government policy currently promotes further integration of BBO and MBO to achieve greater coherence and to provide the widest possible range of education, in response to the specific needs of students. In this context, the industry-education consultative bodies of the MBO and the national bodies for the apprenticeship system were merged in 1993, in order to create a clear organisation for structuring and controlling the entire hierarchy of qualifications within vocational education.

a) The vocational education act

This Bill passed the Dutch Parliament in May 1992, and came into effect in August 1993. Its aim is to establish coherent arrangements for the structure, quality and funding of the apprenticeship system, the part-time MBO and the special training schemes for the jobless, in harmony with the new legislation on full-time MBO. The main aims of the Bill are to increase the autonomy of institutions, to improve the links between education and the labour market, to increase flexibility and to achieve a more integrated approach to educational development and quality control throughout the secondary vocational education system. This Bill replaces the Apprenticeship Act and parts of the Secondary Education Act.

Higher Vocational Education (HBO)

Although certain forms of HBO in the area of technical and art education date back to the end of the nineteenth century, the great expansion in the number and variety of HBO programmes is a post-war phenomenon. Since 1970, the number of HBO students has increased sharply. While past government policy tended to maintain distinction between HBO and university education, during the 1970s, closer harmonisation, and even integration, of HBO and university education was announced on several occasions; the aim then was to create a broad and more differentiated form of higher education including both more practical and more theoretical, research-oriented programmes. This idea has since been abandoned and the uniqueness of HBO is currently being emphasised.

Prior to 1986 there were some 350 HBO institutions, each with an average of a few hundred students, offering education in only one or two disciplines. These institutions were considered to be too small. In September 1983, a policy document concerning subject

19

specialisation and concentration of disciplines in higher vocational education set out three goals:

  a) the creation of larger institutions through amalgamation;

  b) an increase in the institutions' individual responsibility with regard to financial expenditure, staff policies and teaching arrangements, requiring management strengthening of the institutions;

  c) greater efficiency in the use of resources by having larger groups wherever possible, by concentrating expensive apparatus and other facilities, and by streamlining and, wherever possible, combining programme units.

This operation led to the creation of some 90 HBO institutions, with student enrolment varying from 600 to over 11 000. The majority of the institutions have around 3 000 students. Around a third of them, especially the primary teacher training colleges, confine their programmes to a single discipline while the others provide education in several different ones.

The expansion of institutions' individual responsibility and their increased autonomy was the outcome of policies formulated in a 1985 policy document concerning the whole higher education system. Institutions were given a greater measure of managerial freedom, and allowed, for example, to set up new programmes without the prior consent of government. Along with this greater freedom the institutions were to be responsible for setting up a quality control system to safeguard the quality of education. In addition to this system of self-evaluation, an umbrella evaluation committee and the Education Inspectorate would safeguard the quality of higher vocational education by means of regular monitoring.

Another major change in HBO was the introduction of the Higher Vocational Education Act on 1st August 1986. Prior to that date, HBO was under the Secondary Education Act. With the creation of the large HBO institutions, a system of detailed regulation was regarded as no longer consistent with the general philosophy of control and a new system of funding was introduced. The system of detailed regulations gave way to a model whereby educational institutions, within certain limiting conditions, could exercise discretion in spending the funds made available by central government.

The institutions' funds are now based on the number of students. A distinction is made in this context between students leaving the institution with or without qualifications. For the first group the educational institution receives a total of 4.5 years funding, but for the dropouts only 1.6 years funding. This system encourages the institution to ensure that as many students as possible actually complete their programmes, and in the shortest possible time.

The increased autonomy of the HBO institutes and their changed relationship with central government has repercussions on their relationships with the business community. The college itself is responsible for organising such contacts and attainment targets. This is done in consultation with the business world although there is no statutory provision to this effect. Each institute has its own advisory councils or occupational committees for advising on curriculum development in relation to trends in the labour market. The task of such committees is primarily to gauge the extent to which the programmes meet the demands of the labour market and to promote regular contact with the occupational field. Almost half of the institutes now have such a committee for each field of study.

In addition, a large proportion of the colleges have an industry/occupational advisory council at institutional level. At national level, a central HBO consultative body (known as the Council on Higher Vocational Education) operates under the aegis of the whole community of HBO colleges.

On-the-job-learning is important in HBO. The current HBO curriculum therefore includes a period, generally lasting between a few months and a year, during which students gain practical work experience through a placement in a company or institution. This is frequently a first introduction to actual work practices, and is considered of great importance for vocationally oriented programmes. In addition, there are many part-time HBO programmes. Almost a quarter (23 per cent) of all first-year HBO students study part-time. Over the past few years interest in part-time commercial and business programmes has increased. A special type of part-time education allows students to have their on-the-job experience count towards their degree. Known as "concurrency education", this form of education is particularly prevalent in social and community work training. Students in programmes of this kind are required to undertake work relevant to their studies for at least twenty hours a week. Policy agreement concluded in 1990 between the HBO institutes and the Minister for Education and Science includes a decision to examine the potential for introducing "co-operative education", in which a foundation year would be followed by alternating six-month periods of work and study lasting for a period of four years.

Other legislative developments

January 1, 1991 saw the introduction of the Manpower Services Act. A key section of this Act provides for an administrative, financial and statutory framework within which central government and the social partners bear joint responsibility for implementing policies on employment strategy. The aims of the Act include the preservation and expansion of employment and an adequate supply of labour. This employment strategy framework is "tripartite" in composition, made up of representatives of the employers, trade unions and central government. The bodies responsible for implementation are the Central Manpower Services Board (CBA), which operates nationally, and 28 Regional Manpower Services Boards (RBA) spread throughout the country.

The employment strategy framework allows for the formulation of national employment policies, which are then interpreted and implemented at regional (RBA) level. One of the main tasks of the employment strategy framework is to promote training among job seekers. The training schemes proposed by the employment strategy framework constitute a fixed element in long-term national and regional policy planning. By this means it is hoped to harmonise the various training schemes and gear them to labour market needs.

It is intended that educational institutions should also be used to provide training programmes in the context of the employment strategy. MBO schools have been able for some time now to offer services to private enterprise on a commercial basis; the RBA can act as an intermediary in this respect. An attempt is also being made to introduce greater harmony with adult education (for example part-time MBO).

21

Some figures

The population data in Table 1 provide an overview of the total numbers of students attending institutions of vocational education. The LBO schools are increasingly integrated with combined schools offering several different types of LBO and/or AVO/VWO. A proportion of LBO/AVO/VWO combined schools have mixed LBO/AVO transition classes. The students in these transition classes are included in the statistics for AVO/VWO; this produces an artificial underestimate of the number of LBO students. The SVM operation led to a sharp reduction in the number of MBO schools as of August 1, 1994, a process that happened earlier in HBO.

Table 1. **Population data**

			1989/1990		1991/1992
LBO Total enrolled 1989/1990	Male		152 814		135 760
	Female		99 404		88 612
	Total		252 218		224 372
Schools:	LBO unisectoral		395		254
	LBO multisectoral		194		191
	LBO/AVO combined		116		212
	LBO and/or AVO + MBO		73		34
	total		807		692
MBO Total enrolled 1989/1990	Male		159 882		152 398
	Female		134 550		132 006
	Total		294 432		284 404
Schools:			438		144
BBO/Apprenticeships					
Total enrolled BBO 1988/1989		Total	147 998	Male	100 233
				Female	42 464
				Total	142 697
with apprenticeship agreements			110 092		129 841
HBO Total enrolled 1988/1989	Male		120 929		122 985
	Female		103 013		118 163
	Total		223 942		241 148
full-time			168 925		193 986
part-time			55 071		47 162
Number of institutes 1991					80

A particularly significant development since 1970 is the proportionate change in the figures for general and vocational education, affecting the relationship between AVO/VWO and LBO during the early years of secondary education. Selection in the transition class(es) results in many students abandoning AVO/VWO in favour of LBO; moreover students in joint LBO/AVO transition classes are included in the total for AVO/VWO. For this reason, the figures given in Table 2 are for the second (1970,1975) and third academic year (1980, 1985, 1989). The main conclusion is that the proportion of students in LBO has declined. This development has not however been a gradual one. Sudden changes can be seen between 1970 and 1975, succeeded – at least for the boys – by a decade of stability; for the girls, participation in LBO gradually declined over this period. After 1985 there was a further sudden fall, which widened the difference in participation in LBO between boys and girls.

Table 2. **Proportions LBO-AVO/VWO, second/third year of programme**

	1970	1975	1980	1985	1989	1991
Male						
AVO/VWO	52.9	58.4	54.8	55.6	60.0	61.7
LBO	47.1	41.6	45.2	44.4	40.0	38.3
Female						
AVO/VWO	58.4	64.6	66.8	69.0	71.9	72.5
LBO	41.6	35.4	33.2	31.0	28.2	27.5
Total						
AVO/VWO	55.5	61.4	60.6	62.1	65.7	66.9
LBO	44.5	38.6	39.4	37.9	34.3	33.1
Absolute Figures:						
Total						
AVO/VWO	132 302	168 087	165 996	163 919	137 103	129 477
LBO	106 226	105 687	108 032	100 189	71 433	64 078

1970, 1975: proportions for population in second year of programme.
1980, 1985, 1990: proportions for population in third year of programme.

Table 3 shows the distribution of student numbers in the different types of schools in the second stage of secondary and the first level of higher education. Figures for 1975 are incomplete, and thus not given. The particularly striking feature is the growth in participation in education by 18, 19 and 20-year-olds, especially after 1980. MBO and part-time vocational education (particularly including the apprenticeship system) have gained from this increasing participation. The percentage of male students in HBO and university education has changed little in almost 20 years. For females, however, a sharp increase is observed. In general, the pattern of male and female participation has become less unequal over this period.

Table 3. **Percentage participation by 17, 18, 19 and 20-year-olds**

	1970							
	17		18		19		20	
	Male	Female	Male	Female	Male	Female	Male	Female
(V)SO	0.6	0.5	0.5	0.4	–	–	–	–
AVO/VWO	27.5	20.0	15.6	7.7	6.8	2.3	2.8	0.6
LBO	13.2	2.0	6.8	0.9	4.3	0.5	2.9	0.3
MBO (ft)	9.2	9.1	10.0	5.5	7.8	3.1	4.7	1.4
MBO (pt)	20.3	6.3	18.2	4.7	12.5	3.1	5.5	3.2
HBO	1.9	2.0	5.0	5.0	8.1	6.4	8.6	6.0
university	1.2	0.3	4.1	1.2	6.5	1.9	6.7	2.0
none	26.1	59.6	39.9	74.5	55.4	82.8	68.9	86.9
	1980							
(V)SO	1.4	0.9	1.2	0	–	–	–	–
AVO/VWO	34.6	37.0	19.9	17.2	16.5	5.7	3.3	2.6
LBO	17.4	7.9	5.4	1.8	1.2	0.4	0.5	0.2
MBO (ft)	15.9	19.7	17.8	15.0	14.6	7.6	9.5	3.0
MBO (pt)	12.8	7.9	13.3	5.5	9.7	4.2	6.7	3.3
HBO	1.3	1.4	5.2	5.7	9.2	8.7	10.4	9.1
university	0.1	0.0	3.5	2.0	6.3	3.6	7.5	4.1
none	16.5	24.9	33.9	52.2	50.6	69.8	62.0	77.7
	1987							
(V)SO	2.4	1.3	2.1	1.4	–	–	–	–
AVO/VWO	32.5	36.7	17.5	18.1	7.5	7.1	3.2	2.8
LBO	16.5	8.3	4.9	1.9	1.2	0.5	0.4	0.2
MBO (ft)	26.7	30.1	30.8	30.0	25.0	19.5	16.0	9.3
MBO (pt)	12.3	7.2	13.8	6.3	11.5	5.3	9.6	4.3
HBO	1.0	0.1	4.5	6.0	9.2	10.0	11.6	11.2
university	0.0	0.0	4.2	3.0	7.5	5.4	8.3	6.1
none	8.5	14.9	22.1	33.0	38.1	52.2	51.0	65.9
	1989							
(V)SO	2.5	1.4	2.1	1.4	–	–	–	–
AVO/VWO	32.6	36.9	16.1	16.2	5.6	4.1	1.3	0.7
LBO	15.4	7.6	4.7	1.9	1.1	0.4	0.3	0.2
MBO (ft)	28.0	30.4	32.5	32.0	26.2	21.5	16.6	10.1
MBO (pt)	11.7	7.4	14.1	6.9	12.0	5.9	10.0	4.8
HBO	1.1	1.9	4.7	6.7	9.6	11.2	12.7	12.6
university	0.0	0.0	4.3	3.3	7.9	6.4	9.2	7.0
none	7.8	13.2	20.0	29.4	35.5	47.8	47.6	62.2

(V)SO: special education - MBO (ft): full-time MBO - MBO (pt): part-time MBO, including day-release/apprentice-ship schemes and part-time non-formal education for young school leavers.
AVO/VWO, LBO, HBO, university: both full-time and part-time.
1975: figures for university attendance not available.
Source: CBS, *Young people in the Netherlands and their education.*

In very general terms, it may be concluded that:

– in the first stage of secondary education, great changes occurred in the 1970 – 1975 period. These can be seen in relation to the continuing effects of the social changes during the 1960s, the introduction of the Secondary Education Act and the raising of the school-leaving age during this period. After 1985, there was a renewed increase in the pace of change, related to the economic recession and the rapid decline in school enrolment;
– in the second stage, there was a tendency to continue longer in education, particularly after 1980. This too can be seen as in context of the recession. Girls still tend to leave school earlier than boys, but the difference has become less marked. Participation in MBO has increased in both relative and absolute terms (despite the declining population of young people). The differences in patterns of participation between boys and girls have decreased.

2. Policy Debates over the Period 1968-1991

Main lines of policy development

This section considers the time period immediately following the introduction of the Secondary Education Act in 1968. The main lines of policy development since then, which provide a basis for analysis are:
– expanding and restructuring the vocational education system,
– structural integration of vocational education within the system,
– increasing the effectiveness of the system of vocational education,
– improving the responsiveness of vocational education.

Expanding and restructuring the vocational education system

Since the mid 1960s, vocational education has grown dramatically. This is a result of expanding student enrolment in HBO and MBO and contracting enrolment in LBO. Initially, many new types of schools appeared, producing a highly differentiated system of vocational education. During the 1980s, both MBO and HBO underwent restructuring processes characterised by sector formation, i.e. combining related types into sectors, and expansion of scale. These processes were completed at the end of the decade with the integration of various "stray elements" into the new, more orderly system of vocational education.

Structural integration of vocational education in the education system

The Secondary Education Act of 1968 regulated all education beyond primary education, with the exception of the universities. In addition to general secondary education, it embraced three levels of vocational education (LBO, MBO and until 1986 HBO). This comprehensive approach has encouraged the integration of vocational education into the education system. LBO has come more closely to resemble general secondary education thereby changing from directly vocational to pre-vocational education. The apprenticeship system and MBO have become the standard forms of education for skilled workers in lower and intermediate grades, while HBO has come more closely to university education, as a form of higher education with practical applications.

Increasing the effectiveness of the vocational education system

Another prominent issue in the policy debate is that of the system's effectiveness in terms of students successfully completing programmes and the efficiency with which the various forms of education interact with each other. Opportunities for vertical and horizontal mobility within the education system accommodate different styles of learning. The range of pathways have, however, been increasingly reduced due to budget constraints.

Improving the responsiveness of vocational education

During the 1980s, government policy focused on the responses offered by vocational education to labour market needs. The business community expressed their concern that the general education element in the curriculum was at the expense of the acquisition of directly applicable skills. During the 1980s, the social partners became more directly involved in policy making aimed at improving links between education and the labour market. This led to extensive work-study arrangements in vocational education.

Policy developments in LBO

Even before the Secondary Education Act came into force in 1968, there was pressure for radical structural change in LBO. Arguments were advanced for abolishing the distinction enshrined in the Act between vocational and general secondary education, for further generalising the LBO curriculum and for extending the length of programmes from 3 to 4 years.

During the 1970s, education policy debates were dominated by the question of designing an integrated system of secondary education, an issue that eventually polarised public opinion. The controversy was finally resolved in the late 1980s in the discussion to introduce basic education. The emphasis, at this time, was on the social and economic functions of education, rather than on equality.

Structural changes

After 1968, the idea of extending the length of programmes became a serious subject of discussion. One reason for this was unemployment, especially high among youth and in the construction and metal-working industries. Continuing mechanisation and automation was also imposing conflicting demands on LBO. Large-scale industry was calling for broad, technical education, while the small businesses mainly required practical skills. In 1973 LBO became a 4-year programme, the first 2 years being general and introductory. In the late 1960s, LBO certification examinations were not centrally set, and exam regulations differed depending on the type of LBO. The Junior Secondary Vocational Education Leaving Examinations Decree of 1975 recognises the differences between the various forms of LBO only in terms of the possible combinations of exam subjects. Students are allowed to choose from three different levels for each examination subject. The highest level (C) is set centrally, while the A- and B-levels are set by the schools themselves.

The integration debate

Criticism of the education system as it operated in the early 1970s focused mainly on the lack of equal opportunities within education, itself a result of the over-negative selection of students and inadequate opportunities for horizontal and vertical transfer. This criticism was being voiced not only by the education field but also by young workers' organisations and trade unions. Opportunities for intellectual and social development for working-class children thus became a higher priority on the political agenda.

The introduction of the Secondary Education Act triggered widespread interest in comprehensive secondary education, gradually polarising public opinion. In the early 1970s, forces and counterforces were set in motion which encouraged reflection on the functions and design of secondary education. A "Middle School" concept, launched by educators and social organisations, took the centre of the political stage with advocates and opponents roughly divided along left-right lines.

The year 1975 saw the publication of the discussion document *Contours of a Future Education System*, proposing a review of the whole system of secondary education. In contrast to the policy documents which preceded the Secondary Education Act, the "Contours Report" discussed not only the structure of secondary education, but also its functions and objectives. The generalised introduction of the Middle School would probably not be so rapid, but seemed nevertheless inevitable.

However, 1979 brought political changes and the new Minister presented the Secondary Education Development Plan as a compromise between the Secondary Education Act and the "Contours Report". The plan proposed a 2-year transition period on entry to secondary education, together with common examination arrangements for general secondary education and LBO. In effect, this document marked the demise of the Middle School movement (existing experiments were tolerated, but lost their policy significance).

During the early 1980s, the plans for a comprehensive first stage of secondary education were designated as "extended primary education". This term refers to the idea of extending the functions of primary education to the first stage of secondary education, i.e. providing a basic education for all and a period of orientation and preparation for future career and school choices. The principle was that every student should follow the same core curriculum. "Basic education" became a key concept for the future development of the secondary education system.

In a 1986 report, the Scientific Advisory Council on Government Policy argued for raising standards of education across the board, by introducing a common core curriculum for the first three years of secondary schooling. This would include 14 subjects (to be offered at two levels) plus teaching time amounting to 20 per cent of the total curriculum.

Basic education would provide a common and general education in academic, cultural and social subjects, constituting a sound basis for further personal development and equipping students both to function meaningfully as members of society and to make sensible choices with regard to further training or careers. The report recommended that this basic education be introduced in both LBO and general secondary education. It left the existing structure intact, while expressing the expectation that existing distinctions would lose practical significance.

Pre-vocational education

The concept of pre-vocational education was developed in relation to LBO in the second half of the 1980s. This means that the first two years of LBO were further harmonised through integration of the curriculum, while the programme is rounded off by a choice of options in the later years. The vocational character of the second half of the programme is emphasised, with students able to choose from a maximum of 16 vocational options within a departmental structure.

In anticipation of the introduction of basic education, the curricular aspects of this proposal were introduced in 1990 following consideration by parliament. Changing the name of LBO to Pre-vocational education (VBO) in itself indicates that explicitly vocational qualifications will need to be obtained through further education.

Both the law on basic education and on Pre-Vocational Education were passed in Parliament in 1992 and took effect in August 1993.

Policy developments in MBO and the apprenticeship system

Expansion and restructuring

Restricting the expansion of student enrolment and structuring the range of programmes offered are achieved within MBO mainly through sector formation and the amalgamation of school. An early example of sector formation can be seen in the restructuring of home economics (MHNO) and social work (MSPO) programmes in the mid 1970s.

Restructuring of these types of education was thought necessary due to: growing enthusiasm for these types of schools among 16-year-olds and the need for occupational mobility; differences between existing training programmes with regard to entry requirements, the type and length of programmes, work experience schemes and location; developments within the first stage of secondary education and the movement towards the new style of higher education.

The restructuring of MHNO and MSPO was completed in the early 1980s with the introduction of senior secondary personal and social services and health care education (MDGO). This process was duplicated in the late 1980s in the operation to achieve sector formation and innovation (SVM) in MBO as a whole.

Sector formation includes providing interrelated programmes within a single institution. The amalgamation of institutions should guarantee the creation of a differentiated range of programmes, while innovation is intended to achieve a broad and differentiated range of training able to respond flexibly to both education and labour market needs.

Participation trends in the apprenticeship system are extremely sensitive to the economy. The higher the level of industrial activity, the more apprenticeships firms will offer. The more unemployment there is, the more young people need apprenticeships. The asynchronous reactions of the supply and demand sides to the the economic situation make complementary provision by the vocational education system a necessity.

An example of this sort of provision was the Short MBO (KMBO), which provided a response to the changing character of LBO by providing directly vocational qualifications through a form of pre-vocational education. In practice, students in LBO and MAVO could not transfer to MBO. The purpose of KMBO was to fill this gap in the provisions of the Secondary Education Act.

The introduction of KMBO was preceded by the development of day-release education. A year after the Act came into force, a committee set up by the Minister for Education proposed the development of day-release schemes aimed at more practically inclined students in parallel with full-time school-based education for those of a more theoretical and academic inclination. The day-release experiments set up after 1975 were absorbed in KMBO pilot projects in 1979.

The close relationship between trends in the apprenticeship system and the state of the economy is clearly demonstrated by the statistics on apprenticeship agreements. The effects of the oil crises in the early 1970s are reflected in the number of apprenticeship agreements; these declined to 50 000 by the mid 1970s. Following a slight recovery in the second half of the 1970s, apprenticeships further declined during the recession of the early 1980s.

Improving responsiveness

At this time the government initiated a consultation process on industrial policies, involving social partners and the education field. One of the recommendations which emerged from this was to double the number of apprenticeships, a measure actually implemented in the second half of the 1980s.

Since the early 1980s, the social partners have been allowed a greater role in education and training, and as from 1985 they have been represented in the consultative body on secondary education serving the Minister for Education. In addition, bodies have been created in each branch of business, with the social partners involved in drawing up attainment targets for vocational education.

In the late 1980s, the government appointed a committee to improve the links between education and the labour market. The committee advocated the introduction of more extensive dual work-study arrangements in vocational education and the creation of a closer relationship between schools and the business community. The increased independence of educational institutions allows firms to play a greater role in determining the product of education.

The heart of the report is the idea that government, social partners, the education world and individuals should all share responsibility for a system of "lifelong education" and for ensuring that every individual entering the labour market possesses at least basic starting qualifications. The government responded positively to the committee's recommendations and, among other things, introduced a special budget for people up to the age of 27 wishing to acquire minimum starting qualifications.

Policy developments in HBO

The universities have traditionally concentrated a number of different disciplines within a single institution. HBO programmes, by contrast, were dispersed among many different colleges in response to the specific needs of the labour market. University programmes have generally concerned full-time students. HBO, on the other hand, has a strong tradition of part-time education for those who are already working. The development of a unified system of higher education has brought changes to both types of education. HBO has seen increases in the size of institutions and the universities have introduced more part-time programmes. There has also been harmonisation and demarcation in the content of HBO and university programmes. Despite the shift towards a unified system of higher education, however, HBO and university education continue to preserve their separate identities (HBO continuing to be more practically oriented).

The proposals of the late 1960s and early 1970s with regard to higher education focused largely on the integration of HBO and the universities. A 1975 Policy Document on the Future of Higher Education signalled a new phase in the debate. This policy document advocated enhancing the status of HBO by amalgamating existing colleges to form combined institutions (to create HBO institutes comparable to the universities). The document proposed a programme structure in which the foundation (propaedeutic) stage would allow the possibility of transfer either way. This proposal led in 1979 to the Higher Education Transfer of Students Act.

That year also saw the publication of a draft HBO bill. This appeared at a time when the organisations representing Higher Vocational Education had just given their views on higher education development. In 1980 the Council on Higher Vocational Education identified the following as key features in its ideal for the development of higher education: the introduction of a two-tier structure, self-allocation, broader curricula and differentiation. Against this background, the draft bill adhered too closely to outdated structures. In 1981, however, a new bill was submitted which met the wishes of the education field.

This bill was passed by parliament in 1984 and came into force in 1986. The Higher Vocational Education Act of 1986 brought considerable changes to the planning and funding systems. As a result of higher establishment and closure norms, the number of HBO institutes has decreased substantially and those remaining have been given greater funding responsibility, matching the situation already existing in the universities.

3.   Main Stages in the Developments of the VOTEC System

The aim of this section is to outline a number of key trends over the last twenty years. These trends are the outcome of the historical evolution of the vocational education system and policy developments over the last two decades.

The relationship between general and vocational education

One clearly identifiable trend over the last 20 years concerns the changing relationship between general and specifically vocation-oriented education. A distinction can be drawn here in the relationship between general secondary education and vocational education (within the education system) and the relationship between general and specifically vocational teaching within the various types of vocational education. It is possible to distinguish two periods of thinking. During the first period, which lasted until the early 1980s, thinking was heavily influenced by the ideal of equal opportunity, and the aim was to reduce as much as possible the differences between general and vocational education. During the second period, still under way, interest has centred by contrast on employment opportunities and the need to meet the demand for "skills", with greater emphasis placed on the specific character of vocational education.

In the first period, attention focused on opportunities for transfer, not only from the first to the second stage of secondary education (removing barriers to MBO), but also between different types of vocational education, and from senior secondary to higher vocational education. There was a strong emphasis on the principle that vocational education should not be a dead end, but should offer students at least some of the same opportunities as general education. This idea is taken to its logical conclusion in the first "Contours Report" (1975), which proposed a reorganisation of the entire second stage of secondary education by social sector. Within the proposed "senior school", more pre-tertiary and more pre-vocational "routes" would be available. Later plans, however, have consistently been based on a separate development of general and vocational education and the principle described above has generally been translated into curriculum harmonisation and the creation and maintenance of transfer opportunities. The Short MBO's aim of offering underqualified students leaving the first stage of secondary education a second chance to enter MBO was, at least officially, as important as that of offering them a complete vocational training. During the same period, there was also emphasis on providing opportunities for those successfully completing apprenticeships to transfer to MBO.

The second period is linked to the economic crisis of the 1980s. Dominant themes of the period were the need to find a solution to youth unemployment and the desire to tailor the content and structure of qualifications to match changes in the country's economic structure. This implied that vocational education must become more specific. It gave rise to new ideas about managing the relationship between education and the labour market, and establishing a more direct relationship between education and clients. This theme is prominent in the Wagner and Rauwenhoff reports, both of which dealt with the issue of how to strengthen the involvement of industry in vocational education. The new views on the relationship between education and work are reflected in the SVM Act, which for the first time in the history of the Secondary Education Act defines the role of the client system in determining the structure and aims of education.

The same periods can be distinguished as concerns the relationship between general and specialised education within the various types of vocational education. During the first period, great importance was attached to the introduction of more general academic subjects in vocational education, a more general approach to vocationally oriented subjects, and forms of teaching and organisation similar to those found in general education. This may have been due to the higher status of general education, the wish to ensure equality of the two sub-systems (see above), and the vocational training demands from industry and commerce. Concepts like versatility, anticipation of more rapid changes in job content and preparation for lifelong learning were prominent.

The second period, by contrast, brought a stronger emphasis on the specific demands on vocational education and the direct employability of those leaving it. It is not clear however, to what degree this actually brought about a change in teaching style. In any case, there was a change in the themes dominating public discussion of vocational education during the period. One might advance that, as ground gained during the earlier period was consolidated, attention now turned more to curriculum development and teaching methods in relation to demands from the business world.

Contacts between education and the business community

A turning point in the early 1980s can also be seen in relations between education and the business community. During the first period, these contacts were organised in a similar way to those that existed between general and higher education: that is, via bodies set up by central government, in which the "clients" (business and higher education) acted together with representatives from the field of education to advise the government. Such bodies were established not by statute but on an ad hoc basis by ministerial order. Their advice often focused on the examination syllabuses, the only means by which the Dutch government could directly influence the content of education. The Netherlands' unique political consensus on freedom of education means that although examination syllabuses are ultimately set by the central government, they are usually decided in accordance with the advice of the education field and "clients". Another feature typical of this first period is the tendency to administer general and vocational education by means of the same policy procedures and according to the principles of the Secondary Education Act.

During the second period a gradual divergence emerged in policy approaches to general and vocational education. In vocational education, there has been a tendency to organise closer links with the business community. As regards the curriculum, this new approach is reflected in the arrangements laid down in the SVM Act regarding consultation with individual industries and the role of such consultation in the creation of attainment targets and units of certification. Although many features of the previous period remain unchanged, (joint recommendations from "clients" and the education field, and the ultimately decisive role of the Minister), this Act for the first time makes statutory provision for the arrangements, meaning for example that the Minister is now obliged to hear such advice before he can set the content framework for MBO. This, therefore, formalises and guarantees the involvement of the business community, a situation which had already existed for some time in the apprenticeship system through national bodies. This development can therefore also be described as a convergence of MBO and the apprenticeship system, superseding the convergence of general and vocational education seen in the preceding period.

The relationship between individual schools and the business community also changed. There have always been contacts between schools and companies or industry organisations, varying in extent from school to school and between the different types of vocational education and individual industries. The 1980s saw an attempt to create closer contacts. One way to achieve this is to increase the policy freedom of the individual school so that it can arrange its curriculum directly with its client system. If, during the 1970s, the autonomy of schools (in both vocational and general education) was seen more in light of freedom of education and therefore of allegiance to a particular identity, religious or otherwise, during the 1980s this autonomy was seen as a precondition allowing schools to respond flexibly to the needs of their direct "clients". This was reflected in a change in terminology, from one strongly influenced by education (pedagogical and ideological identity, philosophical and organisational freedom, child-centred education) to one drawing heavily on the business world (client- product- and service-centred education, yield and efficiency. The Rauwenhoff report goes so far as to see the school exclusively as an enterprise producing qualified workers, omitting any mention of the concept of "freedom of education" and its constitutional consequences. Finally, MBO and HBO institutions were allowed to provide education under contract beyond the forms regulated and funded by government. HBO institutes are also allowed to carry out research under contract, where this relates to business practice and applications.

Current policy is directed at creating large, autonomous institutions at regional level that provide both MBO and apprenticeship programmes The trend over the last few years will likely continue and the cultural difference between general and vocational education will be further magnified. Within HBO there has been a similar trend of increasing involvement of the business community. The difference is that the institutions themselves bear responsibility, given their different administrative relationship with the central government.

On-the-job training

The 1980s saw a reassessment of the value of on-the-job training, as demonstrated by the attempt to introduce dual systems more widely into senior secondary vocational education. In the context of industrial restructuring, an agreement was made with the business community to double the number of apprentices in the system. The target figure was achieved and participation in the apprenticeship system continued to increase until recently.

As regards LBO, the law on pre-vocational education which came into effect in 1992 makes it possible to include (short) introductory work placements. This too marks a contrast with the preceding period, during which LBO became more general; the present proposal relates to education for those below the school-leaving age.

More recently, a debate has begun regarding the design of vocational education itself, and its dual structure. In a number of respects, there is evidence of a convergence between MBO and the apprenticeship system (institutional concentration, arrangements for attainment targets, unification of the national bodies).

Changing administrative relationships

Since the early 1980s the administrative relationship between the central government and schools has also been a subject of interest. This relationship has long been dominated by the twin concepts of freedom of education and financial equality between publicly and privately run schools. These two factors implied, on the one hand, a considerable degree of government caution regarding the aims and content of education, but on the other, close involvement in the structure of education, the establishment of schools and funding. This resulted in a comparatively detailed set of regulations.

During the 1980s there was a general increase in criticism of government intervention, which had spillover effects on education policies. The key themes emerging at this time were deregulation, meaning a reduction in detailed regulations, and increased autonomy, an attempt to create educational institutions with wider powers to manage their own affairs. Decentralisation, the transfer of powers to lower (local) levels of government, was not a major issue in the education field (except in adult education).

In this area, higher education has led the way. The 1983 policy document which gave the go-ahead for institutional amalgamation of the HBO institutes also identified as goals an increase in individual institutions' responsibility for allocation of financial resources, staff policy and the organisation of teaching. This increased autonomy is evident in HBO regulations since that date and was elaborated in a 1985 policy document on autonomy and quality in higher education. The institutions themselves were to have primary responsibility for setting up a system of quality control. Apart from this self-evaluation, an umbrella evaluation committee and the Education Inspectorate were to safeguard the quality of higher vocational education by means of regular monitoring.

The 1986 HBO Act introduced a new system of funding. The system of detailed regulations gave way to a model allowing more scope for the educational institutions, within certain limitations, to exercise their own discretion in spending the funds made available by central government. The institutions receive a fixed sum based on student numbers ("block grant funding"). In secondary education this trend emerges particularly in the SVM operation, (where a number of the same elements recur), though the autonomy of the schools is less extensive than that enjoyed by the HBO institutes. The setting of attainment targets is, however, a feature unknown within HBO.

Increasing efficiency

The economic crisis and the associated government budget constraints led the theme of efficiency in education to attract considerable interest during the 1980s. When studying the trend towards greater efficiency in education, it should be remembered that the

Netherlands is characterised by a relatively academic system. That is, most training leading to vocational qualifications takes place within the context of educational institutions. Dual forms of education are relatively rare in the vocational training system.

A major feature of the restructuration of the vocational training system has been increasing the size of educational institutions. Both in HBO and MBO there have been specific exercises (known respectively as the STC and SVM operations) to form larger units. The aim is on the one hand to create a more flexible system and on the other to increase the rate of profitability. This involves both increasing the effectiveness of financial expenditure and improving the output of the system of vocational training.

Both the aims and the organisation of the SVM operation were clearly based on those of the restructuring operation that took place in HBO. Here too, for example, a process management team from outside the ministry oversaw the process of amalgamation and concentration in education.

In the first stage of secondary education, the attempt to form larger units is part of the introduction of basic education. One aim of this policy is to form combined schools, to better guide students and help them select programmes.

4. Aspects of Responsiveness

Vocational or general secondary education

In almost all European countries there are two sectors of secondary education, vocational and general, generally with different historical roots. The vocational sector often grew out of initiatives by workers' or employers' organisations and aimed at improving the knowledge and skills of particular groups of workers or at raising the educational level of working-class youths. The more general or academic forms of secondary education have their roots in the schooling originally provided by religious authorities and later taken over and expanded in the 18th and 19th centuries by the State.

The relationship between the two sectors of secondary education has always been uneasy: parents and students are faced with deciding which offers the best prospects for later life, while government must decide which should be given priority. Employers contribute to the tensions of this uneasy relationship (by the organisation of the processes and structure of work) (Maurice *et al.*, 1980). The relationship is subject to constant change as a result of social and economic changes in society and changes in the education system. The responsiveness of the vocational sector to changes in the labour market and within firms must be understood in the context of the relationship between vocational and general education.

Unequal status

The vocational and general sectors of secondary education do not enjoy the same esteem. General programmes have higher status and are more attractive to students and their parents than vocational programmes at the same level, especially in initial education.

The result is that the former have tended to squeeze out the latter in lower secondary education (12-16 years of age) with junior vocational (LBO) schools taking students whose academic attainments at the end of primary school are such that a general secondary education is not judged suitable for them. This also occurs in schools providing general as well as vocational programmes. The main explanation for the disparity of status does not lie in differences in the job prospects of qualified school leavers of comparable intellectual capacity and background, since the outlook for youths with an LBO qualification is similar to or better than that of youths with a general qualification, at least at the start of their working life (Meesters and Einerhand, 1986; Baeten *et al.*, 1990). Rather the disparity is explained by the range of options open to young people with vocational and general qualifications: the school leaver with a general qualification has a wider choice of further education and training programmes than does someone with a junior vocational education certificate, so that students and their parents are wise to select the programme which leaves most options open. The general sector of secondary education thus increasingly functions as a preparation for further education or training.

Final or transitional?

Despite the higher status of general education in the Netherlands, the vocational sector has expanded considerably at upper secondary (16+) and higher (17/18+) level, mainly because general education is increasingly seen as transitional rather than final in nature. Individuals' general education level determines their starting position in the labour market, but vocational education is often the channel for their entry.

This is evident from the pattern of young people's educational careers in recent years. The apprenticeship system and the senior secondary vocational (MBO) sector are taking increasing numbers of students with general education certificates at junior (MAVO) or senior (HAVO) level, while colleges of higher vocational education (HBO) are taking more and more VWO graduates. This is replacing the previous pattern of vertical progression whereby 16-year-olds leaving junior vocational schools entered the apprenticeship system and those from MAVO schools embarked on an HBO programme while HAVO-certificate holders enter an HBO college at 17 and VWO graduates go on to university at 18.

This new relationship between general and vocational education and the labour market has caused MBO and HBO to expand and the LBO sector to shrink. The view of general as transitional and vocational as final is reflected in the recent proposals of official bodies such as the Rauwenhoff Committee, which defined qualifications obtained in vocational education in terms of "minimum initial qualifications".

The institutional gap

General and vocational education are linked by the flows of students within and between the "combined" school sectors but the institutional gap between the two subsystems is wide. Combined schools offering junior vocational and general secondary programmes existed but were not common, though this is changing now as a consequence of the introduction of basic education.

Indeed, the institutional gap between the general and academic (HAVO/VWO) streams of upper secondary education and the vocational streams(MBO) has grown wider in recent years, due to the sector formation and renewal (SVM) programme in vocational education. Following the SVM operation, general and vocational provision at this level function in institutional frameworks that differ more than ever.

Providing vocational and general programmes in the same institutional framework is no guarantee of improved co-ordination between the two subsystems. Where hierarchically ranked school types are brought together in a combined institution there is a tendency for the whole to be dominated by the ethos of the highest type (see Reynolds and Sullivan, 1987). The residual nature of pre-vocational education thus risks being further emphasised in a broad-based multilateral school.

The gap between general and vocational secondary education derives from the individual logic of opting for the highest attainable school career with the widest range of options, including a vocational programme as the final phase. The existence of the gap thus needs not impede flexibility of response, provided there are sufficient opportunities for linking general and vocational education.

"Learning to learn"

The significant difference between vocational and general curricula lies in the degree of orientation towards particular sectors of the labour market rather than in the degree of emphasis on theoretical as opposed to applied knowledge. General secondary education has grown more transitional and less final in nature, tending to focus on progression to a subsequent phase of education. Vocational curricula, in contrast, put the emphasis on preparation for entry to the labour market. "Learning to learn" is, however, now a responsibility of both sectors: the only difference is that in general secondary education "learning to learn" cannot normally be located in any specific context, since it is not yet clear to what later occupational practice the activity should be geared. On the vocational side, "learning to learn" can take place in a much more specific context, since the range of later occupational practice to which it is geared is much more limited (see Moerkamp and de Bruijn, 1991).

The vocational sector thus has greater opportunities to include "learning to learn" in the curriculum with fruitful results, not by making the curriculum more general but by using appropriate educational methods, such as simulation and a project approach in a vocational setting.

The common core of learning

The differing status of general and vocational education and the differing degree of orientation to the labour market mean that the common core of learning is not large. General and vocational education curricula nevertheless broadly complement one another, first, because MBO and HBO admission requirements may specify sets of subjects in which prospective entrants must have passed the examinations. Such requirements are not only of relevance to the knowledge and skills that will be assumed in the vocational programme; they also play a part in the selection of youths with general qualifications on the criterion of "learning to learn". This function is not to be underestimated; it explains the ease with which horizontal transfers from general to vocational programmes have replaced the official pattern of vertical progression.

The second link between general and vocational education relates to the skills for which foundations are laid in general education (but not in specific contexts), since it is on these foundations that vocational programmes must build as they prepare participants for their future occupations.

Problems in the transition from general to vocational education tend to arise when the regulations governing that transition become outdated, when selection in general education changes or when there is crowding on the general side which modifies the nature of the intake on the vocational education side.

Specialist or generalist?

No general rule can be laid down for the relative roles of specialised expertise and broad, vocationally oriented basic knowledge or the possibility of combining them. Given the great diversity of firms, it would be unwise to argue that schools and colleges should concentrate on broad vocationally oriented knowledge, leaving the more specialised knowledge to be acquired through on-the-job training or employer-provided programmes. First, only a small number of mainly large employers are in a position to organise and finance training, on the job or otherwise. Second, not all production processes lend themselves to learning on the job; small- and medium-sized enterprises in particular need people with vocational qualifications who also have specialised knowledge.

The responsiveness of vocational education is often curtailed but sometimes extended by its changing relationship with general education. The responsiveness of the vocational sector has been improved mainly through the acquisition by senior secondary and higher vocational education (MBO/HBO) of final status, completing educational pathways begun in the general sector; the vocational sector's closeness to the work world gives it greater opportunities to respond to employment and labour market developments. As developments on the labour market are unpredictable, an overemphasis on either specialised skills or broad, vocationally oriented, basic knowledge will inevitably reduce the responsiveness of the education system as a whole.

Broadening or deepening?

A broad vocational education is seen as appropriate to changes in firms and the jobs in them. Jobs are steadily becoming more complex (through task integration) and are subject to dynamic processes of change. There is a growing need for workers who are flexible because they know how to learn. Broadening then implies, first, extending the knowledge base (increasing breadth rather than depth) and, second, learning how to use that knowledge in different situations (cognitive skills, flexibility). This interpretation of broadening naturally raises the question of the relationship with general education, and particularly the relationship between vocational education and the common curricular core now being introduced in the early years in all types of secondary schools.

Core curriculum, core skills

The debate in the Netherlands regarding a common curriculum in secondary education for youth under 16 led in 1992 to the formulation of attainment targets for a number of disciplines. These can be reached over periods ranging from two to four years, and the least academically inclined youths, who enter junior vocational schools at age 12, will work towards them (in combination with pre-vocational subjects) over the full four-year period.

The fourteen subjects making up the common curriculum can be taken at different levels, to be determined by the schools. Some variation in the knowledge base is therefore possible, potentially causing problems in the transition to occupational practice or to further study. Moreover the content of the core curriculum includes little or no introduction to the world of work.

The question to be addressed is whether between the ages of 6 and 16 students acquire the foundations needed for further progress in their studies or at work. Where general instrumental skills are concerned (mathematics, Dutch, foreign languages, communication skills, familiarity with scientific concepts and theories, technical understanding) certain foundations can be assumed, but are they sufficient? The introduction of the common curriculum may simply ensure lower average attainment levels in a wider range of subjects.

Many of the students who enter pre-vocational schools at age twelve are likely to have difficulty with this wider curriculum, especially if it is associated with a strongly cognitive bias and a higher level, including greater stress on theories and models than on applications and contexts. This problem can be alleviated if teachers are trained to exploit vocationally relevant aspects and specific student-related characteristics. Teacher exchanges between vocational and general secondary schools could be a useful way of making staff more sensitive to the various types of problem and possible approaches to their solution. The policy towards combining schools in first stage secondary education (see Section 1) stimulates this.

Basic skills relating to discipline, the work ethic, safety, social security, technical processes, the planning and distribution of work, complex activity, communication patterns, and the goals of firms increasingly become a matter of the second stage. This can be covered using dual approaches or simulation techniques (practice businesses, computer simulations).

Skills and skill concepts

Studies have shown that vocational education at any level now focuses on formal qualifications rather than mastery of a field of activity, and on the new practitioner or novice professional. What this constitutes is not always clear: it cannot be defined with precision by either educational institutions or employers and is moreover affected by employers' in-house training facilities: small- and medium-sized businesses have significantly less capacity in this regard than do large firms. If the "new practitioner" is the starting point for many firms, then the question of what level this implies and whether basic skills can be defined become urgent.

These questions were addressed in a study carried out in 1985 (Nijhof and Mulder, 1986) covering office practice (included in junior secondary programmes in business and clerical studies, LEAO) and mechanical engineering (included in senior secondary technical programmes, MTO). Through analyses of young people completing these programmes, their places of work, curricula, innovative firms, etc., a series of skills were defined in relation to training facilities. Basic skills were defined as the broad knowledge, skills and attitudes of qualified school and college leavers which had transfer value in related occupational fields and which were essential for the performance of various tasks. An attempt was made to formulate learning targets for both spheres which could serve to operationalise transferable basic skills. An analysis of the learning targets reveals that many are of a technical instrumental nature; non-technical targets are also mentioned, such as communication skills, precision in execution, and resistance to stress.

In an attempt to tighten the definition of basic skills, Nijhoff and Remmers (1989, 1990), following on from this study, proposed a new definition: basic skills are cognitive, communicative and group process skills which have transfer value and are necessary if the future worker is to be able to learn to learn and to build more than one career. This definition stresses "transition qualities", the ability to learn to learn (Perkins and Salomon, 1989, mention three skills: self-regulation, self-monitoring and self-control) and the manner in which the three groups of skills are linked with task areas.

There are moves under way in vocational curricula at senior secondary level (MBO), to define learning targets as basic skills. This implies a rationalisation of subjects, that is, eliminating outdated targets, reorganising goals into new bodies of knowledge, and adding new goals. Sometimes this happens on the basis of a new technological concept or integrative principle. In electrical engineering and electronics, for example, new learning targets have been defined and legitimated by reference to system concepts rather than components, which was normal practice until recently (Peters et al., 1991). This shift generates new skills and hence new programme syllabuses and applications.

The concept of basic skills has been analysed in relation to the challenges of new technologies. Information technology in particular requires new forms of thinking and abstract reasoning. The ability to give a virtual or abstract description of a product or process with the help of information-processing systems is cited as an example of a new skill. This is an example of a basic skill implying a development of the capacity for abstract thinking. It is a skill which can be used in both business and clerical education and technical education in the design of freely programmable links. These new skills need to be analysed and tested in various task domains.

The integration of general and vocational elements of education in the basic education stage is desirable, provided students' preferences and capacities are taken into account and a variety of pathways through the system allowed. Integration as such does not imply the existence of only one pathway but rather multiple learning contexts. Thinking in terms of selection and specialisation still predominates in Dutch education, and integration can help break this down.

The foundations for the future can, however, only be secured if integration is accompanied by a better understanding of the relationship between cognitive skills and contextual problems. The need here is thus for deepening rather than broadening.

Since cognitive skills have the greatest instrumental value, it is vital to focus attention on how they can be used. For everyone these form the most powerful foundation for the future. The use of technology may determine what happens: for the representation of knowledge, for bridging different contexts and for the interactive solution of problems (Pea, 1988; Nickerson, 1988).

Learning pathways will nevertheless have to be determined contextually. Further research and development is required to determine optimum pathways. The success of integration will depend on the acquisition of good methods of problem solving in a variety of spheres.

Communication between the worlds of education and work

Communication between the worlds of education and work is the first requirement for ensuring that vocational education corresponds with its social and economic environment. Key concepts here are complementarity and collaboration between the two worlds in preparing people for work. This section considers the extent and nature of communication between the worlds of education and work.

Shifting roles at central level

In the past, the role of industry – employers' organisations and trade unions – in vocational education was marginal: the emphasis was on full-time college programmes whose goals and structure were decided by the Ministry of Education and Science in conjunction with the educational institutions. With the exception of the apprenticeship system, where industry's role has always been much stronger, this is still the case in initial vocational education. In the early 1980s, however, vocational education became a major theme in economic and social debate, and industry was attributed a role in decision making. There were two reasons for this (Van Dijk *et al.*, 1988).

The first impetus came from the Wagner Committee, a body set up by government to advise on industrial policy. The Committee's report led to agreement between government, industry and the educational institutions to allow industry a greater say in vocational education, in exchange for providing an adequate supply of work-training placements. Industry exercises its influence in two ways: through the representation of employers' organisations along with trade unions on the central consultative bodies and through their representation in sectoral consultative bodies involving educational institutions (see Section 1).

The second impetus, which relates mainly to the apprenticeship system has come from national agreements in which industry promises to maintain employment levels and provide training in return for trade unions moderating their wage demands. In the 1980s, such collective agreements increased the number of apprenticeship training placements.

41

Increasingly, collective agreements also provide for continuing training of the employed (DCA, 1990). This trend towards greater industry involvement at central level is also recognised in the Employment Services Act which came into force at the beginning of 1991.

Central level instruments of management and control

Industry's expanded role in the apprenticeship system and continuing training is enhanced by its umbrella organisations, and the research and development funds these provide has led to a variety of new work-study combinations in the practical component of apprenticeship programmes (Frietman, 1990). Industry's involvement in full-time vocational education is more modest, though the newly created sectoral consultative bodies may yet allow industry to influence curriculum content in particular sectors. In 1993, these consultative bodies were incorporated into the new National Bodies in Vocational Education, which bring together the formerly separate structures of the apprenticeship system and senior secondary vocational education (MBO).

Greater regional and local autonomy

Until recently, contacts between firms and colleges were largely limited to firms' representation on college governing bodies and ad hoc accords for apprentice and teacher placements, simulation projects, and contract education (whereby publicly funded institutions sell training services to firms). There is little evidence of a systematic strategy of collaboration between MBO colleges and firms. Recent legislation is however likely to lead to greater autonomy for individual colleges, more customer- or market-oriented approaches and a closer focus on regional markets. The independent body set up by government to co-ordinate the process of sector formation and renewal (SVM) in senior secondary vocational education (MBO) emphasises the desirability that colleges embarking on renewal should work from the outside in, that is, they should start from the requirements of target groups and users (students and their future employers) (SVM Report 54). The establishment of Regional Training Centres (ROCs), colleges providing MBO and adult education programmes geared to participants' and employers' needs, will represent the final phase of the process (White Paper on Regional Training Centres, 1991). The Rauwenhoff Committee's call for greater freedom of manoeuvre for the actors at regional and local level, allowing colleges and firms to develop effective pathways through vocational education to employment, is a further encouragement to strengthen contacts between education and industry. Moves to create a dual structure in MBO programmes fit into the same framework.

The opportunities created by recent legislation are not being fully exploited, and certainly not utilised to the same extent in all regions. Indeed, it is questionable whether individual colleges and firms can do much together without assistance; their relative bargaining positions – what they can offer one another – may not be sufficient for the establishment of permanent and systematic contacts unless suitable frameworks are created at the collective level. Moreover the government did not adopt all the Rauwenhoff Committee's recommendations, and notably retains a national structure of qualifications. In some sectors, central agreements have been reached on the balance between national and regional elements in the qualification structure (in printing, for example, the ratio is 3:1).

Recent research on renewal in upper secondary vocational education has found that 38 per cent of colleges are intensifying contacts with industry (Pelkmans and De Vries, 1991). The ultimate result of the movement towards greater autonomy for vocational colleges will depend in large measure on how they use their policy freedom and notably its effect on their position vis-à-vis local and regional industry.

A preliminary evaluation

There is a clear trend in vocational education away from centralised management and control and towards a greater role for the two sides of industry. Key themes are sector formation and regionalisation. The employers' and unions' central umbrella bodies have been given a greater role in decision making, particularly in policy development at sector level. At the same time, greater emphasis is being placed on freedom of manoeuvre for the regional and local level actors: colleges, industry, employment services, etc.

This trend does not imply merely marginal adjustments but rather quite fundamental changes to the vocational education and training system. The processes now under way should help lower the barriers between the worlds of education and work. Already institutions of vocational education are becoming less isolated pedagogically. There is also a better understanding of mutual needs and different interests. New structures are being created at the interface between education and work, including sectoral bodies for the development of national qualifications, and regional agencies for career counselling.

Further co-operation between the education and working worlds in the near future will depend on:
- co-ordination between the processes of sector formation and regionalisation, enabling educational institutions to make the most of their geographical spread;
- open relationships between sectors within vocational education;
- a balance between national and regional elements in the qualification structure, with due emphasis on occupational themes as the foundation of vocational education;
- a balance in the distribution of powers and responsibilities among employers, unions and government, in particular between employers' and workers' interests and between the general and occupational elements in vocational education;
- stimulation of the capacity for change of individual educational institutions, encouragement of contacts with industry, maintaining the distinction between initial education and training services provided under contract, and using experience from the latter as a basis for innovation in the former.

Teaching staff: training, work and employment conditions

The qualifications, motivation, deployability and availability of teaching staff are major elements in the process of educational development. Factors currently relevant to vocational education are:
- the introduction of greater flexibility in the conditions of employment of teaching staff in vocational education at senior secondary level (MBO), with teachers being

deployed more flexibly and greater use being made of people from industry who are not qualified teachers, in the context of the shift to devolved (college-run) budgets;

- the strengthening of MBO college management through the formation of senior management teams;
- a shortage of teaching staff, notably in the technical and business fields, which has led to plans to allow the payment of higher salaries to teachers of these subjects.

Flexibility of conditions

The regulations governing the rights and responsibilities of people working in education are perceived as being too rigid: new teachers entering the profession at the beginning of the salary scale know precisely what they will be earning until retirement.

The legislation which began the SVM (sector formation and renewal) exercise brought radical changes in the regulations governing staff rights and responsibilities: some decisions formerly taken centrally are now taken at college level. Institutions determine their own staffing policies and can respond flexibly to their needs. Colleges, for example, can decide who to employ and, within limits, how much they are paid.

Teachers

An MBO teacher must have successfully completed either a teacher training or other relevant programme at higher vocational or university level followed by an MBO teaching diploma programme. College authorities decide where to employ teachers; under the previous arrangements (similar ones still apply in other sectors of education) there were separate appointment regulations for each subject, with the right to teach a given subject depending on possession of an official certificate of competence for that subject. In the MBO sector, responsibility for assessing teachers' competence in their subjects now lies with college authorities; to facilitate the filling of vacancies, the standard conditions of appointment need not be applied for a teacher's first two years in a post.

5. Instruments of Responsiveness

Organisational flexibility and effectiveness

Organisational flexibility, a feature of the education system as a whole and of vocational education in particular, is an umbrella term referring to a set of instruments, regulatory and feedback mechanisms, capacities and effects. For example the flexibility of an MBO college, in terms of the different learning pathways it offers, can be seen as an effect of national policy. More open legislation gives colleges greater autonomy in the way they perform their function, enabling them to enter into contracts with customers. This is, in part, a result of a change in the government's policy instruments.

The SVM (sector formation and renewal) programme is an example of a policy instrument used to bring about a number of innovations in vocational education. The programme and its co-ordinators well illustrate the interplay of institutions involved: the State sets goals and provides facilities; an intermediary guides and co-ordinates; and the colleges decide their own internal and external policies. The whole operates through a policy of accommodation. At every level, goals, resources and effects play a part in enhancing flexibility in the education system, in the relationship between the worlds of education and work and in the relationship between education systems as well. The processes of co-ordination involving government, intermediaries and colleges are complex and varied. There is no clear hierarchy or linear top-down approach, and many innovative ideas from the colleges work their way into government policy.

Centralisation versus decentralisation

Objectives, content, co-ordination, degree of deregulation, support policies and strategies of introduction are largely determined by government, which influences the colleges' teaching and institutional organisation both indirectly through intermediaries and directly through legislation. College amalgamations and expansion and the use of devolved budgets, for example, have a direct influence on the teaching process. Administrative and organisational policy objectives include:
- amalgamations and expansion as a way of achieving other goals, such as greater differentiation of learning pathways and the strengthening of middle management;
- greater autonomy through the use of devolved budgets, contract activities (the sale of training services) and freedom to determine staff recruitment and organisation of establishments;
- stronger management and administration.

The government has also influenced the organisation of education by introducing a new sectoral structure in senior secondary vocational education (MBO), something it had previously done in higher vocational education (HBO) as part of the STC rationalisation programme. It has also issued regulations covering admission requirements, student guidance, learning targets, examinations and certification.

All this implies a centrally directed strategy implemented in decentralised fashion, with a margin of discretion for the various actors. The government has succeeded in setting up temporary intermediary machinery to co-ordinate the process of sector formation and renewal and force colleges to amalgamate. In relation to its administrative and organisational goals, the operation has been a success. It remains to be seen whether the same is true in relation to its renewal goals.

Evaluative studies are under way concerning the effects both of devolved budgets and of contract activities. When resources are scarce, the effect of devolved budgets can be counterproductive; moreover, the financial and other effects of contract activities, such as the sale of training services, is unclear. The establishment of new legal structures – independent agencies – has taken contract activities outside colleges' control and influence, with the result that their innovative impact, e.g. on the curriculum, may be negligible. Strong influence from industry can be expected at local and regional level as a result of mergers and expansion, relative autonomy and provision for contract activities. Nationally set learning targets may take on a regional dimension reflecting the preferences of dominant industries or firms, thereby limiting mobility and the substitution of components of the curriculum.

Public and private education: responsibilities and provision

In the process of the merging and expansion of colleges, a greater role has been accorded to religious denomination than to organisational homogeneity (e.g. concentration by or specialisation in sectors). Self-preservation is the main motivation for this identification. A similar process has occurred in higher vocational education (HBO); multi-site institutions were the outcome, and their co-ordination, management and efficiency are open to criticism. It is possible, however, that the principles of autonomy and externally oriented flexibility will have an affect at each site.

Legislation and negotiation

The purpose of allowing colleges to sell training services was to strengthen and stimulate information flows between colleges and firms and thus promote curricular innovation. It was assumed that industry was more innovative than education, and that contract activities could enable the latter to tap the innovative capacity of the former and elaborate new curricula. The legislation which introduced contract activities is now being evaluated, but speculations about possible negative effects are as follows:

- advanced knowledge relating to products and product development not covered by patents are not released;
- firms do not release sensitive information which could benefit their competitors;
- firms within a region tend to promote the transmission of the kinds of knowledge that will help them to select workers quickly and efficiently, so that the effect of introducing new skills and techniques will be conservative rather than innovative;
- colleges cannot develop innovative products without good equipment and a foundation of solid co-operation;
- commercially innovative and profitable products developed by colleges tend to be removed from mainstream education, so that renewal goals are not achieved;
- high-level expertise is more likely to be sold by colleges than imported through firms;
- the scope for renewal and increased flexibility through contract activities is thus limited and subject to the law of supply and demand.

Legislation governing the structure and content of education (e.g. the learning targets set by the Minister) can be an important tool in the promotion of mobility and substitution. The targets must be both general in scope and amenable to being used in specific contexts within the relevant programmes.

Planning and experimentation

There are many stages in the reform and renewal of vocational education, a process that began in the mid-1970s. The system is changing from one divided into specialist sectors, to an integrated, large-scale and coherent system of relatively autonomous colleges.

There have been pilot projects in vocational education involving participative learning, modular programmes, etc., but their results have been very limited, if not negative. Experiments, such as those regularly taking place in Germany to test out particular ideas, are rare in the Netherlands, aside from the 14 projects involving comprehensive schools for the 12-16 age range and the Open School experiments. The inspiration often comes from below, with individual schools and colleges taking on particular aspects of a given innovation. Controlled innovation involving explicit ideas, for example in the area of simulations, is rare. The effect is that system innovation of the type outlined is influenced little if at all by programme evaluation research; the dominant influence on decision making lies with the political process.

Organisational flexibility and its effects

The ends, means and effects relating to "flexibility" are to be found at at least three levels: central government, intermediary institutions and individual colleges.

a) Government

The government has achieved a number of its objectives through the legislation that has been implemented, including institutional mergers and expansion, devolved budgets, contract activities, and providing senior management with greater administrative powers. Research is currently under way to evaluate the success of these reforms (see for example Brandsma, 1990). Achievement of the goals relating to flexible preparation for work will depend to a great extent on the institutions, and while colleges are taking an active role this is under pressure from the government. Institutions at intermediary level play an active and encouraging role. Whether implementation of a dual system will help ensure that programmes at all levels of vocational education respond flexibly to industry's needs, as the Rauwenhoff Committee suggested, remains to be seen.

b) Intermediary level

Intermediaries in vocational education can play an important role in facilitating implementation of the policies of both government and the colleges. Although colleges still lack the capacity to undertake for themselves development tasks in areas including curriculum, organisation, management and marketing, regional advisory centres for vocational guidance provide vital links between government and the colleges, and between the colleges themselves. In time, however, they will lose their current functions as new consultative structures are formed and the large colleges become self-sufficient in these areas. This has already happened in higher vocational education. In terms of substantive renewal, intermediaries are facilitating the achievement of short-term goals and influencing policy in the medium to long term.

c) The colleges

As far as the colleges are concerned, organisational flexibility affects external factors which influence the colleges' decision-making process. A proactive orientation towards the labour market which actively anticipates and effectively responds to developments, is the main condition for success in terms of providing benefits to society and access to employment or further study.

An infrastructure is needed which can translate information into internal policy. College managements must ensure their organisation's secondary process serves its primary function, the teaching and learning process. This is crucial to the achievement of a flexible and effective response to external factors. The conditions here are however in the primary process. It is noteworthy that this process is largely steered by differentiation principles:

- gearing the provision of education to heterogeneous intakes;

- diversifying provision to allow horizontal transfers and vertical progression through modularisation;

- differentiating final assessment (partial qualification certificates);

- opening access.

Conclusion

The political process has generated a fascinating panoply of regulations and procedures which are proving effective at government level. While the effect of intermediaries is not too clear, it is generally agreed that they play a significant role. The interplay of forces is diffuse and may eventually lose some of its effect, as the large merged colleges take over this function. The true test of effectiveness is through programme evaluation. The sector-formation and renewal operation can serve as a case for examination.

Quality control and programme evaluation

Quality control and programme evaluation are important means of maintaining the responsiveness of vocational education. This is true in at least two respects: in determining the extent to which vocational education meets society's changing needs, and in determining how far the right balance is struck between the different functions – preparation for work, personal development, social and cultural education – of vocational education as a relatively autonomous social subsystem. This section focuses on how quality control and programme evaluation are organised in the Netherlands. Unless otherwise indicated, the discussion relates to initial vocational education.

The initial situation

The notion of quality has traditionally been closely associated with the level and standards of education. Formally, the government set the learning targets for vocational programmes, while the ultimate instrument of assessment is a national examination. The

Education Inspectorate has a statutory duty to monitor standards, among other things by ensuring that learning targets can be met. The government's influence on programme content is in fact relatively slight; in practice, quality control, notably as regards process rather than product, lies with the teachers.

The importance of learning targets as an element in product quality control is clear. The curricula that colleges ultimately delivered were derived from framework curricula compiled by various organisations and committees with links to the provider institutions. While their status was purely advisory, the framework curricula were generally adopted with no changes.

Sectoral consultations and learning targets

During the sector-formation and renewal exercise, sectoral consultative councils were established to draw up learning targets; this followed publication of a policy statement entitled "Job profiles and curriculum development". Since then, industry has been given a more explicit role in this process, with employers' organisations and trade unions both involved in the "royal road" leading from occupational profiles to learning targets. Responsibilities have been clearly divided, in that industry (including both employers and unions) compiles occupational profiles while industry and education together draw up learning targets.

The sectoral consultative councils submit their recommendations to the Minister of Education and Science, who is ultimately responsible for setting learning targets. This effectively formalises earlier practice. The formulation of learning targets by the sectoral councils replaces the formulation of examination syllabuses by ad hoc committees.

There appear to be at least two possible sources of tension here:
– The relationship between nationally set learning targets and the colleges' margin for discretion, which depends, among other things, on how detailed the learning targets are. This will in large part determine the degree of national uniformity or regional differentiation. The tendency seems to lean towards national targets defined in broad terms.
– The criteria applied in translating occupational profiles into learning targets (which in some cases differ from one sector to another). The "power relations" between the various parties involved and views as to the degree of autonomy of vocational education vis-à-vis current occupational practice are two factors that will influence the selection of criteria.

Greater emphasis on quality control

The rapid growth of interest in quality control in vocational education is the result of two developments (see also Pelkmans and De Vries, 1991):
– market forces have compelled industry to place greater emphasis on the quality of finished products (and to rationalise production processes);
– a new management philosophy has taken root in vocational education, whereby the colleges themselves now have greater responsibility for the quality of the education provided.

Quality control has recently been stressed in various quarters as a central concern in vocational education, with a growing emphasis on the college level. Of relevance here are the Rauwenhoff Committee's recommendations for the establishment of systems of internal and external quality control by the colleges on the basis of agreements with their customers (i.e. employers). The Committee also proposed inspection visits by external experts and a system of funding based on results.

The Rauwenhoff proposals relating to quality control are patterned on the system developed in higher education, with an additional role allotted to sectoral organisations. While generally accepting the Committee's recommendations, the government has opted for national qualification requirements. The system of quality control is to comprise three elements (Pelkmans and De Vries, 1991):
- exploratory studies, to be carried out by the sectoral organisations concerned, which will produce material used for example in the development of learning targets;
- internal evaluation and external accountability through a system of annual reports (including information on success rates);
- regular inspection visits by committees of experts.

Initial annual public reports points to a widespread need for better college record keeping and greater expertise on the part of the system's users. Recent research on renewal in senior secondary vocational education (MBO) has shown that the development of quality control at college level is still in its infancy and moreover that there is considerable disagreement as to what quality control means (Pelkmans and De Vries, 1991). Among the colleges surveyed, eight per cent claimed to have a system of quality control or that detailed plans for one had been drawn up, 44 per cent replied that plans were being developed and the other 48 per cent stated that planning had yet to begin. The colleges tend to focus greater attention on internal than on external quality control, giving highest priority to planning, internal evaluation and reporting. So far, less use is being made of quality-control instruments oriented towards the colleges' economic and social environment.

Conclusion and evaluation

Quality control and evaluation were, until recently, unexplored territory in Dutch vocational education. However, they are now a central focus of attention in policy documents, for example, in the context of educational renewal. Although quality control in vocational education is very recent it is possible to make some general conclusions:

i) The statutorily prescribed procedure ("the royal road") for translating occupational profiles into learning targets is dominated by the "direct match" strategy. This strategy seeks to improve the fit between what education delivers and what industry requires by matching learning targets directly to industry's needs. However, it has certain limitations: insufficient attention is paid for example to processes of *Verberuflichung* and *Entberuflichung* (the appearance of new occupations and disappearance of old ones), to the existence of very divergent sub-markets and to competition from other programmes (with a possible crowding-out effect). Furthermore, the innovative potential of vocational programmes vis-à-vis employment structures is underestimated. This does not necessarily imply automatic support for a strategy of flexibility as the central policy instrument for improving the education-employment fit; moreover, scope for such improvement already exists, thanks to the emphasis on regionalisation, the encouragement of contacts between colleges and employers and moves towards dualisation. Because the flexibility strategy gives no clear guide to the substance of vocational programmes or to changes needed in it, a basic principle is needed to determine the content of initial vocational programmes.

ii) The recent concern with quality control in institutions providing full-time vocational education does not extend to dual forms of training, particularly their practical component. Greater emphasis on quality control is needed in this area, not least in the light of the declared policy of dualising elements of full-time vocational education.

iii) With regard to quality-control criteria, it is noteworthy that little or no explicit attention is focused on the relationship between the vocational and general components of vocational education.

iv) Despite the fact that the quality of education has always depended in practice on the teachers, heavy responsibility is being placed on college management without any explicit reference to their power to influence teachers' professional autonomy.

Certification

Career aspects

Certification plays a major role in Dutch general and vocational education, in relation to progression to further study and entry into employment. Access to virtually all forms of post-compulsory (i.e. post-age-16) education is dependent on entrants possessing certain certificates and having reached certain levels. Even elementary training programmes to junior practitioner level, whether in the apprenticeship system or senior secondary vocational education (MBO), generally apply admission requirements. However, access to shorter MBO programmes (KMBO) is by law open, and bridging programmes are therefore provided to bring entrants without qualifications up to the necessary level for elementary training. Such bridging programmes also form part of training policy for older unskilled workers and non-traditional target groups such as women returning to the workforce and immigrants.

Certification is not only relevant to admission to vocational programmes: in the hierarchical structure of Dutch education, certificates also play an important role in progression through the system. Entrants to most vocational programmes at upper secondary or higher level must hold a vocational qualification for the preceding level or a post-16 general qualification. This applies both to the publicly financed system of vocational education and to the various programmes provided by firms or groups of firms.

The qualifications obtained in mainstream initial education play an important role in entry into employment: the level youngsters reach in their education determines, to a great extent, the level at which they begin their working lives. This starting level is not a fixed variable: in his thesis, Teulings (1990) showed that the state of the economy also has a major impact. In the first half of the 1980s, holders of junior vocational education (LBO) certificates were pushed into marginal areas of the labour market marked by unskilled work and high unemployment rates. By 1991 the LBO certificate and its image had yet to recover from this blow. This is one of the reasons why small- and medium-sized manufacturing and craft enterprises are having great difficulty in recruiting employees at junior practitioner level.

The value and effect of the qualifications obtained in mainstream initial education thus cannot be expressed in terms of absolute levels; rather, they determine individuals' competitive position in the struggle for decent first jobs and career prospects. An alternative route is provided by the dual system, in which apprentices spend part of their time working and learning on the job. Van der Velden (1989) has shown that the employment position of holders of advanced apprenticeship certificates is actually better than that of those with MBO qualifications, although there are more practical obstacles on this route.

While formal qualifications thus play a major role, particularly at the start of people's working lives, they are gradually becoming less important as work experience and employment history take a more important place. In statistical terms, however, the effect of qualifications persists, given their considerable influence on individuals' starting position.

Implementation

Schools and colleges have a statutory responsibility for the conduct of examinations and issuance of certificates. The national bodies for the apprenticeship system and MBO colleges appoint examining boards and decide examination syllabuses on the basis of the learning targets which the Minister of Education sets. The examination and examination syllabus may be divided into sections, corresponding to certification units. These units are also determined by the Minister, on the recommendation of the national bodies; moreover, they must relate to clusters of skills and areas of knowledge which are separately identifiable in occupational practice. Certificates are worthwhile only if they bring some benefit in employment terms. In practice, industry and education must agree at the national level on the targets of the various vocational programmes, relying on the advice of the national bodies, with the colleges monitoring and maintaining standards through examination procedures. The colleges then generally obtain further help from industry by including external experts in their examining boards.

Examination procedures vary sharply from one programme to another, particularly as regards the place of practical work. In the apprenticeship system, theory and practice have equal importance in the final mark, and candidates must pass in both. Written procedures are used in the theoretical section, while on the practical side candidates work through a book of assignments which are marked by the employer and the national commission consultant. Practical work has a less prominent role in MBO short and regular programmes; the work placement is only one of the certification units of the examination syllabus, although a pass mark for the placement is often required before a certificate can be issued. Students transferring from senior secondary to higher technical education do not have to complete a work placement and are therefore often issued with a certificate covering the theoretical section of the programme only, rather than a full diploma of senior secondary technical education.

Renewal

The division of examination syllabuses into certification units, a fairly new phenomenon in the Netherlands, is a response to pressures for greater flexibility in vocational education and the associated modularisation of syllabuses. It can, however, be argued that moves to increase flexibility in initial vocational education can also be justified on internal educational grounds (see for example Meesterberends-Harms and Nieuwenhuis, 1989): a more flexible, modular approach is needed to accommodate students' individual requirements and capabilities, while shorter curricular units are said to enhance the motivation and commitment, particularly of the less able.

There are, however, indications that industry does not entirely welcome attempts to achieve a flexible match between education and employment through greater differentiation of school-leaver profiles. Firms suggest that differentiation is jeopardising both the transparency of qualifications and college leavers' employment prospects. Nonetheless, both sides of industry benefit from clarity as to the meaning of qualifications and programme certificates. Employers have an interest in relation to market position (particular qualifications are a statutory requirement in many sectors), and nationally recognised certificates show what knowledge and skills new employees can be expected to possess. Employees benefit because clear and familiar qualifications strengthen their position on internal and external labour markets; qualifications also affect individuals' career and promotion prospects, notably where specific provisions in this area are included in collective agreements. Both employers and unions, therefore, favour uniform and complete initial training programmes.

Such uniformity has value not only in relation to initial education and training: unambiguous qualifications are often also desirable in continuing training, and in various industrial sectors private programme provision must have a "stamp of approval" issued by the sectoral organisation if it is to receive sectoral funding. Employers are, of course, free to buy training services elsewhere, but here too, both employers and workers benefit from clear formulation.

Qualifications in the form of national diplomas and certificates limit the flexibility of the education and training system, in that they imply fixed assessment procedures and consultative bodies in which agreement has to be reached, but both employers and workers argue that the labour market benefits from a system in which at least some qualifications take this form. The necessary flexibility of qualification can be achieved in two ways: by ensuring that colleges and consultative bodies respond quickly to changing circumstances in the workplace and modify syllabuses accordingly, and by developing a diversified and responsive system of continuing training on and off the job. If programmes and qualifications are to be of value to the individual and to society, some measure of inflexibility is inevitable.

Funding sources and systems

Sources

This section focuses on ways in which changes in funding systems can help enhance the responsiveness of vocational education. First, however, we look at the various sources of finance. Education is divided into two main sectors, the "public" and the "private". The public sector is funded chiefly through taxation, although a small but growing contribution comes from fees and charges of various types. Some of the schools are publicly funded but privately run institutions, which often levy charges on parents and may have resources of their own.

In recent years public institutions have increasingly earned income of their own through the sale of training and research services. The universities and colleges of higher vocational education have been able to engage in such contract activities for some time; furthermore, similar powers have recently been given to institutions at the upper secondary level. The public sector also includes certain types of adult education, some of them also funded by other ministries such as Economic Affairs, and Social Affairs and Employment.

The private sector includes various forms of work-based training and private institutions offering face-to-face and distance tuition. The sources of funding are various. The private institutions are entirely funded from fees paid by programme participants (or often by their employers), while work-based training is generally funded by employers.

Systems

The different parts of the public sector are served by different funding systems. A common feature is that separate arrangements exist for the three main spending categories, namely staff, buildings (capital costs) and operating costs (books, equipment, heating, maintenance, management, administration etc.). Funding for a given category of institution depends on: *a)* numbers of students, *b)* the average length of study programmes, *c)* group size, *d)* teachers' salary levels.

Two funding models can be distinguished; one in which formulas based on general criteria determine the amount of funding, and one in which actual expenditures are defrayed, subject to a set of rules. Institutions' freedom to decide how their budget is used is greater under formula-based systems, and recent years have seen a clear trend towards these. The system of block grants introduced into senior secondary vocational education (MBO) under the legislation governing the sector-formation and renewal operation is an example of formula-based budgeting. The shift from cost defrayment to formula budgeting is discussed below, looking in turn at staffing, capital and operating costs.

Staffing costs

In the coming years, staffing costs in vocational education will be covered by two systems: establishment-related budgets in pre-vocational education (formerly junior vocational education) and block grants elsewhere. Under the establishment-based system, schools receive a certain number of units which they can use to "buy" posts of varying value. These are then funded on the basis of the actual costs incurred. Compared with the previous system of cost defrayment, this gives schools greater freedom, in that they can now transfer funds between different categories of posts, which was not previously permitted. Under the block-grant system, institutions receive a sum of money based on certain objective criteria to cover their staffing costs; they can then use it as they see fit, subject to certain minimum requirements.

Operating costs

Operating costs are covered by block grants in all forms of vocational education. Major elements in the formula used to determine the size of an institution's grant include numbers of pupils or students and the floor area of the premises in square metres.

Equipment costs

Equipment costs are covered by block grants based on approved budgets. A novel element in the system is that, except in pre-vocational (pre-16) education, the State sells or will sell the buildings to the institutions, which are able to borrow money for this purpose. The notion is that if colleges receive a fixed sum to cover accommodation they will use their buildings as efficiently as possible. The burden of management at national level is thereby also relieved.

Spending freedom

The introduction of formula-based block grants has thus given the great majority of vocational schools and colleges greater freedom in the use of their budgets in all three spending categories. Institutions may transfer funds from one area to another according to their needs. They can thus make their own decisions, responding to their economic and social environment; the development of contract activities, such as the sale of training and research services, fits into this framework. Such reforms mean that colleges increasingly operate as open systems interacting with their environments. Combined with the changes in the regulations governing staff rights and duties, they give the institutions greater opportunities to gear their activities to particular needs and to give people working in industry a direct involvement in education.

6. Sectoral Analyses

As part of the Dutch VOTEC project, research was done into the changing role of vocational and technical education and training including case studies of developments in four sectors, showing how the education system has sought to respond to or guide these changes. The general analysis of developments in Dutch vocational education of the preceding chapters is thus complemented and deepened with the help of analyses of the relationship between vocational education and its associated occupational fields. The case-study findings are summarised below.

Trainers, markets, occupations

As in industry and employment, there are sectoral divisions in vocational education. These divisions are not always clear-cut. Some vocational programmes are geared to a specific category of occupation, defined and identifiable as a coherent set of occupational activities; others are geared to a market sector, defined and identifiable as a network of institutional actors. In many but by no means all cases there is overlap between occupational categories and industry sectors. Programmes in such areas as business studies and office practice are geared to occupations in many industrial sectors, for example, while tourism programmes focus on one industrial sector with various occupational categories.

The dynamic nature of industry and employment and economic, organisational and technological developments mean that old sectors are destroyed and new ones created, while the boundaries between occupational categories often become blurred. The advent of new technologies, particularly in the information field, have given rise to new occupational categories, for example, while the growth of the welfare State and private affluence has generated new markets. Vocational education responds to such developments; it can also play a part in determining new boundaries.

It follows from the above that the role of vocational education in meeting employers' needs can only be analysed in specific sectoral contexts. One must first define the occupational category or industrial sector to which a particular programme or set of programmes relates and then consider its stage of development. An occupation can be seen as a coherent domain of knowledge and skills, a unified set of activities, for which individuals can be formally prepared. Sectors, and their stage of development, can be determined based on to the extent to which such coherence and unity exist. Changes can be seen chiefly as shifts in the pattern of occupational activities, with corresponding shifts in the knowledge and skills needed (which may be followed or initiated by vocational institutions).

An occupation can also be seen as a means for practitioners to secure their interests (with a vocational qualification as formal recognition). In this case sectors and their stage of development can be determined (based on the recognition they receive from competing occupational groups). Changes must then be seen as aspects or effects of a strategic interplay of forces and process of institutionalisation (within which vocational education is itself a major actor).

Specific training is thus an instrument both for achieving a certain unity of occupational activity and for defining and maintaining that unity. Where unity is manifested both as a coherent set of knowledge and skill domains and as a defined institutional network, the role of vocational training programmes is clear. Specific training legitimates the existence of the sector by preparing people for a particular occupation or occupations. In most cases, however, the two defining aspects of an occupation or sector do not coincide, with the result that its unity is constantly under threat. In new sectors there is unity in neither aspect, and the role of vocational education is mainly one of definition and recognition; in diffuse sectors, where there are widely different jobs and tasks, vocational education will always have this function. In long-established sectors, where there is greater unity of occupational activity, vocational education plays a part in maintaining and safeguarding

56

the boundaries. These contextual variations are clearly visible in the sectors studied in this book and are briefly outlined below.

Tourism, the first industry examined, is a growth sector with employment mainly concentrated in the four sectors of hotel and catering, transport and communications, culture and recreation, and commerce. In 1989 some 40-50 000 firms (10-12 per cent of all firms in the country) were largely or wholly dependent on tourism and leisure; in the same year the sector employed around 230 000 people, eleven per cent of the Dutch labour force in the private sector. In the Netherlands two subsectors are normally distinguished, namely the hotel and catering industry and its younger sibling, tourism and leisure; these two subsectors have experienced separate development, including in the training field. The case study focused particularly on the tourism and leisure side, which includes some 13 000 mainly small- and medium-sized firms and has a workforce of 60-70 000.

The printing industry is relatively small and tightly organised. At the beginning of 1990 there were just over 3 000 firms, most of them small. Of the sector's 1990 workforce of 62 000, 65-70 per cent were directly involved in printing work. The sector's boundaries are laid down in collective agreements (CAOs) dating from 1914: it comprises firms and employees whose organisations are covered by the relevant CAO. The boundaries of printing work in the technical sense are harder to define, however, since not all those who engage in it are organised. Economic, organisational and technical developments are causing sectoral boundaries to blur, in that printing work is now also done in other sectors.

The third sector studied is that of installation, a general term covering a range of craft and technical occupations with a long history; its early practitioners included plumbers and tinsmiths, but it now encompasses for example the installation of central-heating and air-conditioning systems and the work of gasfitters, bathroom and kitchen installers and roofers. There are some 4 400 mainly small firms undertaking this type of work; in 1989 they employed almost 44 000 people. Here too, there has been a blurring of boundaries between formerly distinct crafts and techniques, leading to mergers between trade organisations and indeed between training systems.

The final area studied is less a sector as such than an area of process and product innovation in the engineering industry, namely the introduction of computer-numerically controlled (CNC) equipment and flexible automated production. Though highly specific, the impact of this technological development is considerable in terms of its spread through industry and its effects on occupational practice. In 1985 it is estimated that there were 12 500 CNC machines in use in 6 000 Dutch firms. Some 263 000 people are employed in metal machining, around 45 per cent of them in small- and medium-sized firms. Around 20 000, or seven per cent of all workers in this sector, are directly concerned with the introduction and use of CNC equipment.

The match between education and employment

A broad distinction may be made between quantitative and qualitative aspects of the match between the education system's "output" and the needs of industry and society at large: a quantitative mismatch occurs where there is a discrepancy between the demand for and supply of workers with particular qualifications, while a qualitative mismatch exists when the content of qualifications is out of line with industry's needs. The segmentation of the labour market and the heterogeneity of the world of work are such that the two types of mismatch are closely related.

Each sector has its own problems of match. Comparison of the sectors studied illustrates the dynamics involved in the processes and the problems found at the interface between education and employment. Bearing in mind the distinction made above between occupational categories and industrial sectors (and developments in each) this section outlines the links between:

i) economic and social developments and the nature of mismatch problems;

ii) technological developments and changes in mismatch problems;

iii) the speed of and relationships between developments and changes in the nature and structure of mismatch problems.

What follows is not intended as an exhaustive analysis of problems at the education-employment interface; rather its dynamics will be outlined on the basis of noteworthy points from the case studies.

Economic developments

Internationalisation, demand for new products and services, increased competition and higher quality standards all affect the nature of problems at the interface between education and employment. The case studies revealed that economic developments in a sector play a part in determining the nature of the problem.

The relatively new tourism and leisure sector, for example, developed in response to new demand, and its origins are reflected in the problems at the education-employment interface. While tourism and leisure constitute an industrial sector rather than an occupational category (in that the set of occupational activities involved is not unified and unambiguous), the main actors within the sector believe that there are certain activities which characterise it and for which skills and knowledge not relevant to other occupational categories are required. This view is shared by some in the vocational education field as indicated by the development of specific tourism and leisure programmes. The interface problem in this sector therefore relates, first, to the definition of a core of occupational practice and the nature of the qualifications required. Vocational education is "forced" to focus on what is specific to the sector and to develop programmes which are distinct from those geared to other industrial sectors and occupational categories. This process of differentiation is also relevant to the education-employment interface.

In older and more established sectors, such as the technical sectors studied, vocational provision does not need to be so concerned about its distinctive features. Indeed, it may have a vital interest in taking account of developments elsewhere: in printing and installation, for example, providers of education must be alert to parallel developments in other sectors, since by incorporating them into programmes they strengthen their own position. Here interface problems are more likely to be expressed in terms of "workers who are not flexible enough or whose training is too narrow".

58

Interface problems, and indeed the extent to which something is seen as a problem, are also affected by the economic situation. Here too, there are variations from sector to sector, with tensions in the relationship between education and employment being much more sensitive to the economic situation in the installation sector than in printing. The recession of the early 1980s persuaded employers in the installation sector that greater efforts and investment were needed in education and training: current shortages of well-trained and experienced practitioners partly reflect past neglect in this area. In the printing industry, both employers' and workers' organisations have always placed great emphasis on education and training and their activity has been less affected by the state of the economy. The difference here is between preventive and curative action; to some extent it is one of timing.

Technological developments

In the technical sectors studied, technological developments have caused new tensions in the relationship between education and employment. In many cases technological changes and the associated organisational changes have led to the disappearance of some jobs, the appearance of others and a redefinition of knowledge and skill requirements.

Technological and associated organisational changes may permanently raise job levels and qualification requirements. But the effects are not necessarily all in the same direction: some jobs may become more complex and demanding while the content of others is simplified. There may also be differences between firms and groups of firms. Where the introduction of CNC equipment extends the machine operator's job to include programming, the level of knowledge and understanding required is maintained or raised; where programming is not included in the job, such knowledge and understanding may lose importance as compared with operating skills.

The speed of technological change appears to create a tension between the traditional core of occupational practice and new demands for knowledge and skills. This has been particularly evident in the case of CNC technology and the flexible automation of production, but similar tensions are visible in the printing industry. Product and process innovations appear to be leading to a different definition of "professionalism": the printing sector opted in the first instance to retain the hard core of print craftsmanship together with an outer layer which is adapted as developments require and to which qualification requirements are geared. The engineering sector has responded to CNC and flexible production automation by formulating a new "professionalism".

In all cases, however, tensions remain between specialist and generalist and between the exercise of more abstract understanding and skills on the one hand and operating skills on the other.

Rates of change and interactions

Organisational and economic as well as technological developments lead to changes in occupational practice, and where all three coincide, their interaction reinforces their impact. Moreover the rate at which developments succeed one another shows no sign of slackening. Both the speed of changes and the interaction between different kinds of changes affect the nature of problems at the education-employment interface.

First, rapid technological and other developments are leading to greater points of similarity between jobs, both in the same sector and in different sectors: there is growing convergence between occupational categories. This trend is visible in the printing industry, for example, mainly as a consequence of process innovations. In installation, overlap between subsectors is growing as a result of product innovations: where formerly subsectors were marked by specific job activities, nowadays it is common for similar methods, materials and equipment to be used throughout the sector.

Second, it is becoming increasingly difficult to draw a line between knowledge and skills acquired in initial education and training and the requirements of occupational practice; this reflects the fact that particular sets of knowledge and skills are now only useful for relatively short periods. The 1980s and 1990s have brought increasing changes in job content, while mobility, both within and between firms, has also increased.

A cautious conclusion might be that the problems at the education-employment interface arise chiefly from the fact that workers are increasingly required to possess a combination of transferable skills (knowledge and skills which can be applied in a variety of situations) and transfer skills (the ability to apply them to new situations). The challenge facing the education system is to find an appropriate response to this trend and to meet new qualification requirements; employers must then make full use of the knowledge and skills with which their workers have been equipped by taking appropriate measures in such areas as the quality of work, the quality of training policies etc. Industry and the education system together face the task of shaping learning processes that focus on transferable skills and the ability to transfer skills.

Tackling problems at the education-employment interface

Various instruments exist for dealing with problems of mismatch at the interface between education and employment. These instruments include quantitative estimates of personnel requirements, analyses of changing qualification requirements, the supply of work and training places, the restructuring of training provision, curriculum innovation and quality control. The nature of the instrument depends on the nature of the problem identified, the specific sectoral context in which it is to be used and on decisions as to the most effective problem-solving strategy. In each case instruments may be geared either to achieving an exact match between educational qualifications and industry's needs (direct matching strategy) or to breaking down barriers between vocational programmes and occupational practice and developing an intermediary system (flexibility strategy). Both the nature and the purpose of the instruments are considered.

Quantitative estimates of personnel requirements

Instruments have been developed in all sectors to estimate the present and future supply of and demand for qualified personnel. Such estimates provide a basis for the management of the labour market and are particularly useful to employers. In the printing industry, the estimates are an important guide for all concerned; such consensus has its roots in the tight institutional network that prevails in the industry (see below).

Sectors vary in the extent to which account is taken of dynamic elements in the relationship between supply and demand. In tourism and leisure, for example, a somewhat rigid calculation was made of supply and demand on the basis of definitions included in an agreement which was very much the product of a particular time. In this young industry it is very difficult to assess the supply side, since employees operate satisfactorily with a variety of both vocational and non-vocational qualifications. It is also difficult to estimate the industry's future need for trained workers for the same reason, and moreover, in a sector seeking to develop an identity of its own, an acceleration can be expected in the demand for staff with specific qualifications. This point is also made by the training institutions who argue that there is as yet no surplus of people with tourism and leisure qualifications, although organisations within the industry have warned that the situation as they see it is one of serious oversupply.

Estimates of present and future supply and demand are also used in other sectors. Such estimates appear more useful in, for example, the installation sector, where occupational patterns are reasonably clear and stable, though here too some crystal-gazing is involved: as similarities between occupational categories grow, should those who complete programmes outside the sectoral training system also be included in supply calculations? And how far can the demand for workers at a particular level be quantified when experience shows that, as in the case of technological innovations, it may not become clear for a long time at what level jobs should be evaluated? Such estimates can serve only strategic goals, while a fixation on figures may adversely affect the training system's flexibility.

Analysis of changing qualification requirements

The definition of changes in qualification requirements is a very complex matter; the speed of economic, organisational and technological changes, parallel and successive, has focused growing attention on this point in the last ten years. In many cases the worlds of education and industry have commissioned analyses from outside experts. In the Netherlands, occupational analyses have been carried out for many occupational categories and industrial sectors with a view to charting qualification requirements and the changes taking place therein; the results are intended to provide educational institutions with a basis for the formulation of learning targets and design of training syllabuses.

An initial problem in the cases studied concerned the boundaries within which occupational practice should be analysed. In the printing industry the boundaries are set by the collective agreements between the relevant employers' organisations and unions. On the grounds of strategic considerations, adjacent vocational areas are also covered (to cover the field as a whole).

In the installation trades the demarcation process was used in part to confirm the merger of two sectors. The new sector boundaries can be traced back to the old craft occupations, and only firms whose main activities are in installation are considered part of it. Here again the types of work which characterise the installation sector are also found outside it; there are also similarities with other occupational categories such as engineers. Related vocational fields are not, however, included in the analyses.

In the case of tourism and leisure the problem was more substantive. The boundaries of the tourist industry were set in relation to production (tourism and leisure spending); opinions differed as to the definition of tourism. All firms contributing to that production were counted as part of the sector, along with their employees, and the characteristic features of work in tourism and leisure were left somewhat ill-defined. One tourism and leisure subsector, the hotel and catering industry, could be clearly identified, since it had developed as a sector in its own right with its own training system; the remaining elements were designated as a separate sector under the name tourism and leisure (visits and excursions, travel and holidays, swimming and water sports, agency services). It remained unclear what should or should not be included as occupational activities within the sector, which lacked the kind of job-classification system that existed elsewhere. The sector's boundaries were eventually settled through a prolonged process of negotiation among the parties concerned. The consensus achieved is rooted chiefly in agreement as to what the sector is not (how it differs from other sectors and occupational categories) rather than what the sector and its occupations are.

A second problem concerns the manner in which occupational practice is analysed. While detailed surveys were made of occupational practice in all cases, the analyses did not always clarify the picture of the knowledge and skills required. The occupational profiles found mainly show the changing tasks performed by practitioners on the basis of evaluations of their occurrence. Even though economic, technological and organisational developments are leading in many cases to the integration of jobs and increasing similarities between occupational categories, the occupational analyses generally produced a considerable number of different profiles (10-20 within a sector), even though unskilled work and the jobs done by higher education graduates were largely excluded.

What emerges is the complexity of formulating qualification requirements at a level that transcends the requirements of particular jobs. If vocational education is to use occupational profiles as a support a measure of breadth is needed: initial vocational education is not geared to specific jobs. The importance of breadth in the initial phase is underlined by the speed and nature of developments in occupational practice as workers are increasingly required to possess specific knowledge and skills, of changing kinds, which initial education could not (and should not) seek specifically to impart. Most occupational profiles are not formulated at a level transcending specific jobs, however; most comprise a summary of concrete tasks which the job holder must be able to perform, and these tasks tend to be specific to a particular job at a particular point in time. Qualification requirements are not normally included in occupational profiles.

Work and training placements

Moves to alleviate problems at the education-employment interface include measures by and aimed at the world of education which are designed to adapt the "product" (knowledge and skills as attested in formal vocational qualifications) to the "market" (the knowledge and skills required by employers). At the same time many employers are taking measures to make better use of the "product", building on it or developing it further. Here the role of work and training placements will be considered.

In three of the four sectors studied, there are both full-time college-based programmes and apprenticeship programmes combining four days of work and one day of study each week. While both types of programme exist in printing and installation the emphasis continues to be on training through the apprenticeship system. In the engineering field there are roughly equal numbers of students in apprenticeship and full-time programmes. No apprenticeship programmes exist in tourism and recreation, where all training is provided by full-time vocational colleges or commercial training institutions; commercially provided programmes are combined with prior general education and subsequent learning on the job when individuals begin their careers.

A major feature of apprentice training is the provision by employers of combined work and training places. Their number has at least doubled over the last ten years, in the sectors studied as elsewhere. Full-time college-based programmes also include placements in industry of varying length; only in tourism and leisure do colleges sometimes have difficulty in obtaining sufficient placements, mainly owing to the relative newness of their programmes.

Regarding the quality of the work and training places provided for apprentices, the picture is rather less clear. Reflecting among other things employers' growing recognition of the importance of developing effective training policies, the quality of placement supervision appears to have improved. Apprentices may spend part of their placement in special training workshops etc. (particularly at the start of training, when employers feel that apprentices cannot yet be deployed in the production process), but while this may make the placement less realistic its development value need not suffer; indeed, simulated situations are sometimes so well designed that learning while working is more effective than in a "real" job in the production process. Another trend is that work and training places are increasingly provided not by individual employers but by groups of firms co-operating for the purpose; the practical element of apprentice training is thus removed from the individual firm. This is an interesting development in relation to quality control (particularly as regards "breadth") and the issue of transfer value.

Restructuring training provision

Among steps taken to improve the match between education and employment, industrial sectors have often restructured and expanded training provision. The analyses of occupational practice to which reference has been made have in some cases both prompted a restructuring of sectoral provision and generated information for use in the process.

In some sectors initial training provision has been expanded and externalised in recent years, with initial programmes being more closely geared to work in the sector concerned. Training in, for example, installation trades was for a long time largely internal, with the apprenticeship system playing a major role; more recently full-time vocational education has increasingly offered programmes in this field. In tourism and leisure, youth with broad qualifications used to enter the sector through one or more mainstream programmes, short commercial programmes and on-the-job learning; in recent years more specific programmes in tourism and leisure have been offered on a full-time basis in initial vocational education.

Another measure taken by industrial sectors to improve the match between education and employment is the strengthening of co-ordination between different types of training. This is illustrated in the printing industry. The first step was to create a broad programme which could serve as a common base for the many different types of apprenticeship; the second was to improve integration between the follow-up programmes that build on the common base by replacing them with broader programmes focusing less on a limited number of specific occupational skills and more on a field of activity or a section of the production process (within which individual differentiation was possible). The final step in the process of co-ordinating initial training was the integration of full-time (i.e. non-dual) programmes and the establishment of a printing college.

While the emphasis in this example is on co-ordination within a training system serving an individual sector, a shift has also begun towards broadening sectoral provision through co-ordination with other areas of vocational education (and even across the barrier separating general secondary from vocational education). In part this runs counter to the development of distinctive training provision as,for example, in the printing industry (an approach also favoured in installation and tourism and leisure). The blurring of boundaries between sectoral training systems has thus been encouraged mainly by government which has been promoting the establishment of multi-sector colleges of vocational (and adult) education. The growing resemblances between occupational categories have prompted industrial sectors to seek greater co-ordination, provided that their own training systems remain intact and recognisable. There is a clear tension here between the need to respond to developments and the desire of sectors to preserve a separate identity.

A fourth development is the increasing co-ordination between initial and further education and training. Ongoing technological and organisational innovation requires that workers quickly master changing techniques and procedures. There has been, as a result, some broadening of initial vocational education. In addition legislation allows vocational colleges to sell training services; vocational colleges are increasingly running specific training programmes for people wishing to work in particular fields. In the printing, engineering and installation sectors, the growth of a ramified system of further training facilities has been a major development. Regarding the relationship between initial and further education and training, two possibilities exist: either the two systems could function separately, with initial training as the first stage and further training as the second, or there could be an integrated training system in which the boundaries between initial and further training were blurred.

Curricular innovation

Along with measures aimed at the education and training system, curricular reform is seen as a way of responding to the demand for new qualifications. One innovation has been the introduction of greater flexibility in vocational programmes. This has involved restructuring the sectoral training system and increasing co-ordination between programmes (see above) and a restructuring of the content of programmes along with changes in their organisation and delivery: modularisation. The introduction of modular structures, with programme content divided into units covering coherent sets of occupational requirements, offers students individualized routes through the training system.

Modularisation has its roots in the analysis of occupational practice and compilation of profiles. This substantive basis for module construction brings with it certain risks. As noted earlier, job analysis focuses mainly on "visible" activities; less attention is paid to the broader analysis of qualification requirements, which also encompass less "visible" aspects of occupational practice. The result is that modules have a fairly direct link with the task clusters identified in occupational practice. Qualities such as "independence, flexibility, social skills and the ability to work safely, hygienically and with an awareness of environmental considerations" (in the installation sector) may be essential to occupational practice but are not criteria in the restructuring of programme content and thus play no part in the demarcation of modules. In tourism and leisure, the older programmes, which had a fairly large common core (relating to management and finance on the one hand or communication on the other), have been transformed into a new kind of training with a "general base of sectoral knowledge". The practice of gearing programmes to current occupational practice – what the job specifically comprises – may tend to make them somewhat narrow.

A second curricular innovation has been the expansion of the practical component of programmes. This is directly linked with moves to improve co-ordination between college-based learning and learning on the job. In recent years, full-time programmes in particular have allowed greater scope for the application and further development of knowledge and skills in more or less realistic learning situations. As seen in the case of the introduction of CNC technology, provision is increasingly made within programmes for experimentation with the new equipment, particularly through simulations. Such experimentation often takes place in special regional centres equipped with standard industrial machinery, enabling students and teachers, the employed the unemployed, to become familiar with this new technology.

Expanding the practical component of programmes thus does not necessarily imply more time on traditional work placements, as students can apply their knowledge and skills in simulation situations. As indicated, developments of this kind are also under way in the apprenticeship system.

In conjunction with the various moves to enlarge the practical component of programmes, attempts are also being made to improve the link between theory and practice. In full-time vocational education at upper secondary level (MBO), the long continuous work placement is increasingly being replaced with shorter placements spread over the whole programme; this was done some time ago in the case of the shorter MBO programmes and is now being extended to the full-length programmes. Simulations and case studies are also a way to link theory and practice. Modularisation in the apprenticeship system is intended to improve co-ordination between college and firm and between theory and practice: every module has a school and work component; the acquisition and application of knowledge and skills are more closely integrated, and the same module is covered simultaneously in college and on the job wherever possible. In some cases even integrated teaching materials and integrated testing have been developed.

More radical curricular reform has so far been mainly restricted to apprenticeship programmes. Curricular innovation, generally preceded by studies of occupational practice, clearly got under way sooner in the apprenticeship system than in full-time post-16 vocational education (MBO), at least in the sectors studied. The MBO sector is quickly catching up, however; the shorter MBO programmes, initially experimental, may play a part in assisting the process.

Quality control

The restructuring of the sectoral training system and curricular reform are both intended to enhance the flexibility of training provision, thereby creating a new framework for the operation of quality control procedures. This review of the measures taken to deal with problems at the interface between education and employment ends with a brief account of the monitoring of learning targets and certification and the qualifications of teachers and trainers.

The new learning targets for the initial programmes in the sectoral training systems have been set by central government. In all cases these targets are the outcome of a process of negotiation involving government, employers and trade unions, based on the results of analyses of occupational practice.

The apprenticeship system provides a complex network of training routes. While an assessment and certification procedure forms part of every module, a full apprenticeship certificate (at elementary, advanced or specialist level) is issued only when set groups of modular certificates have been obtained; this is to maintain the transparency of qualifications and thus their utility to workers and employers. In the installation sector, where training is extensively modularised, modular certificates have no value or recognition in their own right; students are as far as possible guided along comprehensive training routes, and colleges are prohibited for example from selling individual modules to either employers or workers. All sectors wish to ensure that initial training meets certain minimum requirements and that vocational qualifications are widely recognised.

Along with modular structures, tighter procedures are being introduced for monitoring and maintaining the quality, of the practical component of apprenticeship programmes. Students must complete all modules of the practical component, and in this sense modularisation can be seen as an instrument of quality control. While the school component is also affected, the main impact is on the work component: college syllabuses were always reasonably clear, but in the past it was often unclear what precisely had to be covered in training on the job.

In some sectors, specific measures are being taken as regards teachers' skills and qualifications. In tourism and leisure there is strong pressure for a specialised programme of teacher training. In all sectors, teachers spend time on industrial placements and there is extensive in-service training in new technologies. Even so, teachers are often uncertain as to how best to impart what they have learned. At this level, that of curriculum content and delivery (which differ from one college and teacher to another), much work is being done to improve the match between education and employment; it is at this level that the professionalism of education and the main prospects for shaping provision are located.

Networks of actors

Sectors have their roots, on the one hand, in demarcated and coherent occupational activity and, on the other, in institutional networks. The sectors studied differ in the extent to which they have formed such networks; the strength of networks also differs, as does the influence of the various actors. Within each sector, the main actors are the education and training institutions, employer bodies and organised labour; the strength and direction of the measures they take are influenced by the government. The themes of the sections above will now be considered in relation to sectoral institutional frameworks.

One must take into account the stage that a sector has reached in its development to obtain a clear picture of the institutional network that has formed. While the level of organisation is still low in tourism and leisure, in the printing industry it is highly developed. Printing work has long been recognised by outsiders as a distinct occupational category; both sides of the industry have been highly organised since the end of the last century, and since the start of this century, collective agreements between employers' organisations and trade unions have regulated (among other things) access to printing trades and thus provided the basis for the sector's training system. In tourism and leisure, in contrast, there are no national organisations of employers and trade unions and as yet no collective agreement in the sector. Where the printing industry has a publicly recognised status, the tourism and leisure industry has yet to achieve this.

There is also contrast regarding the extent to which "education" can be distinguished as an actor in its own right. The installation, engineering and printing trades are served by long-established and internally coherent training provision within the apprenticeship system, in which employers' organisations and trade unions play a co-ordinating role. While the links with external training (mainstream education) are weaker, they are nevertheless clear. Training provision for tourism and leisure, in contrast, comprises a variety of programmes offered by various institutions, which may or may not claim to belong to the sector; initial full-time training is provided by two institutions which, until recently, were in competition with one another and which have a much shorter history than those in the other sectors. As neither employers nor workers in tourism and leisure are organised, there was no co-ordinating agency covering training matters or the shaping of a sectoral training system. The growing use of training facilities outside the sector and the search for government funding for programmes in tourism and leisure have gradually led to the development of a co-ordinating body; this is, however, weak due to the absence of employer and union organisations geared to the sector and of a sectoral collective agreement (with job-classification systems).

The sectors studied can also be contrasted regarding the roles actors play in identifying and tackling problems at the education-employment interface. The unified training system for installation trades was established chiefly by the sector's employers, for example, with the unions having little input into the restructuring process. Generally, Dutch unions have limited influence on training matters, with the exception of unions in the printing industry.

The training institutions themselves, particularly those offering full-time programmes, have had much less influence on how interface problems are tackled. In part this reflects the loose organisation of vocational education outside the apprenticeship system, which lacks national bodies able to speak for all providers in a particular sector. The umbrella bodies for full-time vocational education are not organised on a sectoral basis, and moreover there are many different organisations with varying degrees of influence. They include college associations on denominational lines and broad sectoral organisations, of which only that covering technical studies has much influence. The creation of national bodies covering senior secondary vocational education (MBO) as well as the apprenticeship system, in 1993, and the formation of a single association of MBO colleges may alter the picture. The less dominant role of the sectoral training system (including both dual and full-time programmes) can also be explained by reference to the message which the training institutions received from all quarters in the 1980s: programmes should be more closely geared to occupational practice, and employers, or both sides of industry, should be more involved in the formulation of learning targets. The result was that the vocational education system as a whole took few initiatives and made few proposals for reform, and most proposals emanated from government; indeed, until recently this division of responsibilities was taken for granted.

While the system as a whole has tended to respond rather than initiate, the colleges themselves have been much more proactive: individual colleges have developed programmes geared to installation work, and established programmes in tourism and leisure. In installation, the move was assisted by the employers' organisation which sought a clear presence in external training provision. In tourism and leisure, external training was developed in the first instance against the wishes of the sectoral organisations but with support from regional employers and government; the government later withdrew its support. In the absence of clear umbrella organisations, individual colleges rarely succeed in propagating their views or exercising influence in the interplay of forces within the sector, except where their activities match generally recognised visions or interests.

The strength of an institutional network or sector is also visible in the extent to which the sector maintains its identity, perhaps despite current trends. Both tourism and leisure and the printing industry, at different stages in their development, can serve as illustrations.

The launch of programmes geared to tourism and leisure in initial vocational education stimulated the emergence of a distinct sector or network of actors. Where industry had been unsympathetic towards mainstream full-time programmes, preferring to take on motivated youth with general qualifications and mould them to its needs, it now sought a place within the system. This gave the co-ordinating unit set up by the sectoral organisations greater influence: training was now an issue for it to tackle. The call for specific initial programmes was reinforced by the large volume of spending on tourism and leisure. Developments accelerated, with the industry and educational institutions consulting on the development of training profiles for various forms of initial vocational education. The industry is now working for the establishment of colleges specialising in tourism and leisure programmes at both initial and further education levels.

In the printing industry, the institutional network is so strong that specialised colleges have now been established and recognised, even though printing activities are spreading through other sectors, and similarities with other sectors are growing (notably through technological and organisational changes). When training provision for the printing trades seemed at risk of losing its separate identity through the government's policy of restructuring vocational education, including the creation of larger institutions, the printing industry responded strongly. Building on previous developments and thinking in the area of training, the print employers and unions got together and set up a college providing a full range of initial programmes. In this way the industry, and specifically its co-ordination unit (which was initially set up to deal with internal training), extended its influence to full-time vocational education.

Whether the developments in these two areas represent the "right" response to current developments remains to be seen. There is a dilemma here. A strong network, whose participants are, as it were, condemned to work together, could mean rigidity, making it difficult to anticipate growing similarities between occupations, new developments etc. Even so, the printing industry seems able to react quickly and effectively precisely because it comprises a tight network with short lines of communication. Perhaps it is easier to take account of other sectors, occupations and developments if one's own position is secure.

Looking at the other sectors studied, it is clear that the installation sector is less able to react quickly and effectively than the printing industry, not least through the absence of a clear union input. Particularly as regards external training, this sector is squeezed by general engineering on the one side and electrical engineering and electronics on the other. While the installation trades include a long-established craft sector with its own internally organised training system, it remains to be seen whether this system can be sustained. Engineering, finally, is such a broadly defined and economically important sector that it is unlikely to lose its distinctive identity despite differentiated occupational profiles.

One of the main conclusions to emerge is that vocational education is under considerable pressure to help maintain sectoral identities. But while the education institutions are taking on this role they tend to follow rather than lead where problems of match between education and employment are concerned. It is difficult to discern how far this also applies at the level of the determination of curriculum content; the scope which exists for innovation in curriculum and qualifications is mainly exploited by individual colleges. The most recent trend observed in the sectors studied is to extend individual colleges' room for manoeuvre.

Shaping the system

The introduction to this part indicated the viewpoints from which the responsiveness of the sectoral training system was examined in the Dutch case studies. A central focus was the extent of flexibility. It must be stressed that this study was mainly concerned with flexibility as an attribute of the supply side, the system of initial vocational education, in relation to changing qualification and training requirements on the demand side and the labour market. Second, the sectoral development of vocational education served as a specific context (and limiting framework) for the consideration of the extent of flexibility; each sector was viewed from two angles, the unity of occupational activities and the unity of the institutional network.

In the Netherlands, problems of match between educational curricula and the needs of employers are generally seen as requiring a response by vocational education to external developments; less attention is focused on what industry might do. The issue of their contribution to initial vocational education, e.g., by providing more work and training places and improving their quality, is increasingly being discussed, at least in the sectors studied. Greater attention could be devoted to possible internal responses within the world of work in relation to job quality, training policy etc. While this matter is partly outside the scope of the study, it is relevant to the innovatory role which vocational education could play in dealing with problems of match. This role will mainly find expression in the product, the range of knowledge and skills – qualifications – imparted. Then the question becomes that of industry's response, i.e., how it uses those qualifications. This issue was not considered in depth in the sectoral studies.

Despite the fact that in the sectors studied most of the measures taken were aimed directly at producing a close match between education and employment, the general result has in fact been to create more flexible routes through training to qualification. This increased flexibility is largely limited to the sectoral training system. The division between initial and further education and training remains, with initial provision delivering a basic package on which further provision can build. A major gain from the new systems is the creation of alternative training routes: college-based alongside work-based, routes combining practical and theoretical learning, shorter and longer programmes, and so on. Moves towards greater flexibility have gone furthest in the printing sector; in the other sectors the process is either just beginning or is limited to only part of the sectoral training system. In some cases intermediary structures have been incorporated into the training system; in the case of CNC, for example, regional centres could play a key role in translating technological developments into training syllabuses and in updating and upgrading the knowledge and skills of workers and job seekers. The sale of training services by colleges (contract activities) can also be seen as a step towards intermediate structures in the training system.

Vocational education has also played a part in the evolution of industrial sectors and occupational categories: the advent of programmes in tourism and leisure has helped give the sector a distinct identity; the printing industry has set up specialised colleges covering all print trades, thus strengthening its own identity; and colleges of vocational education have developed a range of programmes relating to installation trades, confirming the integration between the two training systems within the apprenticeship system and of the formerly distinct sectors.

This strengthening of sectoral boundaries within the training system runs counter to the official policy of horizontal integration; at a time of increasing overlap between occupations it also brings a real danger of rigidity and stagnation in training processes. Perhaps the problem is best resolved at the institutional level. If occupations increasingly overlap and knowledge and skill requirements are shifted by technological and organisational change, then every sectoral training institution will need to focus greater attention on transfer, including both transferable skills and the ability to transfer them. Training syllabuses in different sectors could well begin to show more similarities as a result. However, such skills cannot be acquired other than in specific contexts: they must always be related to particular topics or activities whose substance is subject to change, and in this light the continued existence of sectoral divisions is not an impediment to progress but rather the opposite. Highly developed sectoral training systems are thus fully capable of responding to changing requirements and producing appropriate patterns of qualification.

7. Conclusions

The 1980s saw a growing emphasis on preparation for work in Dutch education. Where in previous years there had been stress on general education, the work-related or occupational element now came more to the fore; programmes designed to give young people a taste of different jobs and guide their study and career choices made a cautious entry into general education. Many programmes were revised with the aim of gearing them more closely to occupational practice and participation in such programmes increased.

The division between general and vocational provision has remained, though general secondary education has increasingly acquired a preparatory role vis-à-vis vocational education. This shift is seen in a new definition of the first and second stages of secondary education. The introduction of a common curricular core for all students aged 12-15 will confirm the new first stage, which will formally include no vocational education. In the second stage an institutional division is likely to persist between general and vocational education. The distinction between preparatory and final provision will increasingly coincide with that between general and vocational education. Even at the highest level, where university is still seen to have higher status than higher vocational education, there is a gradual shift towards equality. The vocational element in university programmes is being strengthened and the vocational sector is increasingly seen as offering programmes and qualifications equal in value to those of the universities.

Bridging the gap between general and vocational education could well prove a central issue in the coming years. The debate is likely to focus not so much on institutional divisions as on the definition of learning targets for the various courses and curriculum design. On the vocational side, this bridging process can be seen in the moves to reshape the pattern of vocational programmes (with combinations of general and work-related elements), and in moves to integrate or broaden traditional job-related programmes.

As the sectoral studies reveal, these shifts in vocational education run parallel to shifts in industry and occupational structures. The studies also show that in some cases the initiative for change came from the colleges. Looking back on the evolution that has taken place in Dutch vocational education over the past ten years, several tendencies can be distinguished which could well dominate discussions of the system's future role and structure.

First in response to the fragmentation of training provision over the last 10-15 years, moves have been made recently to establish a stronger and more coherent vocational provision at upper secondary level, by creating a differentiated system of training pathways. This process is at the core of official policy. The study therefore ends with an examination of the main features of the process and of the challenges involved. It looks at the broadening of vocational education, the dualisation of programmes and the modularisation of syllabuses, all in relation to the need for flexibility, both internal and external. External flexibility is concerned with matching vocational provision to regional training needs (offering the qualifications the employers need), while maintaining overall coherence. Internal flexibility refers to matching regional provision to the wishes and needs of the students.

Broadening

The broadening of vocational education consists of extending provision both horizontally and vertically. The horizontal broadening process has two aspects: dismantling sectoral divisions in vocational education, and transcending the distinctions between general and vocational education and qualifications.

The dismantling of sectoral divisions is a laborious process. The growing overlap between different occupational categories and the blurring of sectoral boundaries by economic, technological and organisational change, pull in one direction. The self-interest (including the economic interest) that sectors have in maintaining or developing distinctive training provision pulls in the other. Greater integration means, above all, that learning targets and training syllabuses will become more similar, perhaps to the point of including common features. In this regard it is encouraging that colleges of vocational education at upper secondary level, which have traditionally been narrowly specialised, have begun in the last few years to offer programmes ranging over several sectors.

The division between general and vocational education is also not seen as an institutional issue: rather, the vocational side is facing the challenge of achieving recognition as a complete and valid form of education. It will be essential for colleges to meet this challenge, broadening their provision in light of the growing demands for understanding, flexibility, the ability to learn, communications and organisational skills, and foreign language knowledge. These are all skills being required of employees at the intermediate level. In this sense the distinction between general and vocational knowledge and skills is in fact outdated. But while this view is increasingly taking hold in the worlds of employment and education (and among students and their parents) its translation into educational curricula will be no easy matter.

These two aspects of the horizontal broadening of vocational education reinforce one another, positively when institutions go beyond sectoral boundaries and support the development of broader-based knowledge and skills. If, however, institutions limit themselves to preparing people for particular job categories, the programmes are likely to have a narrow focus.

Led by top industrialists (Wagner and Rauwenhoff, who each chaired education committees), industry has taken a greater interest in the content of vocational education. In the 1980s, educators, employers and unionists gave extensive consideration to the purpose of upper secondary vocational programmes, whether college-based or in the apprenticeship system. In the case of college-based programmes, sectoral consultative councils were set up for this purpose; in the apprenticeship system the relevant national bodies already existed. Colleges were pressured into focusing on occupational practice in a single sector, but a contrary movement has been visible more recently, with the government working to create multi-sector colleges of vocational education.

The results so far of the reorganisation of upper secondary vocational education illustrate this tension: both single-sector and multi-sector colleges have been formed. Even so, individual sectors are still to be found in separate departments within the multi-sector colleges. Sectoral consultations have led to attainment targets which will be implemented mainly at the level of the individual sectors; it will be left to the colleges themselves to take a supra-sectoral view in designing new courses.

The government's most recent policy goal is vertical and horizontal extension through the creation of colleges providing both vocational and adult education, along the lines of institutions of this type in the United Kingdom and the United States.

The tendency towards vertical extension of vocational education has made itself felt in both the initial and further education phases. Following from the above, it is evident that despite (or perhaps thanks to) the government's drive to create colleges serving several sectors, there is in some sectors a movement to concentrate all forms of vocational education for that given sector in one type of institution. While such an orientation might be expected to produce a certain rigidity, those sectors which have organised themselves in this way, such as printing and agriculture, tend to look beyond sectoral boundaries: developments in other sectors are monitored and, where necessary, incorporated into the curriculum.

Sectoral training systems of this kind comprise a wide framework of courses, including both initial and further provision, with proper co-ordination and efficient transitions. The initial phase is seen as broad and pre-vocational, while the further education phase is specialised and job-oriented. This coherence across initial and further provision makes for a smoother transition from education to employment. In addition, further training is seen as a way of responding to the training aspirations and needs of divergent groups of adult clients, such as people seeking to return to employment or to change career direction, older workers, immigrants, and the unemployed.

Presently, the government strongly encourages the fusion of colleges providing full-time programmes with those delivering the college-based element of apprenticeship programmes. Bringing these different learning routes under the same roof could stimulate innovation on both sides. These fusions also involve institutions for adult education. This leads to both a horizontal and vertical extension of provision.

The establishment of colleges catering for more varied types of learning pathway (short, full-length, college-based, learning-while-working, for the young, for adults) may also give a strong impetus to the development of short further education programmes of a specific nature. Virtually all colleges now provide such programmes, mainly on a commercial basis, for example through contract activities. This represents a first step towards the broadening and extension of regional provision of education and towards improved co-ordination within it.

Dualisation

While dualisation has been a major theme in vocational education discussions in recent years, there are as yet no concrete plans in this direction. Part of the difficulty lies in the fact that the term is used in different ways. There are two core meanings: on the one hand the increased responsibility (including financial responsibility) of industry; on the other hand an increased practical component, notably in full-time programmes. Work placements are being replaced by periods of employment under combined work-and-training contracts.

It is unclear whether dualisation should be seen as a phenomenon in its own right or as a manifestation of the drive for greater external flexibility; in that case the preceding discussion of external flexibility is related to dualisation. The public debate on this theme arose in the 1980s, when generally the emphasis was on the direct matching of courses to employers' requirements and greater course specialization.

If, as has been argued, there is still room for discussion of broadening, both horizontally between sectors and vertically between hierarchically distinguished components of the system, then the theme of dualisation will again be a subject of debate. The dual system runs the risk of evolving towards flexibility but also towards specialization, implying that training is narrow and excessively focused on occupational requirements. Recent developments emphasizing the notion of dual teaching will show whether this type of education will be broadened or whether the movement towards dualization will at some point level off.

Modularisation

Here also, the outcome of developments remains to be seen. The theme of modularisation, like that of dualisation, has been central to the movement towards greater programme specificity and the direct matching of courses to employers' requirements. Modular approaches increase internal flexibility because they allow differentiation in learning routes and the time spent on them, and choices between overlapping learning routes, with a view to meeting the needs and wishes of wider groups of students. In this sense modularisation is a response in keeping with the "hardening" tendency of the 1980s: the emphasis is on hard goals, clearly directed and structured learning routes, the strict monitoring of progress.

The major changes of recent years (sector formation and renewal, the new tripartite structure of employment services, the reform of pre-vocational education for less academically inclined 12 to 16-year-olds and initiatives aimed at further horizontal integration), were all launched in the mid-1980s. They represented responses on the one hand to the education debates of the 1970s (with equal opportunities and integration as the main themes) and on the other to the recession of the early 1980s. They have entailed an emphasis on the direct matching of courses to employers' requirements and greater specificity of course goals, with greater influence accorded to industry. This movement is now reaching its conclusion, and new demands are now emerging. One hypothesis might be that another paradigm shift will take place in the next few years, producing other answers to the question of how vocational education should develop, but there are no clear indications emerging as yet. It might be desirable to repeat the VOTEC study in ten years.

Bibliography

ARCHER, M.S. (1984), *Social origins of educational systems*, Sage, London, Beverly Hills.

BAETEN, J.J.M., VAN CUIJCK-REMIJSEN, A., DRONKERS, J. and VAN'T HOF, L. (1989), "Horizontale differentiatie in het onderwijs en ongelijkheid op de arbeidsmarkt", *Sociale Wetenschappen 32*, pp. 253-262.

BRANDSMA, T.F. (1990), *Achtergronden, toepassingen en effecten van de zogenaamde "naieve" benadering van aansluitingsproblemen onderwijs-arbeidsmarkt*, Subsidieaanvraag t.b.v. SVO-promotiebeurs, Onderzoekcentrum Toegepaste Onderwijskunde, University of Twente, Enschede.

DUMOULIN, T. (1990), "Denken over 'nieuwe' basisvaardigheden", *PRINT notitie*, 15 March 1990, Den Bosch.

FRIETMAN, J. (1990), *De kwaliteit van de praktijkcomponent van het leerlingwezen*, Instituut voor Toegepaste Sociale Wetenschappen (Institute for Applied Social Sciences), University of Nijmegen, Nijmegen.

GOODLAD, J.I. (1984), *A place called school: Prospects for the future*, McGraw-Hill, New York.

HUIJGEN, F. (1989), "Opleiding van werknemers en het niveau van hun werk. De kwalitatieve structuur van de werkgelegenheid 1960-1985", in Gadourek and J.I. Peschar (eds.), *De open samenleving. Sociale veranderingen op het terrein van geloof, huwelijk, onderwijs en arbeid in Nederland*, Van Loghum Slaterus, Deventer, pp. 79-101.

JONG, M.W. de, MOERKAMP, T., ONSTENK, J., BABELLOWSKY, M. (1990), *Breed Toepasbare Beroepskwalificatics in leerplan en beroepspraktijk*, Een probleemverkenning en beroepsanalyse, SCO Amsterdam (SCO-rapport nr. 20), University of Amsterdam, Amsterdam.

MAURICE, M., SORGE, A. and WARNER, M. (1980), "Societal differences in organizing manufacturing units: A comparison of France, West Germany, and Great Britain", *Organization Studies 1*, pp. 59-86.

MEESTERBEREND-HARMS, G.J. and NIEUWENHUIS, A.F.M. (1989), "Beroepsonderwijs in modulen: aanzetten en verwachtingen", *Pedagogische studiën 66*, pp. 7-8.

MEESTERS, M.J. and EINERHAND, M.G.K. (1986), "LBO- en MAVO-schoolverlaters op de arbeidsmarkt", *Tijdschrift voor Arbeidsvraagstukken 2*, pp. 67-77.

MOERKAMP, T. and DE BRUIJN, E. (1991), *Leren voor een loopbaan. Het verwerven van transitievaardigheden in HAVO en MBO*, OSA, OSA-werkdocument 92, Den Haag.

NIJHOFF, W.J. and MULDER, M. (eds.) (1986), *Basisvaardigheden in het beroepsonderwijs*, SVO, Den Haag.

NIJHOF, W.J. and REMMERS, J.T.M. (1989), *Basisvaardigheden nader bekeken* (Basic Skills reviewed), Faculteit Toegepaste Onderwijskund, Enschede.

PEA, R.D. (1988), "Putting Knowledge to Use", in Nickerson, R.S. and Ph.P. Zodhiates (ed.), *Technology in Education: Looking Toward 2020*, pp. 169-213, Lawrence Erlbaum Ass., Hove and London.

PELKMAN, A. and DE VRIES, B. (1991), *De V van SVM*, Instituut voor toegepaste Sociale Wetenschappen (Institute for Applied Social Sciences), University of Nijmegen, Nijmegen.

PERKINS, D.N. and SALOMON, G. (1989), "Are cognitive skills context bound?", *Educational Researcher*, Vol. 18, No. 1, January-February.

PETERS, F.J.M., STREUMER, J.N., NIJHOF, W.J. (1991), *De opleiding van MTS'ers Energietechniek: Naar aanpassing en vernieuwing van eindtermen*, Onderzoek Centrum van de faculteit der Toegepaste Onderwijskunde, Enschede.

REYNOLDS, D., SULLIVAN, M. and MURGATROYD, S. (1987), *The Comprehensive Experiment: A comparison of the selective and non-selective systems of school organisation*, Falmer press, London, New York, Philadelphia.

TEULINGS, C.N. (1990), *Conjunctuur en kwalificatie*, Doctoral Thesis, University of Amsterdam.

van DIJIK, C., AKKERMANS, M. and HÖVELS, B. (1988), *Sociale partners en beroepsonderwijs in Nederland*, CEDEFOP (European Centre for the Development of Vocational Training), Berlin.

van HOOF, J.J. and DRONKERS, J. (1980), *Onderwijs en Arbeidsmarkt*, Van Loghum Slaterus, Deventer.

van der VELDEN, R.K.W. (1989), *De lange arm van het onderwijs; een vergelijkend onderzoek naar de lange termijn effecten van opleiding bij MBO en leerlingwezen*, RION (Education Institute, North Holland), Groningen.

WIELERS, R. and GLEBBEEK, A. (1990), "Worden we echt te slim voor ons werk?", *Mens en Maatschappij 65*, pp. 271-288.

Part II

SECTORAL CASE STUDIES

A. Tourism and Recreation

E. de Bruijn

SCO-Kohnstamm, Institute for Research on Education,
Amsterdam University

1. Introduction

The present report derives from a case study of the way in which vocational education both reflects and helps to shape developments in the tourist industry. The study was based partly on information supplied by thirteen key figures in tourism and the contents of various publications.

The report consists of four sections. Sections 2 and 3 provide a general survey of developments in the tourist and leisure industry over the past ten to fifteen years, with special reference to developments relating to job competences and the changing requirements in this respect, and to developments in the relevant branch of vocational education. Section 4 presents conclusions concerning the relationship between education and industry and the related professionalisation of this branch of industry. The present section outlines the principal developments in, and characteristics of, tourism and the training provided in the Netherlands for occupations in the industry.

Some figures

The size of the tourist industry, an aggregate of businesses of a highly disparate nature, is generally determined by analysis of the market, i.e. of the earnings derived from it. This is likewise the basis for estimating the consequences for employment, which is largely concentrated in four parts of the service sector, namely the hotel and catering industry, transport and communication, culture and leisure, and trade, with other branches of the service sector accounting for no more than 10 per cent of employment in this field. In 1989, according to the Netherlands Research Institute for Leisure and Tourism (NRIT), direct employment amounted to 139 000 man-years, and indirect employment to 38 500. The share of the hotel and catering industry was 84 500 of these 177 500 man-years, which represented five per cent of total employment in the Netherlands. The figures for both categories of employment rose by 10 per cent between 1982 and 1989.

The actual number of persons employed was higher than the estimated number of man-years, for this is a sector employing many seasonal and part-time workers. The 1990 policy document issued by the Ministry of Economic Affairs puts the figure at 230 000, or 11 per cent of the labour force, divided into some 130 000 in the hotel and catering industry and 100 000 in other areas of tourism. More than 40 000 businesses, comprising 9 to 10 per cent of the total number in the Netherlands, are entirely or largely dependent on the tourist and leisure industry. The Consultative Committee for the Hotel, Catering, Tourist and Leisure Industries responded to the policy document with a somewhat different set of figures for businesses and employees. There is some degree of overlap with regard to the tourist and leisure market on the one hand, and hotels and catering on the other, in that the catering side of the former is also included separately in the figures for the latter. The majority are small and medium-sized businesses. Many in the leisure and hotel and catering categories are family businesses, though there are a few large firms in both (Table A1).

Table A1. **The tourist and leisure industry**

1. *Accommodation*

camping sites and bungalow parks	4 560 businesses
water sports centres	1 719 businesses
facilities for day trippers	409 businesses

2. *Transport companies* — 284 *businesses*

3. *Intermediary organisations*

travel agencies	1 200 offices
banks' travel departments	3 600 offices
tour operators	200 businesses
Royal Dutch Touring Club (ANWB)	48 offices
tourist information offices	549 offices

Total: nearly 13 000 businesses and organisations employing 60 000 to 70 000 people
(Centre for Innovation in Vocational Training for Industry, CIBB, 1989).

Hotel and catering industry

beverages (cafis, bars etc.)	19 687 businesses
meals (restaurants)	7 918 businesses
"fast food" (snack bars)	7 394 businesses
accommodation (hotels)	2 990 businesses

Total: nearly 38 000 businesses employing approximately 130 000 people
(Information System for Labour Market Trends in the Hotel and Catering Industry, ISAH, 1990).

Development of the branch

As is apparent from the above, a distinction is made in the Netherlands between the hotel and catering industry and the tourist and leisure industry. This is based on the way in which the two categories have grown and developed their own traditions over the years. Recently, greater emphasis has been placed on the interrelationship of these two component parts of the tourist industry. The distinction must nevertheless be preserved in the interests of the relationship between the industry and vocational education, and its further development.

The growth of the hotel and catering industry in the Netherlands took an upward turn after the Second World War, emerging in a comparatively short time as a separate entity with a professional culture of its own. It achieved general recognition as such, as evidenced by its inclusion in the International Standard Industrial Classification (ISIC) and the Dutch Standard Industrial Classification. It has a "social structure" and industrial board of its own and a separate collective labour agreement.

The tourist and leisure industry, as the other part of the tourist industry is known in the Netherlands, is a fairly recent growth sector which has not yet developed a clear-cut identity in the sense of being formally classified as a separate industrial sector. It may be roughly divided into the three categories of tourist information services, the travel sector (reservations, conducted tours, package holidays) and leisure facilities.

The first travel agencies and tourist information offices were established in the late 19th century in response to the increased mobility (railways, steam trams) of the moneyed classes. With the advent of mass tourism in the 1960s and 1970s, the number of tourist and leisure businesses rapidly increased. Some years ago, the representative branch-organisation of the travel sector, the Netherlands Association of Travel Companies (ANVR), established in 1966, was transformed into a federation of four separate organisations (travel agents, incoming tourism, tour operators, air and business travel). Some 600 firms are affiliated to the Association, of which 100 are tour operators and 500 are travel agents with branches throughout the country.

The tourist information offices have displayed a more gradual rate of growth. The Netherlands Association of Tourist Information Offices (ANVV) was set up in 1915 to co-ordinate the work of the various offices. After the Second World War leisure travel in the Netherlands increased, marking the beginning of 'social tourism' as growing numbers of people became able to afford excursions in their own country. This promoted the growth of the hotel and catering industry and, in its wake, of the tourist information offices, which responded to the new mass tourism by expanding their information and reservation services for both foreign and Dutch tourists.

Like the travel sector, the leisure sector owes its growth mainly to the emergence of mass tourism in the 1960s and 1970s. The Netherlands Association of Leisure Industry Proprietors (RECRON), representing the interests of businesses providing accommodation and day-tripper facilities, has existed since 1969. The accommodation branch has evolved from "a tent in a farmer's field" to professional camping sites and bungalow parks.

The tourist information, travel and leisure sectors have thus developed separately. Nevertheless, in the 1970s and 1980s they were all faced with a need to improve the quality of the services they offered as a result of the more critical attitude and less predictable demands of the consumer. This led to cautious attempts to co-ordinate their activities and to an awareness of the importance of greater professionalism, but they have yet to achieve true cohesion based on employers' organisations, a specific "social structure" and collective labour agreements. The process of professionalisation, of the specification of occupations and jobs, is still under way.

While supporting these efforts, the tourist and leisure industry, and specifically the travel agencies specialising in outgoing tourism, wish to remain distinct from the hotel and catering industry. Domestic tourism brings together hotels and catering, the tourist information and leisure sectors, and incoming tourism. Outgoing tourism, from which the travel agencies derive part of their identity, has the fewest ties with the domestic hotel and catering industry. As far as the practice of these various professions is concerned, however, the leisure, information and travel sectors all claim that their work is substantially different from that of the hotel and catering industry, arguing that the product they sell is much less tangible, much more ephemeral than that offered by the latter, and that they are essentially engaged in "selling illusions".

Developments in education and training

The difference between the hotel and catering branch and the tourist and leisure branch is even more apparent in their training systems. The latter, claiming a different task for itself, feels that this should be reflected in its occupational training.

The shortage of qualified staff after the Second World War led the hotel and catering industry to create a vocational training system geared to its specific needs. The development of its own "social structure" was accompanied by awareness of the importance of training, with the larger concerns, then as now, leading the way. The importance of training for the institutionalisation and formal recognition of the industry was acknowledged at national level and the Centre for Training for the Hotel and Catering Industry (formerly the Association for Vocational Education for the Hotel and Catering Industry, the SVH) has functioned for more than 40 years as the central body for all training activities. Full-time training programmes are currently offered in junior and senior secondary vocational education, apprenticeship training and higher vocational education, and there is a comprehensive system of in-service training and refresher courses.

The large number of commercial training programmes is a conspicuous feature of vocational education for the tourist and leisure industry. Up to the end of the 1970s, training in this area was the exclusive responsibility of the trade schools, run by sub-branch-related organisations and commercial educational institutions. This was especially the case with regard to training for middle-management or intermediate posts[1]. The majority of employees completed a broadly-based or general education before embarking on a specialised programme and/or gaining experience in the workplace. This was considered by the industry itself to be the best preparation for a successful career.

In the late 1970s and throughout the following decade, a greater role was given to the non-profit vocational colleges, in many cases on the joint initiative of schools and sub-branch-related organisations. The need for higher standards in the industry and for more professional staff was a motivating force in this development. Some businesses, however, are not yet convinced of the advantages of incorporating tourism and leisure programmes in non-profit vocational education, and a clear-cut training system is not yet in existence.

Like the hotel and catering industry, the tourist and leisure industry has established a centre for the co-ordination of training under the supervision of the various sub-branch-related organisations. Though it has not yet fully established its status and role as a spokesman, the Centre for Training for the Tourist and Leisure Industry[2] has already played a leading part in the incorporation and recognition of tourism and leisure as a specific programme in senior secondary vocational education. The two centres have recently begun to work more closely together with a view to correlating the further elaboration of their training systems.

Professionalisation of the tourist and leisure industry

Professionalisation is now progressing throughout the tourist and leisure branch[3], but the industry is still in the process of establishing an organisational structure. The majority of those in the branch recognise that clearly defined formal vocational education (provided by the non-profit colleges) is important to its future and will provide it with the necessary identifiable 'banner' of its own. Formal vocational education thus constitutes part of the process of professionalisation now under way, and can help to determine the direction it will take. The precise role it now plays or can play in the future is discussed below.

The scope of this study is mainly on developments within the tourist and leisure branch. The nature of those developments will be of significance for the hotel and catering branch, which is closely related to the tourist and leisure branch, and its training and branch-related organisations are taking an active part in shaping the professionalisation process. Where those developments relate to co-operation between the two branches, the hotel and catering branch is included in the discussion.

2. Occupational Developments

The Netherlands Research Institute for Leisure and Tourism defines tourism as "a phenomenon encompassing all forms of activity that are wholly or partly focused on the desire for recreation in a different environment". It is more difficult to form an idea of the people active in the industry and of the knowledge and skills they possess. Before dealing with present-day economic trends influencing competence requirements, attention will therefore be directed to the product and activities of the industry as a means of portraying the relevant occupations and occupational developments.

The product, the industry and the occupations

What the hotel and catering industry, travel agencies, tourist information services and the leisure sector have in common is a product, to which they each make their own specific contribution. In September 1990 a conference of representatives from the entire sector arrived at the following pragmatic conclusion:

"It is possible to construct a conceptual framework for the industry with the aid of the terms *service, transport, accommodation, consumption* and amusement. Service relates to the firms and governmental agencies performing an intermediary task in tourism, namely tour operators, travel agencies, tourist information offices and the Netherlands Tourist Board (NBT); *transport* to the firms, including car rental firms, which provide the requisite means of transportation, and motorists' organisations; *accommodation* to the businesses providing overnight accommodation; *consumption* to those selling food, beverages and souvenirs, and *amusement* to those offering various amenities and attractions for day trippers".

These five categories are regarded as comprising the tourist industry in the narrowest sense, i.e. those parts of the industry which operate mainly or wholly in this field. In a broader sense, it may also be said to extend to various other categories such as financiers, insurance companies and construction firms.

It will be clear from the above why the official figures on the number of tourist businesses and professional workers within the industry are compiled on the basis of their turnover. Ascertaining whether its turnover derives largely from tourist and leisure activities may however be a useful criterion for the classification of a business in the tourist and leisure category. At the same time, the occupations represented in such businesses cannot all automatically be classified as tourist and leisure occupations, quite apart from the fact that people whose occupations do in fact fall into this category may be employed in businesses where only a small part of the turnover is attributable to tourist and leisure activities.

The principal criterion for the classification of occupations is the nature of the work entailed and the nature of the competences required for such work. It is not applicable when it comes to the question of the main source of income of a particular business. The driver of a holiday coach is first and foremost a driver, just as zoo keepers are employed to care for the animals. But what is the guard in a museum, the manager of a travel agency, the boatman, the children's games organiser in a holiday camp, the camping site manager or the cashier in a theme park? Can these be counted as tourist and leisure occupations, and if so to what extent, and what precisely are the competences involved? The job specification and the competences this demands are one characteristic of an occupation; the other is recognition by the outside world. The fact that neither the tourist and leisure industry nor the occupations within it are to be found in the existing classifications suggests that recognition and institutionalisation are still a long way off.

Occupational profiles

The role of vocational training and the problem of aligning education and industry cannot be properly understood without some knowledge of tourist and leisure occupations. Those inside and outside the branch are agreed that there are certain occupations which may be classed as belonging to the tourist and leisure industry. Owing to the lack of a proper "social structure", however, they have never been officially classified[4]. The same work may be designated differently by different employers; conversely, the same designation may be given to different types of work.

The two surveys of tourist and leisure occupations undertaken in the Netherlands originated in a perceived mismatch between education and industry. The first, conducted by the Netherlands Research Institute for Leisure and Tourism (NRIT), was designed to yield an estimate of the quantitative demand for graduates of full-time training programmes for the tourist and leisure industry. It was commissioned by the Ministry of Economic Affairs, which was concerned about employment prospects for the growing number of graduates of such training programmes in the early 1980s. The survey distinguished between jobs at the intermediate and senior levels for which candidates were required to possess a certificate and/or which were considered by employers to require specific knowledge and skills. Depending on the nature and level of the work, jobs were classed as executive (technical, reception, information and supervision) or policy making/managerial. The executive category, found throughout the leisure branch, was not, as a rule, regarded as specific to the tourist and leisure industry[5]. The survey presents neither an overall nor a detailed picture of occupations and jobs in the industry.

That was accomplished by the second survey, conducted by the Centre for Innovation in Vocational Training for Industry[6]. Its findings now serve as a guideline for occupations and jobs in the industry. This study was commissioned by the Ministry of Education and Science, and supervised at all stages by representatives of the industry's various branches and of closely related areas such as the hotel and catering branch.

Job definitions

The boundaries of the tourist and leisure industry being so indistinct, the study began with a definition of the industry and the jobs it provides. It was decided that occupations specific to the hotel and catering industry would be excluded, but that this would not apply in respect of the hotel and catering aspects of work in the tourist and leisure industry. It was also decided to include family businesses (largely found in the leisure branch) on the ground that it is precisely in such small businesses that vocational training is becoming ever more important. As some parts of the industry, such as the tourist information branch, depend on the work of volunteers, these jobs too were included in the study, as were those of seasonal workers. Tourist and leisure jobs were divided into two groups:

1. In organisations whose activities primarily relate to tourist and leisure services, such as camping sites, hotels, tourist information offices and travel agencies, the jobs geared directly to the provision of such services and perceived as such by the clients, whether individuals or organisations. This group includes tour operator managers (whose services take account of the needs and wishes of the client) but not heads of vehicle maintenance and repair departments (whose work maintaining the coaches is not regarded as primarily relating to tourist and leisure activities). It comprises inquiry desk staff in tourist information offices but not clerical staff in tourist information offices.

2. In organisations whose activities do not primarily relate to the tourist and leisure industry, such as banks, airlines, government departments and railways, the jobs

geared directly to their tourist and leisure services and which determine the quality of those services. This group includes staff of banks' travel departments but not bank managers; it includes managers of department stores' travel departments but not staff of department stores' insurance departments (PCBB report, 1987).

The relationship with the client or consumer thus constitutes the main selection criterion for the 660 occupations arranged in the following major groups:

Proprietors and management:	management of small- and medium-sized businesses
Advisory and support staff:	advisory, training and commercial activities
Information staff and guides:	escorting sightseeing and travel tours, providing information, reception
Travel organisation:	package arrangement, tickets, reservations, handling complaints, travel management
Leisure occupations:	supervision, maintenance, cash desk, amusement, instruction

Job profiles

On the basis of a questionnaire administered to a large number of persons in the above occupations, the relevant tourism and leisure occupations were regrouped as follows:

– central activities within the industry:
   a) policy and management;
   b) administration;
   c) execution (information and supervision);
– central tasks of the industry:
   a) leisure;
   b) travel arrangements and sales;
   c) publicity and education.

The 15 job profiles which emerged and were approved by the branch-related organisations are listed below (see Table A2). The abbreviations on the left signify the present educational level indicated by the branch-related organisations. The right-hand column shows the educational qualification of the respondents who best matched the profile[7].

The discrepancy between the stated and actual educational qualification can be explained in various ways. First, the occupational level is not solely determined by the formal educational background. Previous work experience, the time spent in the present job and the knowledge and skills gained from any vocationally-oriented courses followed are of equal importance. Second, the discrepancy may point to a lack of sound training facilities for the jobs in question, as may well be the case in the leisure branch. Finally, it may indicate a need for greater professionalism and/or stricter qualification requirements, in which case the educational qualification should be regarded as the recommended level. It is probably a combination of all three.

_1._	**_General management profiles_**	
1.	General HBO	53% HO
2.	Administration	31% HO
	MBO/HBO	31% HO
3.	Policy	79% HO
	HBO	
4.	Policy support	56% HO
	HBO	
_2._	**_Leisure branch profiles_**	
5.	Management	20% HO, 30% MO
	MBO (HBO)	30% unknown
6.	Administration	49% LO
	MBO	26% unknown
7.	Reception/cashier	39% LO
	LBO/MBO	34% unknown
_3._	**_Travel agency profiles_**	
8.	Management	51% HO
	MBO/HBO	22% MO
9.	Administration	38% HO, 23% MO
	MBO/HBO	31% unknown
10.	Travel arrangements	23% HO
	MBO	51% MO
_4._	**_Information profiles_**	
11.	Management	42% HO
	MBO/HBO	31% unknown
12.	Provision of information	19% HO, 44% MO
	MBO	20% unknown
_5._	**_Education, publicity and travel guide profiles_**	
13.	Education, publicity	51% HO
	management support	18% MO
	HBO	
14.	Education and publicity	38% HO, 13% MO
	HBO	38% unknown
15.	Travel guides, tour management	78% HO
	HBO	

Jobs in the industry

Statistics on the number of people working in the tourist industry in the Netherlands are scarce, the sole source being the two studies referred to According to the Netherlands Research Institute for Leisure and Tourism (NRIT, 1982), there are a total of 7 970 jobs,

4 445 of which are at intermediate level, and 3 525 at senior level. Jobs in governmental and intermediary organisations (branch and sectoral organisations, research institutes and trade journals) amount to 1 750. These are without exception, classified at HBO or university level (Table A3).

First, it must be noted that voluntary and seasonal workers are barely represented, if at all, in the estimated number of jobs. Neither do the number of jobs include the bulk of the leisure branch (the greater part of the industry) mainly because small businesses were excluded.

Second, the criterion used to define occupations relating to the tourist and leisure industry is not clear, particularly as regards what is to be understood by specific knowledge and skills. This influences the number of jobs, and thereby the demand for persons with vocational qualifications.

In determining the latter, very little account is taken of the possible impact of a large supply of such qualified workers. A demand for their services can be cultivated, especially in an industry such as this, where workers' educational backgrounds are highly varied and the precise nature of the occupational field and of specific jobs has still to be specified.

All in all, it may be stated that the study probably underestimates the number of jobs in the industry, and that its estimate of the demand for workers with appropriate qualifications is based on a somewhat rigid approach to the functioning of the labour market and to its relationship with education.

The Centre for Innovation in Vocational Training for Industry (CIBB) also attempted to ascertain the number of jobs in the tourist and leisure industry by means of a study of the labour market. The figures merely give an approximate indication of the number of businesses and workers in the tourist and leisure industry in the late 1980s; indeed some are based on data collected in 1984 (Table A4).

Table A3. **Jobs in consumer-oriented areas of the tourist and leisure industry**

	Intermediate level (information, advice, ticket offices)	Senior level (policy and management)	Total
Tourist information offices	510	175	685
Travel agencies	2 145	595	2 740
Tour operators	505	500	1 005
Camping sites, bungalow parks*	155	80	235
Hotels*	280	1 140	420
Theme parks, etc.	110	65	195
Boat trips	10	10	20
Ferry companies	45	20	65
Foreign tourist offices	70	35	105
Foreign airlines	130	65	195
ANWB (Royal Dutch Touring Club) offices	485	90	575
Total number of jobs	4 445	1 775	6 220

*Larger concerns only

Table A4. **Number of concerns and jobs in the tourist and leisure industry,
and number of relevance to vocational education**

	Type of concern	No. Jobs	Relevant to vocational education
Camping sites, bungalow parks	4 560	18 000	5 000
Water sports centres	1 719	11 740*	3 600
Theme parks, etc.	409	5 600	1 000/2 000
Guides (self-employed)	200	1 000/2 000*	1 000/2 000
Tour operators	185/200	2 150	2 150
Travel agencies	1 200	2 980	2 980
Banks (travel departments)	3 600	4 300	4 300
Tourist information offices	549	3 000/3 400*	2 500/2 900
Governmental and semi-governmental agencies	–		
Transport companies	346	7 155	3 500
Foreign tourist offices	30	130	130
ANWB (Royal Dutch Touring Club) offices	48	2 600	700

* Including voluntary workers
Source: PCBB/SVATOR (1989).

Using this method, the CIBB arrived at a total of almost 13 000 concerns and approximately 62 000 jobs in the tourist and leisure industry, of which 31 000 are in the category defined above (relevant to specific vocational training). As with the Netherlands Research Institute for Leisure and Tourism figures, the number of jobs varies according to the criterion used.

Shifts

In 1988 the Centre for Innovation in Vocational Training for Industry attempted to estimate replacement demand, studying job changes and turnover patterns in 461 businesses employing a total of 10 991 people (6 610 full time, 4 381 part time), or approximately 18 per cent of the total number employed in the industry. Here, too, according to information supplied by the businesses in the sample, it appeared that the educational background of workers in the same type of job was highly diverse, ranging from general secondary education to senior secondary vocational and higher vocational education and specific vocational training. Only a small proportion of workers had followed a full-time vocational training programme. The changes recorded were as follows:

- Changes in business size in the previous and succeeding five years: 16 per cent had reduced the number of staff, and 56 per cent had increased their workforce (20 per cent by one or two workers, 23 per cent by three to ten, and 10 per cent by 11 to 50). Twenty-three per cent expected a decline in the near future, and 38 per cent predicted growth.

– Changes in the number of jobs in the previous five years: 17 per cent reported a drop, and some 40 per cent an increase. The job losses were fairly evenly distributed in terms of job types. The additional jobs were mainly in the supervisory, information and amusement fields, together with a considerable number in the domestic and maintenance areas (possibly resulting from internal reorganisation). The educational qualifications of the discontinued and new jobs were much the same.

– Changes expected in the number of jobs in the succeeding five years: 6 per cent expected jobs to go, and some 30 per cent expected an increase. Half of the jobs expected to be discontinued related to sports, games and instruction posts (possibly more use of the services of professionals). The expected growth related to all types of jobs, with a relative emphasis on the commercial and information side. Qualifications on the whole would be at senior secondary vocational and senior general secondary level.

– Labour turnover in the previous five years: The outflow was 2 007, and the inflow 2 158. The turnover in information and clerical jobs was high, but lower in management and administration. The inflow exceeded the outflow among guides and those in the commercial and amusement fields, while the reverse was the case with jobs of a supervisory nature. The majority of incoming staff had work experience in a similar business or in a business outside the tourist industry. On the whole, their educational qualifications were higher than those of their predecessors.

The CIBB's calculations of the replacement demand by the businesses in the sample showed an annual outflow of 18 per cent of the total workforce over a period of five years, or 3.7 per cent per year, of whom 0.3 per cent remained in the industry, and 0.3 per cent were eligible for unemployment or disablement benefits or had reached retirement age. As the inflow exceeded the outflow, an annual inflow of 3.7 per cent is conceivable.

Nature of the market

The above survey and a study of the need for training conducted by the CIBB among 327 persons employed in the industry (1990) validate certain conclusions regarding the nature of this section of the labour market. The 1990 research data reveal wide variations in both educational background and experience.

– Some 40 per cent of the 159 managers and 19 per cent of the 240 staff (72 of whom were also managers) who performed other duties, had a higher vocational or university education. With respect to the managers this percentage was the highest in the day-trippers and information sectors (68 per cent and 57 per cent respectively), and the lowest in travel agencies and the tourist accommodation sector (37 per cent and 26 per cent). Of the staff, the majority with such qualifications (38 per cent) were employed in the day-trippers and water-sports sectors.

– Some 41 per cent of managers and 30 per cent of staff had a senior secondary vocational or higher vocational education. Of the former, 55 per cent were active in the day-trippers sector, and 48 per cent in information services, with only 29 per cent in travel agencies. The majority of staff with such qualifications (53 per cent) were likewise employed in the day-trippers sector, with a smaller number in travel agencies and information services (24 per cent and 22 per cent).

– The majority of the respondents had a general vocational education. No more than 13 per cent of managers had qualifications specific to the tourist and leisure industry; most were managers of travel agencies (47 per cent) and tourist information offices (19 per cent), while few, if any, were to be found in the leisure branch. The comparable percentage among staff was slightly higher, 26 per cent of those with vocational education qualifications having followed a programme specific to the tourist and leisure industry and being largely employed in travel agencies (54 per cent) and tourist information offices (43 per cent).

– A substantial number of respondents had general secondary education qualifications, namely 20 per cent of managers and 35 per cent of staff. This was quite frequently the case among travel agency managers (45 per cent), but not among those of day-tripper businesses (6 per cent). The staff figures are similar, showing 62 per cent with these qualifications in travel agencies and 54 per cent in tourist information services, but none in day-tripper businesses.

The predominance of persons with a general education background in the tourist and leisure industry is partly attributable to the fact that in this industry, and the leisure branch in particular, there is as yet little in the way of specific training (see also Section 3). Moreover, the larger firms like KLM and Holland International prefer employees with a broad educational background who can then be given on-the-job training meeting the company's specific needs.

This means that the tourist and leisure sector of the labour market bears a closer resemblance to a business-specific-sub-market (Van Hoof and Dronkers, 1980), where selection requirements are geared to "ability to learn and adapt" and "the right attitude". For this reason, experience is often rated higher than any formal qualification. However, along with the professionalisation of the industry and the establishment of a separate identity, there now seems to be a trend towards an occupational sub-market where occupational qualifications are more important.

Current and future trends

After a slight decline at the beginning of the 1980s, tourism resumed growth in the second part of the decade. Slight to average growth is predicted for the industry up to the year 2000. According to *Toerisme, trends en toekomst* (Tourism, trends and the future), a collection of the findings of ten research projects published by the Netherlands Tourist Board (NBT, 1989), and a study of labour market trends and future developments conducted by the Centre for Innovation in Vocational Training for Industry (1989), the major current trends in the tourist industry are as follows:

Consumers' changing wishes and demands

– Consumers are becoming less stereotyped: demands ranging from "traditional holidays in the sun" to active, individual, faraway and cultural holidays are growing ever more differentiated, necessitating both a wider choice of destinations and a

more individual approach to the provision of information and the arrangement of package holidays;
- present-day consumers are better informed, rendering information and services of a general, non-specialised kind inadequate; .
- consumers are more critical, demanding better-quality information and a more attentive handling of complaints.

Social and demographic trends

- Growth of the "over-50s market" with a concomitant greater demand for specialised information and service (guides/couriers) and comfortable transport and accommodation;
- more leisure time, resulting in more day trips and short breaks;
- increased awareness of environmental pollution, giving rise to a greater demand for good public transport facilities;
- a larger number of young people seeking inexpensive holiday accommodation and amusement.

Organisational changes

- Partial specialisation of the intermediary sector, promoting more effective, professional information and advisory services;
- increasing computerisation of information and reservation systems;
- increased competition, resulting inter alia in expansion of scale, commercialisation and more attention to management, price control and marketing.

Internationalisation

- After 1992, specialisation and a more distinct cultural identity will assume greater importance for the individual European countries;
- a sound knowledge of languages will be increasingly in demand;
- international co-operation and competition will both intensify throughout the 1990s, placing heavier pressure on the products and services of the tourist industry.

Not all of the various sub-branches of the industry will be affected by all of these trends. Generally, however, there is an acknowledged need for better quality. The need for a more professional approach became apparent around 1980, and attention was thereafter devoted to greater efficiency and improved amenities. It was not realised until later that the workers themselves were in need of professionalisation. A notable feature of the Netherlands Tourist Board's 1989 trend reports is their failure to link this point with the need to improve the quality of the tourism product. On the other hand, questionnaires administered to 50 experts by the Centre for Innovation in Vocational Training for Industry and the answers supplied by 461 businesses in the study of labour market trends and future developments (1989) leave no doubt of the perception of the need for professionalisation of the workers in the field.

In many parts of the industry, and particularly in the leisure branch, workers with no more than a primary education have acquired occupational competence through experience.

This is due to the nature and the evolution of the leisure branch, which offers opportunities for pioneers and entrepreneurs who fill 'a gap in the market'. But experience in itself is not always enough, for in some sub-branches, and especially in the leisure branch, and at managerial level in some sectors, the growing number of older persons makes refresher courses essential. While one or two specific areas like languages and computerisation are targeted for professionalisation, the need for upgrading across the board is also pressing.

Developments in the sub-branches

Since 1978 travel agents have been required to possess a certificate in commercial practice and professional competence, qualifying them to run a travel agency business[8]. This statutory obligation was introduced partly in response to the view of the Netherlands Association of Travel Companies (ANVR) that improvement was needed in the sector and that workers should have certain specific qualifications. In the following decade the certificate was increasingly required for intermediary staff as well. The main development in the travel sector in the past ten years is the heavier demand made on intermediary staff, whose principal task of "selling illusions" grows more difficult as consumers become less stereotyped, better informed, and more openly critical. This requires greater knowledge, skills, judgement, imagination, resourcefulness and assertiveness on the part of those dealing with those demands.

The Netherlands Association of Tourist Information Offices (ANVV) also views the demand for better service as the most notable trend in the past few years. For those dealing with the public this implies wider knowledge and more skills, including language skills. A second aspect of better service is better management. Regular sector-oriented further training and refresher courses have become increasingly important for managers, inquiry desk staff and the voluntary workers who comprise more than half of the workforce in the sector. The Association also seeks to foster professionalisation through improved terms of employment and better working conditions, especially for voluntary workers.

In the leisure branch, emphasis is placed on better management, and thus on the task of proprietors. The owners of small businesses have a wide range of responsibilities, but their principal task is that of efficient management. According to the Netherlands Association of Leisure Industry Proprietors (RECRON), this has become highly complex in recent years. Because the leisure branch is linked with other areas of activity (agriculture, the services sector, the hotel and catering industry) it is subject to many rules and regulations which may be expected to proliferate further in the years to come. In addition, competition has become more intensive. The Association considers overall upgrading to be a matter of urgency. The first generation of proprietors, the pioneers who often started out with only a primary school education, must be succeeded by a second generation with senior secondary vocational or preferably higher vocational qualifications. Adequate facilities for further and refresher training must also be available.

The sub-branch related organisations take the view that the quality of the industry's product and the need to provide a better service are closely linked to the need for specific vocational training. Whether the investment required for this purpose will actually be forthcoming is less certain. This point is discussed below.

Social structure

Examination of developments in the structure of tourism reveals to what extent the industry is still struggling to acquire a clear-cut identity, and shows that some of the problems associated with the process of professionalisation are rooted in its social structure.

The first point to emerge is that despite the large number of parties involved in the tourist and leisure branch, they can in no way be considered to be social partners. An employers' organisation does not exist. The sub-branch related organisations view themselves first and foremost as promoting the interests of their members, not as employers' organisations. The employees are represented by the service sector unions of the National Federation of Christian Trade Unions (CNV) and the Federation of Netherlands Trade Unions (FNV)[9]. The trade unions showed no particular interest in the industry until 1990, when the Federation of Netherlands Trade Unions appointed a special official for the travel and leisure branches. Trade union membership is low throughout the industry.

An additional problem is that some workers in the leisure sector are members of the FNV hotel and catering trades union. The hotel accommodation and catering sections of leisure businesses must be registered with the Hotel and Catering Trades Board, so that the terms of employment of the employees concerned are governed by the collective labour agreement for that branch. A representative of the Netherlands Association of Leisure Industry Proprietors states that, owing to the different occupational areas represented in the industry or, in other words, because of its position covering a number of such areas, the Association has to deal with several collective labour agreements. A similar situation prevails in the travel sector, where some workers in the transport branch (tour boats etc.) come under the collective agreement for transport workers, while others have their own collective agreement.

It became clear in the late 1980s that the lack of a social structure was not conducive to professionalisation. Improvements in the quality of the product can be effected only provided businesses are prepared to invest in their personnel and in better facilities. As the majority are small or even one-man businesses with limited financial resources, it would be necessary for them to join forces. The same applies with respect to some sectors, such as the subsidised tourist information services and much of the accommodation and water sports sectors. This is also acknowledged by the sectoral organisations and, for reasons of competitiveness, by the large firms in the travel sector.

Terms of employment and working conditions often leave much to be desired, such aspects as working hours and work breaks in many cases being poorly regulated, if at all, while career prospects and training facilities are generally lacking, especially in the travel sector. The staff turnover in intermediary jobs in the travel sector is high as young women leave after a few years to marry and start a family. The tourist information sector makes intensive use of the services of volunteers, often women returning to work who have little prospect of paid employment. One of the main characteristics of the leisure branch is the hard work it entails, but for many this is offset by the fact that they are self-employed.

Developments in the individual sectors

The realisation on the part of the sectoral organisations and the large firms that in the long term such a situation is undesirable, together with the trade unions' new interest in the position of workers in the industry, is gradually bringing about changes. Negotiations have led to a collective labour agreement in 1994, marking the success of the first activities undertaken by the Federation of Netherlands Trade Unions in the sector. Conducting a campaign which included consultation with Holland International, one of the largest firms in the travel sector, with a reasonable number of union members and an active works council, the Federation forced through a sectoral labour agreement by threatening to draw up a separate labour agreement for the firm's employees, a move which would have been detrimental to its competitive position.

On the initiative of the sectoral organisation for the leisure branch, the possibility of designing a collective labour agreement for the entire branch is now being studied. In addition, a large-scale project aimed to improve management by encouraging participation in training courses is currently in progress.

The tourist information sector, led by the Netherlands Association of Tourist Information Offices, has for some time been considering ways and means of improving the situation, beginning with personnel management. In consultation with the trade unions, specific terms of employment, a job evaluation system and a pension scheme have been elaborated. As from 1992, use of the job evaluation system has become obligatory for all tourist information offices. The Association is also taking steps to improve the management of information offices and thus to strengthen the structure of the sector, with the larger offices functioning as a backbone for the smaller ones. As a result the smaller offices could purchase management from the larger ones, exchanges would be more frequent, and managers obliged to gain practical experience in various types of offices. Furthermore, greater efforts will be made to involve volunteers more closely and offer them training opportunities in the hope that they can eventually be given paid employment with the aid of government subsidies.

Awareness of the importance of training is growing in all sectors. What is viewed as the greatest impediment is the lack of a collective labour agreement for the whole of the industry, which could specify, for instance, the financial amount to be deducted for training. It is doubtful whether a training and development fund of this kind can be established in the short term, for it implies that "wealthy" sectors and businesses would be obliged to subsidise the "poor" ones. The problem is illustrated by the case of the Centre for Training for the Tourist and Travel Industry, whose predecessor, the Advisory Centre for Training for the Travel Industry, was set up by the sectoral organisations in 1972 to represent them in matters pertaining to training and in discussions with the Ministry of Education and Science, and to act as a channel for funds. It has to date received little financial or other support from the industry. The director, for instance, is temporarily paid part of his salary by the Ministry of Economic Affairs, and the Centre does not yet occupy a central position in training for the industry, with powers to introduce compulsory rules and regulations. The branch is still too fragmented, with individual businesses and some sectoral organisations continuing to operate autonomously.

The future

Present indications are that the professionalisation of the tourist and leisure will continue throughout the 1990s. The demand for better services, stemming from growing international competition and a more critical attitude on the part of the consumer, will exert greater pressure on those active in the branch. Training, and specifically vocationally-oriented training, is expected to become ever more essential. It is probable that the competences required for occupations in the travel and information sectors will be substantially different from those prevailing in the day-trippers, accommodation and water sports sections of the leisure branch. For the small- and medium-sized businesses in this branch, management skills will be increasingly important, in much the same way as in agriculture and the hotel and catering industry. The same applies in respect of the travel and information sectors, whose ties with the hotel and catering industry will be strengthened in the process, while the intermediary and informative nature of many of the jobs concerned will remain their dominant feature.

What the future holds for the structure of the tourist and leisure branch is not altogether clear. The various sectoral organisations are likely to be transformed into employers' organisations. The demand for better service, issuing from central government as well as consumers, will focus the attention of the sectoral organisations and businesses ever more strongly on those working in the industry and thus on their terms of employment and working conditions. Quite possibly a number of separate collective agreements will emerge, as it is highly improbable that a single one covering the whole of the industry can be negotiated. That means that some other way must be found to establish a fund for training. The Centre for Training for the Tourist and Travel Industry could constitute a cohesive force in these developments and, for more pragmatic reasons, co-operation with the hotel and catering trades will increase, mainly through closer relations with the Centre for Training for the Hotel and Catering Industry.

In view of these developments, the problems connected with providing competences will come to resemble those characteristic of small- and medium-sized businesses in general (see for example Van den Tillaart *et al.*, on training in small- and medium-sized businesses, 1991). Though expansion of scale will be increasingly common, a substantial number of small businesses may be expected to survive for the time being at least. In the fields of training and management, problems will arise in such areas as professional management and personnel policy, while further obstacles will be encountered in the development of a training policy (lack of funds, outside support and opportunities for training during work hours) and following training courses (businesses' lack of information regarding training opportunities).

3. Developments in Education

There are many different programmes on offer for those interested in a career in the tourist and leisure industry. A guide published by SVATOR (now the Centre for Training for the Tourist and Travel Industry) in 1989 listed 55 institutions that provided tourism and leisure-related programmes. These include programmes at both initial and continuing education level, run by both government-funded (non-profit) and commercial institutions. Rather than attempt to describe all these programmes in detail, this section looks at the main types of programmes available, giving only a cursory treatment of the programmes offered by commercial institutions. An outline is given of developments in the range and content of programmes offered over the last decade. Finally, the future of senior secondary tourism and leisure education is discussed, including the plans produced within the Education and Industry Forum on Tourism and Leisure (BOOB-T/R).

Provision and participation

The first tourism and leisure-related programmes in the Netherlands were set up on the initiative of the industry and commercial institutions. With the advent of mass tourism in the 1950s and 1960s, the major companies, tour operators and travel agency chains introduced internal training courses. The commercial institutions and sectoral organisations (i.e. the ANVR and the ANVV) began running programmes in the 1960s. In the early 1960s the industry founded a college for management training and research, which was funded by government. The late 1970s and 1980s saw an enormous increase in the provision of programmes in both the commercial and non-profit sector. The picture in 1991 is as follows.

Higher vocational programmes – HBO (non-profit sector)

The first vocational programme in the non-profit sector that was geared to careers in the tourist and leisure industry was run by the National College of Tourism and Transport in Breda. Initially, the college was involved in research as well as teaching, until a separate institute, the Netherlands Research Institute for Leisure and Tourism (NRIT, see above), was founded. The programme lasts four years. The college also runs various management programmes and a programme for professional guides. The number of places is limited to 270 on the basis of labour market research. Of the annual intake of students, three-quarters hold VWO certificates and the remainder HAVO or MBO certificates. Between 180 and 200 students graduate each year.

The college recently introduced two-year HBO programmes for specific management posts (tourist information, leisure, travel agents and tour operators). The maximum intake is around 250 students. These programmes are open to holders of HAVO, VWO or senior secondary commercial education (MEAO) certificates. Graduates of the trade schools set up by the industry are exempted from part of the programme. Students who have completed these short programmes can go on to the six-year part-time HBO programmes introduced in 1991.

Since the late 1980s, more and more HBO colleges have introduced programmes or options in tourism and leisure, bringing the total number of colleges offering such programmes at present to 20 (Council for Higher Vocational Education, 1991). Some of these programmes are specifically geared to tourism and leisure, others are in related fields but lead to careers in tourism and leisure. They may fall under social work and cultural studies, applied home economics, forestry, land and water management, commerce (management), teacher training or hotel management. Almost all these programmes offer a limited number of places. At a rough estimate, the total number of graduates per year is about 1 500, of whom around one-third will have specialised in some aspect of tourism and leisure.

Senior secondary vocational programmes (MBO)

Vocational training for posts in tourism and leisure has been provided in the non-profit sector at MBO level since the late 1970s. There are currently 10 colleges in the Netherlands providing senior secondary tourism and leisure education (MTRO). Four of these programmes have their origins in commercial education (MTRO-MEAO) and six in hotel management and catering (MTRO-MHO). Accordingly, the first group focuses more on careers which involve information provision and public relations, and the second group on middle management posts and running a business.

In the late 1980s MTRO became a full four-year programme. The first students graduated in the summer of 1991. These are the 250 or so students now in their final year at five of the six colleges whose MTRO programmes originated from hotel management and catering courses. These six colleges are expected to produce twice as many graduates from 1992 onwards. The four programmes in commercial education were transformed from two-year programmes in tourism and leisure within MEAO to a full four-year programme, a process completed in 1994. These four colleges are expected to produce around 550 graduates each year. The total number of graduates from all ten colleges is expected to be 1 050 per year.

In the last few years, several MBO colleges have introduced programmes with a tourism-oriented option or optional courses in tourism. Although some of these are two-year programmes, none of these colleges have MTRO status. No data is available on the number of students with a qualification including a tourism and leisure option.

Apprenticeship training

There are no apprenticeships in the Netherlands geared specifically to the tourist and leisure industry, although there are apprenticeship places in related areas including: agriculture, (relevant to maintenance work in the leisure branch), motor mechanics, (relevant to the water sports sector), and hotel management and catering (relevant to catering posts in the day-trippers, tourist accommodation and water sports sectors and to reception posts in hotels, etc.)

Trade schools

Until 1990 there were three trade schools partially subsidised by the Ministry of Education and Science via the Centre for Training for the Tourist and Travel Industry[10]. These schools were set up in the 1960s and 1970s by the sectoral organisations, namely the ANVR (which set up the Trade School for the Travel Agency Industry) and the ANVV (Trade School for the Tourist Information Business)[11], and by local industry in the province of Overijssel (College of Tourism). They provide full-time programmes lasting one or two years which are geared to specific posts in the travel and tourist information sectors.

Prospective students must have a HAVO, VWO or MBO certificate. The sectoral organisations and the enterprises regard the trade schools as closer to HBO than MBO level.

The number of students admitted depends on the information supplied by the industry. Between 250 and 300 students qualify each year. Most find work immediately in the sector concerned; some (10-30 per cent) go on to HBO or short HBO programmes.

Vocational courses in the commercial sector

Commercial institutions offer numerous courses. There are at least 65 commercial institutions (Centre for Training for the Tourist and Travel Industry, 1990) most of which prepare students for the state-recognised examinations in professional competence and commercial practice for travel agents. There are far fewer courses geared to jobs in the tourist information sector or the leisure industry. Some of the institutions run daytime and evening classes; many more provide correspondence courses. According to the Centre for Training for the Tourist and Travel Industry, the average success rate on commercial courses is much lower than on the courses run by the sectoral organisations and in-company training courses (35 per cent compared to 70 per cent in 1990).

No exact figures are available on the number of courses or students, although some idea of the numbers involved can be gained from looking at the number of candidates who take the eight state-recognised examinations set by the Centre for Training for the Tourist and Travel Industry. In 1989, for instance, there were 4 000 candidates, most of whom took the examinations for the travel industry. It should be remembered, however, that this figure includes all candidates regardless of the programmes they followed (i.e. including, for instance, those who attended in-company training courses in preparation for the exam).

Company training courses

The major companies in the tourist and leisure industry, such as transport companies, bungalow park chains, tour operators and banks that sell package holidays, arrange internal further training courses for their staff. Rather than being company-specific, some of the courses prepare employees for national examinations and diplomas that are recognised by the branch and by the government. With the increase in the number of external training courses, however, in-company courses are increasingly geared to teaching company-specific knowledge and attitudes. No figures are available on either the number of courses or the number of persons attending such courses.

Continuing education (contract training)

Besides company training courses, commercial courses and the initial training courses run by the trade schools, there are also (commercial) specialised further training courses run by the non-profit sector vocational colleges and the trade schools. One of the main providers of such courses for those already working in the industry is the Tourism and Transport Services Centre, the transfer centre set up by the National College of Tourism and Transport in Breda. The Centre provides tailor-made courses, sometimes in-company, and courses that are open to anyone, usually developed at the request of the sectoral organisations. Some of the courses are developed with the financial support of the Ministry of Economic Affairs. A relatively large number of these courses relate to the leisure branch, a noteworthy fact, in that most courses are geared more to the travel industry than the leisure industry). The trade schools also provide further training programmes for those already working in the industry. These are short programmes which are open to everyone, usually relating to information and public relations posts.

Developments in the training system

The training system for the tourist and leisure industry has been characterised in the last ten years by two main trends:
- the externalisation of training (the shift away from training courses mainly funded by the industry to prior vocational training in non-profit colleges funded by government;
- the increasing importance attached to training, especially continuing education.

Underlying these trends was the need for greater professionalisation described previously.

Vocational training in non-profit colleges

Until the early 1980s, formal training was seldom used as a selection criterion for work in the tourist and leisure industry. Small businesses in particular (especially in the leisure sector) were more interested in entrepreneurial spirit, initiative and flexibility than formal qualifications. The larger companies (for instance in the travel business) preferred candidates with a broad education (HAVO or VWO certificate) and a "customer-friendly" manner (who would then be moulded further to meet the company's standards). This attitude is still common today. Both the trade schools and the non-profit colleges that provide tourism and leisure-related courses had to set about convincing the industry, and especially employers, of their worth. The trade schools had the advantage of having been set up by the sectoral organisations (or local industry). During the course of the decade, the combination of a broad education followed by job-specific training came to be regarded increasingly by large sections of the industry (both in the travel business and the tourist information sector) as the ideal qualification. For the non-profit colleges, especially the MBO colleges, the need felt by the tourist and leisure branches for recognition as a branch in its own right furthered this trend. As a result of pressure from the sectoral organisations and the government, and the increased competitiveness and expansion of scale in vocational education, more attention was focused on the need for mergers of schools for specialised programmes.

A vocational qualification in tourism and leisure from a non-profit college is regarded as essential throughout the industry. Attitudes towards MTRO programmes, in particular, still tend to be a little sceptical. There are three factors involved here: the short history of MTRO; the many other options available, the chief of which are the short HBO programmes at Breda and the courses run by the trade schools; and current thinking on the best way to train young people for work.

Section 2 showed the difficulty of defining specific tourist and leisure competence in the tourist and leisure industry. It was no less difficult for the colleges. Two types of MTRO were developed in the 1980s. The oldest (MTRO-MEAO), which has its origins in commercial education, came about through the efforts of the municipality of Leiden and the travel and tourist information business. The developments in Breda (which also officially belonged to the commercial/economics sector) served partly as an example. At the same time non-profit catering colleges had been set up, which a few years later also showed an interest in developing tourism and leisure programmes (MTRO-MHO) in response to feedback from ex-students and the needs of local industry.

The catering colleges placed a much greater emphasis on entrepreneurship. At that time the industry, the Centre for Training for the Tourist and Travel Industry and the National College of Tourism and Transport in Breda, expressed a preference for MTRO-MEAO[12]; the tourist and leisure branch was anxious to be seen as separate from the hotel and catering branch. The outcome was the development of two different types of MTRO. Both the government and the sectoral organisations feel that these should be combined into one during the next decade.

The question of where or how young people should gain their competences played almost no role in all this. The colleges developed curricula according to their own ideas and in consultation with some parts of the local tourist and leisure industry. For a long time, the overriding attitude of most of the industry was that MTRO was not needed to produce competent personnel. The travel business and the tourist information sector relied mainly upon the trade schools to supply middle management. The leisure industry sought to professionalise its staff through continuing education and tended to recruit from the National College of Tourism and Transport in Breda. Under pressure from the government (which commissioned a job profiles study and subsequently recognised MTRO as a separate training programmes) and the Centre for Training for the Tourist and Travel Industry, MTRO diplomas were increasingly recognised as a worthwhile qualification.

The attitude of the industry remains somewhat ambiguous, however. The college at Breda, for instance, working closely with the various sectoral organisations and on the basis of the job profiles study mentioned in Section 2, has started short HBO programmes specifically designed for middle management. Yet, this is the very field in which MTRO (and MBO in general) claims to specialise, especially MTRO-MHO (hotel management and catering)[13]. The sectoral organisations, however, are not yet convinced that MTRO can deliver graduates of the right calibre and were therefore willing to co-operate with Breda - - with which it has strong links in setting up short programmes. The leisure industry, in particular, has more confidence in the short HBO programmes for entrepreneurial posts than in MTRO (partly because, for a long time, MTRO programmes were not geared in any great measure to the leisure industry).

Generally speaking, MTRO is set to become the main channel for initial training for the tourist and leisure industry. This "externalisation" of training is supported by the industry mainly as a means of promoting the institutionalisation and recognition of the branch. In return, however, employers expect the colleges to produce graduates who have been trained for specific jobs and can be deployed immediately with little, if any, additional training.

Continuing education and training needs

Unlike the tourism and leisure programmes provided by the non-profit vocational education colleges, continuing education has been developed mainly with a view to training and professional development for those already working in the industry. The provision of training throughout an employee's working life came to be regarded as increasingly important during the 1980s and the number of further training programmes grew accordingly, mainly due to the efforts of the Centre for Training for the Tourist and Travel Industry and of sectoral organisations, such as the RECRON.

The transfer centre at the National College of Tourism and Transport in Breda developed during the 1980s as a kind of pivotal point for vocationally-oriented further training programmes for the industry, encouraged by the Centre for Training for the Tourist and Travel Industry and the sectoral organisations. Commercial provision, by contrast, developed more in response to demand from individual students and employees. Newcomers to the market for vocationally-oriented training for the tourist and leisure industry (such as the MTRO colleges and other senior secondary vocational colleges) therefore face competition from two sides and will have to develop their further training programmes largely in response to local demand. For the time being at least, the Centre for Training for the Tourist and Travel Industry sees the transfer centre at Breda and the trade schools as forming the backbone of high-quality continuing education.

The Ministry of Economic Affairs, in its policy document published in 1990, concluded that the tourist and leisure industry received a relatively large proportion of the funds made available by the Ministry for training under its three subsidy schemes (one for training in industry in general, one for entrepreneurial training and one for small- and medium-sized businesses). Both the various sections of the industry and individual employees and companies make use of these schemes. The figures are comparable to those for the average small or medium-sized business in the Netherlands (Tillaart *et al.*, 1991).

Programmes partially subsidised by the Ministry of Economic Affairs and the Ministry of Social Security and Employment in the last few years include a course in strategic planning and forward-looking business management, a course in social skills and a course for leisure workers. A total of some 1 100 people took part in the first two of these courses between 1985 and 1988 (Institute for Social Science and Economic Research – ISEO, 1989).

Educational developments

The emergence of tourism and leisure programmes in non-profit vocational education and the growth in further education have added to the range of programmes available. In senior secondary vocational education, in particular, various new programmes were created in the 1980s. There have also been changes in course content and design, with the incorporation of more practical elements and the introduction of modular programmes. These measures are a result of the trend towards a dual system of training (combining theoretical and practical components) and a better alignment of training and work. Both the trade schools and the non-profit colleges now place more emphasis on the work environment which is reflected in various ways[14].

Practical component

The practical component in senior secondary tourist and leisure education (MTRO) has expanded considerably since the Ministry of Education and Science gave MRTO permission to become a department in its own right. Previously, courses had to take the same form as other courses run by the "parent college", so that the tourism and leisure element could not be given the emphasis it deserved. This was especially true of MTRO-MEAO in the early 1980s. The courses had a commercial basis, work placements were limited to six weeks and the majority of the teachers were from MEAO. Efforts were made to gear courses more to the tourist and leisure industry by organising visits and study trips and hiring visiting lecturers. The MTRO programmes set up by the catering colleges (MTRO-MHO) were separate four-year programmes from the outset and could therefore be geared to jobs in the tourist and leisure industry right from the start. Since the MTRO-MHO programmes are recent and MTRO-MEAO is still in the process of switching to a four-year programme, it is only possible to give an initial impression of the practical component of each.

The old three-year MTRO-MEAO programme included a six-week work placement. In the four-year programme, the fourth year is practical with students going on two long placements. In addition, up to 24 days can be taken up by compulsory excursions, and study trips which are "programme units". In the first year they will go on one in the Netherlands and one abroad (visiting several cities); in the second year they will visit a foreign summer resort and in the third year a ski resort. Students will be tested on the content of each study trip (and day trips/excursions). Some study trips will form part of the practical component of the examination. For the others, tests will be held in the various subjects taught by the lecturers responsible for the content of the trip.

In MTRO-MHO students have to spend at least two weeks in a tourism or leisure-related business in their first or second year, outside school time. In the fourth and final year they are required to spend 40 weeks in industry. There are plans to introduce a requirement that students spend at least half of their work placements abroad. Visits are organised throughout the programme. Simulations also allow students to apply and build on the knowledge and skills they have learnt in the classroom (just as in other MHO programmes).

The curriculum in the trade schools is strongly geared to the students' future work. In the mid-1980s, placements and visits become a more important element of the programmes. The one-year programme at the trade school for the travel agency business, for instance, originally included only two weeks of practical experience. The programme is now longer and includes two periods of work experience: four weeks in the first year and three months in the second year.

The short programmes recently introduced at the National College of Tourism and Transport in Breda include mainly practice-oriented courses (comparable to some extent with the type of subjects taught at the trade schools). The last part of each programme involves a ten-week placement.

Apprenticeship training

With regard to the development of a dual system of training, i.e. training which is more application-oriented, there has been discussion (by the Centre for Training for the Tourist and Travel Industry) of introducing apprenticeships for tourism and leisure-related occupations. In 1990, the CIBB conducted a study of the feasibility of such a course of action. The study concentrated on two possible types of apprenticeship:

- inquiry desk staff/receptionists/travel advisers (the report described this as an apprenticeship at elementary level for holders of a HAVO certificate; the latter would however imply training at secondary or tertiary level);
- managerial staff (given the admission requirements – MTRO/trade, school/ apprenticeship – this would be at tertiary level).

A survey was conducted by telephone among 581 businesses (tourist information offices, travel agencies and businesses in the day-tripper, tourist accommodation and water sports sectors)[15] and a number of key figures were interviewed. Of those questioned, 72 per cent were interested in the apprenticeship for inquiry desk staff and were prepared between them to offer 217 training places per year, mainly in tourist information offices. Some 50 per cent were interested in the apprenticeship for managerial staff. However, almost 60 per cent of the businesses selected had no interest whatsoever in apprenticeship schemes and another 17 per cent could not be contacted. It should also be noted that many companies in the tourist and leisure industry have no real idea of what apprenticeship training is about. With regard to setting up a national body for apprenticeship training for the industry, opinions are divided: 58 per cent of the respondents were in favour of such a body, but 25 per cent of the businesses in the accommodation sector preferred to join the training body for the catering sector; 24 per cent of the businesses questioned were undecided.

The Centre for Training for the Tourist and Travel Industry concluded on the basis of the survey that there was sufficient interest to set up an apprenticeship scheme for the tourist industry, even if this were only at further training level. It decided against having a separate system (partly because the government was not in favour of it). If apprenticeship schemes are created, they will be placed under the umbrella of the Centre for Training for the Hotel and Catering Industry. There are signs that the ANVV (Trade School for the Tourist Information Business) is interested in an apprenticeship for inquiry desk staff, partly because of the shortage of applicants in their own trade school.

Modular teaching and vocationally-oriented subject matter

In the 1980s, many programmes (notably apprenticeship training programmes) were given a modular structure. A modular programme is one which has been organised in self-contained units or modules, mainly with a view to improved efficiency. The modules are checked to ensure that there is no overlap of subject matter, which must be arranged in a clear fashion. Modular teaching was seen as bringing about greater efficiency and flexibility (in terms of the rapid replacement of outdated components) and bringing the curriculum more into line with the reality of work. The latter objective means that the modules created must form units which are relevant to the profession for which students are being trained. In this sense, modular teaching can encourage innovation in the curriculum.

As far as tourism and leisure programmes are concerned, no steps have yet been taken in this direction, although the possibility is being investigated in MTRO. Teaching is still based largely on separate (commercial) subjects, with, however, an increasing emphasis on tourism and leisure. In MTRO-MEAO, modern languages are given a relatively heavy emphasis, focusing on terminology in the travel business. MTRO-MHO concentrates more on business economics with the programme focusing specifically on three elements: economics/commerce, communication skills/languages and specialised knowledge and skills.

The curriculum at the trade schools consists of a combination of specialised subjects (e.g. the Dutch countryside and travel agency administration) and subjects of a more general nature (such as languages and economics), which are taught in blocks. Information technology was recently included in the curriculum (as it has been in MTRO); the emphasis here is on learning to deal with the kind of programmes and systems used in the branch. The trade school for the travel agency business is the only one with a modular (thematic) structure, the more general subjects being combined with specialised subjects within broad themes, such as commercial business administration and general travel knowledge. A modular structure was introduced largely for efficiency reasons. The industry wanted students to have more specialised training. Modules (differentiation) have therefore been introduced mainly in the second year. They also had to be suitable for further training.

The short programmes offered at Breda are similar in structure to the programmes run by the trade schools. The subjects are mainly practice-oriented, but are dealt with in greater depth than is the case at the trade schools. Teaching is divided into blocks of ten weeks, each of which is concluded with an examination. Three types of subject are taught: tourism and leisure subjects, economics and management subjects, and communicative skills and languages. There is as yet no theme-based teaching as there is at the trade school for the travel agency business.

The 1980s saw very little change in tourism and leisure programmes in terms of curricular innovation, especially as regards the structuring of subject matter and course design. Instead, the emphasis was on the range of courses available. Educational curricula will be given more attention in the next few years, especially in MTRO where the exit qualifications fixed by the BOOB-T/R (see below) will have to be translated into a curriculum.

Towards colleges of tourism

In its action plan "Vocational education for the tourist industry. A structure for the 1990s", the Centre for Training for the Tourist and Travel Industry concluded inter alia:

"If the tourist industry wishes to see courses of a sufficient standard to suit its needs, it will have to establish a qualification structure to make those needs apparent to the education world, and a qualification structure for the industry cannot exist without a matching system of tourism-related education."

Given that no such structure or system yet exists, the Centre for Training for the Tourist and Travel Industry – which will presumably be the initiator of both – still has a lot of work to do. The rest of this section looks at the work of three fora which play an important role in improving the structure of the training system.

The Education and Industry Forum on Tourism and Leisure (BOOB-T/R)

This national consultative body was set up by the Ministry of Education and Science in early 1989 to translate the job profiles that had been drawn up into training profiles, exit competences and credit units for senior secondary vocational education. The BOOB-T/R comprises six representatives from industry (three from the sectoral organisations and three from the service industry unions, the CNV and the FNV) and six from education (four from the organisations of school boards and educational personnel and one each from MTRO-MHO and MTRO-MEAO). In addition, there is an observer from the Education and Industry Forum on Hotel Management and Catering and more recently an observer from the National College of Tourism and Transport in Breda (HBO). The chairman of the forum is a member of the staff of the Union of Non-denominational School Boards (ABB) and the secretariat is provided by the head of the Centre for Training for the Tourist and Travel Industry.

This was the first time that education and the tourist and leisure industry, or even the sectoral organisations and trade unions, had come together to discuss training, and the professionalisation of the industry, and conducting the talks was frequently a difficult process.

The training profiles for MTRO are as follows:

– Programmes will last four years.

– There will be a general core with nine possible options: four "information" profiles (information officer, information and publicity officer, managerial posts, information officer with responsibility for tourists from abroad); three travel agency/travel business profiles (assistant travel adviser, travel adviser, managerial posts) and two leisure profiles (leisure staff, managerial posts). Three separate profiles are also being developed for guides, receptionists and couriers. This reduces the 39 job profiles to 12 training profiles or profiles of competences to be provided by MTRO.

– There will be eleven credit units. The basic unit, which should be the same regardless of the option chosen, is "basic knowledge about the tourist and leisure industry". Another four units will be geared to various aspects of management. A qualification in "hospitality skills" has been added at the insistence of MTRO-MHO. In this way each programme will comprise between two and seven credit units.

– In principle, all MTRO colleges will provide all the possible options, although certain options may be emphasized more in one region than in others (this will be determined jointly by the sectoral organisations and colleges).

Some representatives have criticised that entrepreneurship/management is not given sufficient attention or should be more obviously a core part of the programme. The trade unions feel that students' career prospects will be limited as a result, while the sectoral organisation RECRON argues that entrepreneurship is central to the leisure industry and should therefore form the core of all training. Finally, the MTRO-MHO colleges say that the programmes they provide, of which entrepreneurship is a central part, are not adequately reflected in the training profiles; they would like to see programmes with a different basis and more scope for various types of MTRO: "It is not clear why there has to be only one type of MTRO, given the diversity of the field of work. Moreover, the training profiles place too much stress on blocks of knowledge and skills and on certificates. When I say, for instance, that the entrepreneurial element is too weak, they reply by saying they will add a management module." Other parties commented that the training profiles have too few cross-links with other branches and programmes, for instance in catering. The training profiles were being modified in light of these comments.

A new structure for the 1990s

In 1990 the Centre for Training for the Tourist and Travel Industry, with financial help from the Ministry of Economic Affairs, published a plan for a new structure for training. Two action points were proposed. First, job classification systems must be developed, using the same methods throughout the industry (to make modular teaching possible). Secondly, a cohesive structure, encompassing the trade schools, MTRO and apprenticeship training, must be developed. In addition, all courses, including those in the commercial sector, should in future have official approval. The Centre envisages the creation within five years of "colleges of tourism", in which the trade schools will focus on specialised further training and MTRO mainly on initial training. Apprenticeship training would come under the umbrella of these schools with the MTRO staff providing the off-the-job part for apprentices. The Centre would play a co-ordinating and supportive role. Two other important areas that require attention are the development of teaching material and the training of tourism and leisure teachers.

With regard to (part-time) industrial training, the Centre also plans to use the occupational profiles (see Section 2) to develop further training profiles. It will be established for each profile what courses are necessary to improve provision. The existing courses will be analysed and restructured, and any gaps filled. Every programme will need to have a modular structure to help prevent any duplication and improve co-ordination.

Committee for the Hotel, Catering, Tourist and Leisure Industries

In 1985, the sectoral organisations and trade unions in the hotel/catering and tourist/leisure industries set up a committee to improve the co-ordination of training and to give the two industries more political clout. In 1990, the committee drew up an action plan in response to the policy document, "Enterprise and Tourism", published by the Ministry of Economic Affairs. The plan indicates that there will be greater co-operation between the two branches, notably as regards putting the expertise of the hotel and catering branch (i.e. the Centre for Training for the Hotel and Catering Industry) at the service of the tourism and leisure branch (the Centre for Training for the Tourist and Travel Industry). The points for action are:
– labour market analysis: comparison of the occupational/training profiles and research into the possibility of transferring the labour market survey methods used in the hotel and catering sector to the tourism and leisure branch;

- education and training: the cohesive development of colleges of tourism and colleges of hotel management and catering; the formulation of a plan for national and international recognition of diplomas; promoting the development and distribution of teaching materials; co-operation on the development of apprenticeship training courses, for which purpose the Centre for Training for the Hotel and Catering Industry will make its facilities available for tourism and leisure-related courses; the development of a training structure for permanent education for workers in the tourist and leisure industry, with the use of the facilities belonging to the hotel and catering industry.

This joint action plan highlights the importance of practical co-operation for the further development of both branches, particularly as far as training is concerned. After a period in which the emphasis has been on the differences between the two branches, it now looks as if there will be a much greater degree of co-operation. This is indeed more or less essential with regard to the streamlining of the tourism and leisure training system, all the more so given that the policy of the Ministry of Education and Science is geared to the integration and broadening of industry-wide training systems and consultation.

4. Professionalisation of the Branch

The last section of this report looks at the relationship between the tourist and leisure industry and the education world. First, the different types of problem which can lead to a mismatch between education and industry are discussed. This is followed by an examination of the role of the various actors involved and the steps that have been taken to improve the alignment of education and industry. In each case, both the past and the future are discussed. To begin, a brief account is provided of the nature of the relationship between education and industry in the tourist and leisure industry.

The word which best describes the developments of the past few years is professionalisation. Some refer to the "maturing" of the industry. One of the major steps in this process was the occupational analysis described in Section 2, in other words the identification of those tasks which can be regarded as belonging primarily to the tourist and leisure industry. By classifying and grouping together the many jobs and tasks that occur in the industry, it was possible to produce 15 job profiles. These tasks and occupations which have been claimed by the branch need, however, to be recognised by the outside world as well. A job is, after all, identifiable as such firstly because it forms a cohesive group of actions for which a certain body of knowledge and skills are required and secondly because it is recognised by society as a self-contained unit of actions and requirements.

To give an adequate picture of the relationship between the industry and the education field, it must be considered in the light of the ongoing process of professionalisation. The public sector vocational colleges play an important role in the definition and recognition of tourism and leisure-related occupations. First, the exit qualifications of their courses and the design of the curriculum influence the way in which jobs are performed; they deliver graduates with particular competences. Secondly, the colleges give the industry a public profile, which results to a certain extent in institutionalisation and, hence, recognition.

The mismatch between education and industry

As far as the interface between education and industry is concerned, a broad distinction can be made between quantitative and qualitative problems. The former relate to discrepancies in the demand and supply of persons with a particular profile of competences. The latter concern discrepancies between actual and required competences. In many cases, these two problems occur in combination with each other. Taking the quantitative approach, the simplest explanation for the emergence of tourism and leisure courses in public-sector vocational education would be that there was a shortage of persons with competences which were appropriate to the tourist and leisure industry. Such an argument, however, takes no account of the dynamic nature of the labour market and the relative value of and influence that can be exercised over the competences that are required at any given time. At the same time the question remains of what constitutes an appropriate profile of competences, i.e. in what way applicants' competences are inadequate. Finally, no account is taken of the background or other factors which can play a role (vested interests, agreements, etc.). The way in which qualitative and quantitative problems intermesh has become clear as the tourist and leisure industry has tried to give itself a higher profile.

In the 1980s, the tourist and leisure industry and parts of the education establishment placed a heavy emphasis on the quantitative mismatch of education and industry. It was repeatedly maintained that there were too many college leavers with tourism and leisure qualifications, without however making any attempt to distinguish between sectors and/or types of job. Nor was any distinction made between the various types of training: the problem was simply seen in terms of the public and commercial sector institutions and trade schools between them producing too many qualified people. This approach was both static and one-sided.

First, a distinction should be made between sectors (and also jobs and types of business). The travel industry was very popular among students in the 1980s, and the majority of programmes, too, in both the public and private sectors, were geared to this sector. Large numbers of students took the national examinations in professional skills and commercial practice for travel agents. The supply of persons wishing to work in the travel business is likely to fall in the future, however, owing to the fading of its glamorous image (partly because of protests against poor terms of employment and working conditions) as well as demographic trends. There is already a shortage of qualified personnel in the tourist information sector. Although the terms of employment are fairly generous and the job calls for a broader range of skills and knowledge than in the travel business, students seem to find this sector less attractive to work in. In the leisure branch, finally, the supply of qualified personnel (for entrepreneurial posts) more or less matches demand, although this sector is given little attention in the various programmes. The main problem faced by the leisure branch is finding enough seasonal staff with the right competences[16].

Secondly, one should distinguish between types of training, or rather differences in the competences offered. Simply referring to a surplus of qualified personnel would imply that there were no differences between them or the courses they had completed. A HAVO certificate holder with a diploma in commercial practice for travel agents (awarded after a short programme at a commercial institution) will be regarded differently and deployed in a different way to someone who has completed a four-year MTRO programme. This is primarily a question of quality: what competences are required, what sort of competences do programmes lead to and to what extent are a person's competences made use of?

No definition of the competence required

As this report has repeatedly shown, it is more or less impossible to find a single definition which embraces all tourism and leisure businesses and in particular all those working in this field. A general description of the industry as encompassing travel, tourist information services and leisure does not adequately cover the many jobs and activities involved. Nor is there any uniformity of job descriptions: different businesses may or may not use the same title for the same job. All posts (and there are a great many) fall into the services category.

The occupational analysis carried out by the CIBB was an attempt to bring some order to this vast array of jobs and bring the number of job categories down to a more manageable figure. Initially, 39 job profiles were identified. These were eventually reduced to 15.

However, the CIBB report fails to define what the most essential competences for work in the tourist and leisure industry are and to say what makes an occupation a tourism and leisure-related one. Some people mention very specific skills and knowledge, while others say it comes down to a particular attitude (which you either have or do not have, so that vocational training has nothing to do with it). For many jobs no particular educational qualification is required, although employers increasingly expect applicants to be as highly educated as possible. Given the diversity of the tourist and leisure industry, it is also extremely complicated to indicate precisely what competences are required and how these differ from the requirements in related industries or comparable occupations. Indeed, what distinguishes many of these jobs is the very fact that they combine various activities and specialisations found within the branch. This is particularly true of the entrepreneurial posts in the leisure sector and of middle management posts in the industry as a whole, to which MTRO programmes are geared. At this intermediate level employees are expected to perform a wide variety of tasks and to manage others (and understand and direct all the work that goes on).

Apart from the diversity of the branch and the variety of tasks which the employee is called upon to perform, there is a second element which complicates the issue of competences. As well as specialised knowledge and skills, employees must possess competence of a general kind (e.g. a good command of modern languages, business knowledge).

Given that the debate on profiles of competences and paths of training is still going on and that the education establishment is one of the main actors in this process (partly because of the status it can confer on the industry), there is, in principle, considerable scope for the non-profit sector vocational colleges to influence the outcome of the debate.

The parties involved and the interests at stake

The picture presented by the tourist and leisure branch in the 1980s, as far as relations between the various actors at the interface of education and industry are concerned, is one of a great many groups between whom there is very little co-operation. Within the industry there are several sectoral organisations and a number of large companies which act more or less independently; at government level, various ministries are involved, while on the education side there are numerous institutions with an interest in this field. Because of the links which the industry has with other branches and because the branch itself is composed of several sectors, intermediaries from outside the industry and various employers' organisations and trade unions are also keen to have a say in the development of the industry and training matters.

The role of the various actors can be best illustrated with reference to the development of senior secondary tourism and leisure education (MTRO; see also Section 3). The first stage was, mainly, to achieve recognition of the importance of non-profit sector vocational education geared specifically to the branch of industry. With no clear answers as to what distinguished the industry from any other or what gave it its distinctive nature, two types of education each staked a claim to part of the field. Although each programme was set up after consultation with the local tourist and leisure industry, they were, in fact, developed more or less independently of the industry. There was, to some extent, a gap in the market because of the emerging demand for professionalisation, which the non-profit sector colleges were able to fill. The government was more or less responsible for reversing the attitude of the industry towards these programmes. Until then there had been little interest in MTRO-MEAO, as reflected by the constant shortage of work experience placements for instance. When the Ministry of Education and Science, followed by the Ministry of Economic Affairs, suddenly switched its preference from MTRO-MEAO to MTRO-MHO, the industry felt that its position was being undermined. Association with the hotel and catering industry was tantamount to denying the separate identity of the tourist and leisure industry, a status which the industry was justified in claiming, if only because of the situation in higher vocational education where there was a college for tourism and transport (economics sector) as well as hotel management schools. Accordingly, the sectoral organisations, the Centre for Training for the Tourist and Travel Industry and the National College of Tourism and Transport in Breda opted en masse to support MTRO-MEAO in response to the Ministry's move.

The second stage in the history of MTRO involved a struggle for the institutionalisation of the branch. Under pressure from the government, which wanted to know once and for all what profiles of competences students on the various MTRO programmes were being trained for, and with a certain amount of opposition from the industry, which remained sceptical (especially the sectoral organisations), the MTRO colleges and the Centre for Training for the Tourist and Travel Industry attempted to develop an initial training path. Because of the government's shift in policy, the two types of training programme ended up in competition with each other. The "battle" was fought mainly at national level through the job occupational research, which was supervised by the industry, and in the joint Education and Industry Forum on Tourism and Leisure (BOOB-T/R). The formulation of training profiles and exit qualifications for MTRO would protect the respective identities of MHO and MEAO programmes. The trade unions supported MTRO because of the enhanced status that a vocational training course in the non-profit sector could confer on its members. The sectoral organisations remained largely undecided. Eventually all the parties represented in the BOOB-T/R talks decided to support the further development of MTRO.

The third stage, which is still a long way from being realised, will be to win proper status for MTRO in the education and training system. The form and content of the programmes will be discussed more extensively. Moreover, the colleges must be given the chance to have a say in the nature of the jobs for which their students are being trained, thereby justifying the existence of MTRO and winning recognition for it.

In retrospect, the emergence of MTRO – precisely because of the rivalry between the two programmes and the policy of the government – has acted as a kind of catalyst in the process of professionalisation within the branch of industry. The existence of specific initial training means, from the point of view of the branch, that it is recognised as such. The developments regarding MTRO have also led to a pooling of interests. Although the forerunner of the Centre for Training for the Tourist and Travel Industry had been representing the combined interests of the sectoral organisations of industry since 1972, it was not until the 1980s that the Centre's position was consolidated. It has in many cases played a mediating role between the colleges, the trade schools, the sectoral organisations of industry and government, giving impetus, for instance, to the development of a social structure in the branch.

A kind of network seems to be developing, within which joint action is becoming more common. This can be seen, for instance, in the increased level of consultation and co-operation between the Centre for Training for the Tourist and Travel Industry and the Centre for Training for the Hotel and Catering Industry. This is taking place at a national and institutional level. Whether individual companies are following suit is another question; the major companies in particular continue to go their own way. At local level, the impetus for co-operation and consultation will have to come from the ten MTRO colleges. Their interest is to strengthen their status in the occupational field (of branch) and in the education system. For local industry (especially small- and medium-sized firms) co-operation with the colleges will reap benefits with regard to the supply of manpower and the professionalisation of the existing workforce. The latter advantage will be all the greater once MTRO colleges can offer tailor-made contract teaching.

Measures to achieve a better alignment of education and industry

As indicated earlier in this section, the problems in the alignment of education and industry are related to the need for professionalisation of the tourist and leisure industry. The measures taken to date in an effort to remedy these problems have focused primarily on giving structure to either the industry as a field of employment or the training system. A better structuring of the industry, in particular, can lead to better interaction between education and industry. Other measures which have been taken by the actors involved have been geared to achieving a quantitative match of supply and demand (labour market research) and, more recently, to the form that training takes.

Structuring the branch

Attempts to structure the branch have included, firstly, initiatives to develop a social structure and a policy on terms of employment and secondly, efforts to map out a job structure. The transition to a fully-fledged branch of industry, with distinct employers' organisations and trade unions, a job classification system and a collective agreement (CAO) which includes deductions for training, is proving difficult because of the fact that the branch does not form a single unit. Initiatives are certainly being taken in the various sectors, as indicated in Section 2, but it is not inconceivable that in a few years time there will be several unions and employers' organisations in the industry and several CAOs. This will make it difficult for the Centre for Training for the Tourist and Travel Industry, as the only combined spokesman of the branch as a whole in training matters, to strengthen its position. The only solution in the Centre's view is that every CAO should provide for deductions for training and development (a training and development fund), from which the Centre could be funded. Whether this can be put into effect soon is uncertain. The Centre is trying to devise a funding system, whereby the development costs and revenue would be shared among the various parts of this branch of industry. The Centre hopes that this will encourage more parts of the branch to invest in programme development.

Job classification systems are also devised mainly within individual parts of the industry. This is a very recent development, however. The Centre is trying to encourage this by impressing on the industry that in order to have a proper training system it must first produce a job structure and identify the competences that are required. The disadvantage of formulating competence requirements at the level of the individual parts of the branch is that vocational courses are primarily expected to train students for specific jobs. The job profiles produced by the CIBB study, which were devised for the purpose of defining the content of training, are highly differentiated, and consequently make it almost inevitable that programmes should be equally differentiated. If the colleges want to provide programmes with a broader scope, they themselves will have to make a link between the job profiles.

The Centre for Training for the Tourist and Travel Industry could play an important supportive role in translating the profiles of competences formulated at sub-branch level into more integrative branch-wide requirements. Areas of overlap with related branches of industries (hotel management and catering, transport and agriculture) would have to be taken into account. In this way the recent conciliation between the tourism/leisure sector and the hotel/catering sector as parts of the tourist industry can serve to widen the horizons.

Training system

During the 1980s a lot of energy was put into streamlining the training system for the tourist and leisure industry. It is only in the past two years that a structure has become clear. This is to some extent because the rivalry within MTRO has ended and MTRO now plays a central role in initial training.

Industry has set itself the task of giving greater structure to short training programmes by linking them to the 15 occupational profiles which have been developed. The branch aims to create a vertical training structure: the schools of tourism which are to be set up within the next five years will offer full-time education, combined on- and off-the-job training (dual system) and continuing training, to be provided by the MTRO colleges and trade schools. The level of these courses will lie somewhere between junior secondary vocational level and higher vocational level. Higher vocational education will continue to be organised separately. This plan means that the principal actors in the branch have opted for a particular training route, i.e. initial vocational education geared to the industry followed by further training courses. General secondary education followed by part-time training will consequently fall partially by the wayside as a means of qualification. In everyday practice, qualification via this route will still be common because individual firms are not yet convinced of the value of non-profit branch-related vocational training and they are as yet under no legal obligation (imposed by a CAO with an approved job classification system). The decision to include a dual route (apprenticeship training) in the new schools of tourism serves, however, as a formal confirmation of the value of the traditional means of qualification via short training programmes combining work and learning.

The vertical structure of the training system (which is designed to institutionalise the individuality of the branch) is to some extent at odds with the general policy of the Ministry of Education and Science which is aimed at broadening and integrating vocational education and bringing together training systems for different branches of industry. A departure from this policy would seem to be in the best interests of the tourist and leisure industry. The Ministry of Economic Affairs, for instance, believes that the creation of a recognisable initial vocational training system like that for technical occupations would be advantageous for the industry. If integration with other branch-related training systems takes place too soon, this may hinder the process of professionalisation of the branch: a distinct identity of its own is necessary for integration.

Labour market research

As a result of the emphasis placed on the quantitative alignment of education and industry, research has been conducted at various levels into the demand for personnel with tourism and leisure-related competences. The National College of Tourism and Transport in Breda and the trade schools run by the sub-branch-related organisations of industry in particular have gone to great lengths to regulate the number of graduates they turn out. Various estimates have also been made for the industry as a whole (see Section 2). The MTRO colleges have made regional estimates, but do not adhere completely to these figures. The MTRO-MHO colleges, in particular, believe that there will be a surge in demand for people with tourism and leisure-related competences in the broadest sense.

The form and content of training

In the tourist and leisure industry "general" competence (such as imagination, a customer-friendly attitude, initiative and a knowledge of foreign languages) is seen as essential for the work involved, while job specific competence is regarded as being of secondary importance only. At the same time the industry emphasizes the importance of practical experience. The colleges providing tourism and leisure-related initial training programmes are consequently faced with the task of linking up all these requirements and producing graduates with a sufficient grounding and sufficient prospects to develop their skills competence further during their working life (and not, for instance, remain "trapped" in a small part of the industry because of a training which was too job-specific).

Paradoxically, it now seems as if the non-profit sector colleges with their new programmes will be "forced" (by the professionalisation of the branch) to focus on job-specific competence. The BOOB-T/R has decided that a "basic tourism and leisure-related knowledge" unit should form the core of every programme. Students will then choose one of a number of options in which general elements (e.g. management, mediation, provision of information and hospitality) will be given a job-specific orientation. Because it is not clear what exactly is meant by basic tourism and leisure-related knowledge, its position as the core of the course is likely to have the effect of "narrowing" the content of the training. It has yet to be seen whether the MTRO colleges will succeed in encapsulating in this part of the programme what it is that constitutes the common factor in tourism and leisure-related work, in other words its essence.

In the existing MTRO programmes the core of the programme is rather broad (related to more than one job). The programme which originated from hotel management and catering education (or more broadly speaking, tradespeople's education) focuses on the business economics side of the work. The programme which grew out of commercial education, although more specialised, emphasizes the communication aspect of jobs in tourism and leisure industry. In the format proposed by the BOOB-T/R, these two elements follow the unit "basic tourism and leisure-related knowledge" and need to be more job-specific. Only when the training profiles and credit units have been given definitive shape by the ten MTRO colleges will it be possible to say whether the broad core of the existing programmes has been combined with the specific core of the programme proposed by the BOOB-T/R in such a way as to produce MTRO graduates with a vocationally-oriented rather than a job-specific profile of competences. Some important factors in this respect are, of course, the form that co-operation between industry and schools will take, the use that is made of application-oriented or practical learning situations, and what form these take, and the training lecturers have had or will receive.

In conclusion, it can be said that most of the measures which have been taken with regard to the relationship between education and industry in the tourist and leisure industry have been aimed at achieving a "seamless" link between them. This has largely been the efforts of the (actors within) branch to establish a distinct identity of its own. Looking at the outline of the training system and the prevailing views on paths of training, there would however seem to be ample scope for the development of a flexible system of initial and continuing vocational training.

Notes

1. Training for senior management posts was provided at the National College for Tourism which was established in Breda in the early 1960s.

2. Three organisations merged to form the Centre: the Advisory Centre for Training for the Travel Industry (SVATOR, 1972), the Examinations Centre for the Travel, Tourist and Leisure Industries (SEPR, 1978) and the Centre for Preparation for Careers in the Tourist and Leisure Industries (BETER, 1983, set up to develop teaching aids and training courses).

3. The term 'tourist branch' is used in this study to refer to the sector as a whole. Its component parts – the tourist and leisure branch and the hotel and catering branch – are designated separately.

4. A job classification and evaluation system has recently been developed for the tourist information branch. The sub-branch related organisations in the leisure branch, and specifically that relating to the water sports sector, are currently developing a job classification system.

5. The leisure branch was largely excluded from the study from the outset as only businesses employing more than 10 people were included. No more than 15 of the 300 employers in the sample provided accommodation and day-tripper amenities, even though such businesses together with the water sports branch make up more than half of the tourist and leisure industry.

6. Formerly the Educational Advisory Centre for Vocational Training for Industry (PCBB).

7. The three educational levels are LO: primary education and junior secondary vocational education; MO: junior and senior general secondary education (MAVO/HAVO) and senior secondary vocational education (MBO); and HO: pre-university (VWO), higher vocational (HBO) and university education (WO). The disadvantage of the system is that there is some overlapping of the educational levels, and it makes no distinction between vocationally-oriented terminal and general preparatory education.

8. The Ministry of Economic Affairs plans to abolish this requirement shortly or to replace it with more flexible regulations.

9. In 1990 the employees of the tourist information offices transferred to a public service union, demonstrating the lack of organisational unity among workers in the tourist industry.

10. Since the start of the 1990/1991 school year the three trade schools have the status of senior secondary vocational education under the Accredited Educational Establishments Act but also paradoxically no longer receive a subsidy from the Ministry of Education and Science.

11. Without a subsidy from the Ministry of Education and Science this trade school was unable to continue as an independent college and in 1991 was attached to the National College of Tourism and Transport.

12. This choice was forced upon them by the unclear policies of the Ministry of Education and Science, which initially gave MEAO (commercial education) the sole right to develop tourism and leisure courses and in the mid-1980s suddenly gave MHO (hotel management and catering) that right.

13. Some MBO colleges claim that Breda developed these short courses to maintain its leading position in the market (having itself had to overcome opposition from some sections of the industry in order to build up this position in the first place) and that this was done mainly in response to the creation of tourism and leisure departments in MHO colleges.

14. This section concentrates on senior secondary vocational education. No reference is made to higher vocational education, apart from the short programmes offered at this level.

15. Apart from the tourist accommodation sector (for which a random sample of 40 per cent was taken), the survey covered the entire population. However, one-half of the tourist information offices, travel agencies or day-tripper businesses approached and 70 per cent of the businesses in the water sports and accommodation sectors did not wish to take part in the survey because they felt that apprenticeship training was not relevant to their business.

16. Social legislation is partly to blame for this. Extensive use is made in the leisure industry of seasonal labour, not only for the simpler jobs, but also for more responsible posts. Until recently seasonal employees could return to the same employer every year, but this is now prohibited by law. As a result, staff are unable to gain experience with one employer and employers will be less willing to invest in training for seasonal staff.

Bibliography

Action plan for tourism education policy in the 1990s (1990), Plan drawn up by the Consultative Committee for the Hotel, Catering, Tourist and Leisure Industries following the publication of the policy document "Enterprise and Tourism" on the tourism policy of the Ministry of Economic Affairs in the 1990s, Zoetermeer.

Algemene Arbeidsvoorwaarden voor VVV's (General Terms of Employment for Tourist Information Offices), Amersfoort, ANVV, 1990.

ALLAART, P.C., KUNNEN, R. and van STIPHOUT, H.A. (1990), *Trendrapport Vraag naar arbeid 1990* (Trends in the demand for employment 1990), Organisation for Strategic Labour Market Research (OSA), The Hague.

ALLAART, P.C., KUNNEN, R., OURS, J.C. van and STIPHOOT, H.A. van (1987), "OSA-Trendrapport 1987" (Trends 1987), *Current information on the labour market*, Organisation for Strategic Labour Market Research (OSA), (OSA preparatory study no. V 18), The Hague.

Association of Colleges of Higher Education (1991), *Rapport vooronderzoek hbo-opleidingen "toerisme en recreatie"* (Report on a preparatory study of HBO tourism and leisure courses), The Hague.

BOECKHOUT, I.J. and VOSKUIL, R. (1989), *De toeristische sector in macro-economisch perspectief* (The tourist industry from the macro-economic viewpoint), Study carried out for the Tourism Policy Document Project Group, Ministry of Economic Affairs, Institute of Economics, Rotterdam.

BOOIS, H. de (1990), "Vakkundig het toerisme en de recreatie in met MEAO-MTRO" (A good start in tourism and leisure with an MEAO-MTRO qualification), *Hoofdzakelijk, Tijdschrift van de Economische Sector Groep*, year 1 (no. 4), pp. 11-13.

BRANDSMA, T.F., NIJHOF, W.J. and KAMPHORST, J.C. (1990), "Kwalificatie en curriculum" (Qualifications and the curriculum), *An international comparative study of methods of setting qualifications*, Swets and Zeitlinger, Amsterdam, Lisse.

Centre for Training for the Hotel and Catering Industry (1990), *Waar zijn ze gebleven* (Where did they go?), Study of appointments and career opportunities.

Centre for Training for the Hotel and Catering Industry, *1989-1990 Annual Report*, Zoetermeer.

DIEDEREN, J. (1985), *Beroepentheorie en methoden van beroepenstudie* (Occupational theory and methods of occupational study), Basis for a comparative study, Institute of Applied Social Sciences, Nijmegen.

Eindrapport Haalbaarheidsonderzoek Leerlingwezen (Feasibility study of apprenticeship training, Final report), Centre for Training for the Tourist and Travel Industry, Hilversum, 1990.

European Institute of Education and Social Policy (1991), *Education for Careers in European Travel and Tourism*, American Express Foundation.

GEURTS, J. (1989), *Van niemandsland naar beroepenstructuur* (From no-man's-land to an occupational structure), A study of the relationship between education and employment at the level of junior skilled worker, Institute of Applied Social Sciences, Nijmegen.

GEURTS, J., HÖVELS, B. and van ONNA, B. (1987), "Autonomie in de aansluiting tussen onderwijs en arbeid" (Autonomy in the alignment of education and employment), in Akkermans, M. *et al.*, *Autonomie als arbeidssociologisch vraagstuk*, Zeist, Kerckebosch.

Haagland College (1991), "Contractonderwijs" (Contract teaching), *Prospectus,* The Hague.

HESSELMANN, A. (1990*a*), "MEAO-MTRO and MHO-MTRO naast elkaar" (MEAO-MTRO and MHO-MTRO side by side), in *Hoofdzakelijk, Tijdschrift van de Economische Sector Groep,* year 1 (no. 4), pp. 16-17.

HESSELMANN, A. (1990*b*)," Van Meateam naar Meatour naar York Minster" (From Meateam to Meatour to York Minster), in *Hoofdzakelijk, Tijdschrift van de Economische,* Sector Groep, year 1 (no. 4), pp. 14-15.

Information on MEAO-MTRO courses, Leiden, Maastricht, Utrecht, Zwolle.

Institute for Social Science and Economic Research (ISEO)(1989), *Evaluatie Toeristisch Onderzoek and Cursussen* (An evaluation of tourism-related research and courses), Report presented to the Ministry of Economic Affairs, Bussum.

LINDNER, P., BODEWES, T., GIJSBERTSE-LANTING, H., DUIM, V.R. van der, and WAMMES, G.J. (1991), "Toeristisch vakonderwijs naar het jaar 2000" (Vocational education for the tourist industry: towards the year 2000). *Recreatie Reeks* no. 12, Association for Outdoor Recreation, The Hague.

MTRO/MMO senior secondary tourist and leisure businesses education, Curriculum, Examination regulations, Examination syllabus, c. 1990.

MEVISSEN, J.W.M. and VERHAAR, V. (1988), *De andere kant van flexibilisering. De Horeca* (The other side of flexibility. The hotel and catering industry), A study of the background, motives and opinions of flexible manpower), Regioplan, Amsterdam.

NAFZGER J. (1989), *Beroepenanalyse toekomst- en arbeidsmarktonderzoek Toerisme en Recreatie* (Occupational analysis, Study of future developments and labour market trends in the tourist and leisure industry), with tables, SVATOR, PCBB, Hilversum, Den Bosch.

NAFZGER, J. (1990), *Scholingsbehoefte onderzoek t.b.v. werknemers in toerisme en recreatie* (A study of the training needs of employees in the tourist and leisure industry), Centre for Training for the Tourist and Travel Industry, CIBB, Hilversum, Den Bosch.

NAFZGER, J., TILKIN, J.M.W.J. and WOLTERMAN, H. (1987), *Beroepenanalyse* (Occupational analysis), Report of preparatory study, SVATOR, PCBB, Hilversum, Den Bosch.

National College of Tourism and Transport (1990), Higher vocational course in management training for the tourist and leisure industry, Breda.

National College of Tourism and Transport (1991), *Kort Hoger Beroepsonderwijs voor Toerisme en Recreatie* (Short Higher Vocational Education Courses in Tourism and Leisure), Breda.

Netherlands Research Institute for Leisure and Tourism (1982), *De economische betekenis van toerisme en recreatie in Nederland* (The economic significance of tourism and leisure in the Netherlands), NRIT, Breda.

Netherlands Research Institute for Leisure and Tourism (1984), *Toeristisch onderwijs, Op zoek naar samenhang* (Tourism education. Looking for cohesion), NRIT, Breda.

Netherlands Research Institute for Leisure and Tourism (1990), *De behoefte aan toeristisch-recreatief onderwijs in Nederland* (The need for tourism and leisure-related education in the Netherlands), A quantitative estimate and summary of the report, NRIT, Breda.

NEVE, J. (1988), *De andere kant van flexibilisering. Het Reiswezen* (The other side of flexibility. The travel industry). A study of the background, motives and opinions of flexible manpower, Regioplan, Amsterdam.

Notitie Definitie/Afbakening Toeristische Sector (Policy memorandum on the definition and delineation of the tourist industry), 1990.

Ondernemen in toerisme (Enterprise and tourism). Policy memorandum. Lower House, 21 525, SDU, The Hague, 1989-1990 session.

Samenvattende rapportage beroepsanalyse Toerisme and Recreatie (Summary of an occupational analysis of the tourist and leisure industry), job profile study, labour market study and potential future developments regarding the alignment of tourism and leisure education with the reality of work, SVATOR/PCBB, Hilversum, Den Bosch, 1989.

SCHOLTEN, P. (1990), "Ondernemersonderwijs voor de bedrijfstak Toerisme en Recreatie" (Entrepreneurial education for the tourist and leisure industry), *Hoofdzakelijk*, Tijdschrift van de Economische Sector Groep, vol. 1 (no. 4), 1990, pp. 9-10.

SVATOR (1990), "Werken in Toerisme en Recreatie" (Working in the tourist and leisure industry), *Training opportunities*, Hilversum, (brochure).

TEULINGS, C. (1988), "De grenzen van beroepsdeelmarkten" (Boundaries in the job market), Classification of occupations on the basis of labour market criteria, *Tijdschrift voor Arbeidsvraagstukken*, vol. 4 (no. 4), pp. 46-61.

Toerisme, trends en toekomst (Tourism, trends and the future), Netherlands Tourist Board, Leidschendam, 1989.

Toeristisch Vakonderwijs (Vocational training for jobs in tourism), A structure for the 1990s. Hilversum, Centre for Training for the Tourist and Travel Industry, 1990.

Toeristisch produktbeleid, integratie en sectorbeleid, (Tourism product policy, integration and sectoral policy), An evaluation of the main points of the Policy Document on Tourism Policy for 1985 to 1989, Final report. Bussum, ISEO Research.

Toeristisch Informatie Medewerker (Tourist information officer), 1991/93 prospectus of the ANVV vocational training course for tourist information office staff.

van DELFT, A. (1990), *Informatiesysteem arbeidsmarktontwikkeling Horeca (ISAH)* (Information system for labour market trends in the hotel and catering industry), Hotel and Catering Trades Board.

van GEUNS, R.C., MEVISSEN, J.W.M. and NEVE, J.H. (1987), *De andere kant van flexibilisering* (The other side of flexibility), A study of the background, motives and opinions of flexible manpower, The Ministry of Social Affairs and Employment, The Hague.

van MIDDELAAR, H. (1990), "Je verkoopt geen hotelkamer of een busreis, je verkoopt een illusie" (You're not selling a hotel room or a coach trip, you're selling an illusion), *Werking*, year 1 (no. 16), pp. 8-11.

van RIETBERGEN, T., BOSMAN, J. and de SMIDT, M. (1990), "Internationalisering van de dienstensector" (Internationalisation of the services sector), *Dutch businesses from a worldwide viewpoint*, Muiderberg, Coutinho.

van den TILLAART, H., FRIETMAN, J. and van den BERG, J. (1991), *Ondernemen met perspectief* (A business with prospects), a study of staff training in small and medium-sized businesses, Institute of Applied Social Sciences, Nijmegen.

van der HAUW, P.A. (1990), "De beroepenstructuur in het MKB" (The occupational structure in the small and medium-sized businesses sector), *A preparatory study of the period 1979 to 1985*, Institute for Small and Medium-sized Businesses, Zoetermeer.

van der STELT, D. and VELTHUIJSEN, J.W. (1989), "Vraag en aanbod op de toeristische markt" (Demand and supply in the tourism market), *The feasibility of a simulative model*, Economic Research Institute, Amsterdam.

van 't HOF, A.J. (1990), *De plaats van de AVR-Reisbureau Vakschool* (The role of the AVR trade school for travel agents).

VISSERS, A.M.C., VISSERS A.M. and SCHEPENS, T. (1986), *Arbeidsmarktgedrag ten tijde van massale werkloosheid* (Labour market behaviour during periods of mass unemployment), The initial results of a national study, Organisation for Strategic Labour Market Research, The Hague.

VRIES, B. de and HÖVELS, B. (1991), *Afgesproken!* (Agreed!), A study of the effectiveness of collective agreement arrangements on training, Institute of Applied Social Sciences, Nijmegen.

WAMMES, G.J. (1990), "Het BOOB Toerisme/Recreatie" (The Education and Industry Forum on Tourism and Leisure), *Hoofdzakelijk,* Tijdschrift van de Economische Sector Groep, vol. 1 (no. 4), pp. 5-7.

WIELDERS, P.J.A. (1990), *Beschrijving en waardering VVV-functies* (The description and evaluation of jobs in tourist information offices), ANVV, Amersfoort.

B. The Printing Industry

B. Hövels and J. van den Berg
Institute for Applied Social Sciences
Nijmegen

Introduction

This study analyses the responsiveness of the system of vocational training in the printing industry vis-à-vis developments in the outside world. The first sections provide a description of historical developments. Section 4 analyses these historical developments in relation to the central question of the responsiveness of the system of vocational education. Responsiveness is understood here as meaning the ability of the vocational education system to respond to developments in the world around it, in particular in the workplace. This may denote any of three different abilities: the capacity to adapt, to anticipate or to innovate. The question of responsiveness is broken down into a number of key components: important regulatory factors, the range of instruments or strategies employed to cope with current or predicted problems, and the role of the various actors. Section 5 attempts to answer the question of responsiveness against the background of the preceding sections.

The printing industry historically has occupied a unique position in the Dutch economy and it has been viewed as a role model for other sectors in the implementation of the government's plan to restructure the education system.[1]

1. Position of the Printing Industry

The printing industry provides an example of a sector in which technological innovation is taking place at a rapid pace. The invention of typographical printing in around 1450 (the famous Gutenberg Bible was printed in 1456) and the description a century later (by Vanoccio Biringuccio in his book *De la Pyrotechnica*) of how letters were to be cast from lead alloy laid the foundations for the relief and letterpress methods of printing which were to predominate in the succeeding centuries. It was only after 1798 – with the invention of lithography by Alois Senefelder – that offset printing developed. In 1879 Karl Klietsch invented the rotogravure method. Thereafter, the pace of change increased. Over the last century, the main techniques of printing – relief, planographic and gravure – have all been perfected, and special techniques such as flexography, screen printing and die stamping have made their appearance. Particularly since the late 1960s, electronics and computers have accelerated the pace of technological development and presently the printing industry can be regarded as one of the most technologically advanced sectors.

It also occupies a notable position in Dutch industry from another point of view, namely as regards its system of industrial relations. The first collective labour agreement for the printing industry, which was drawn up in 1914 and was the first collective labour agreement in the Netherlands, contained provisions relating to the introduction of the closed-shop system. The collective labour agreement of 1917 laid down that an "industrial diploma" was necessary for any form of technical work in the printing industry. These provisions have had a major influence on the design and development of vocational training in this field. Even today, they are still part of the collective labour agreements for the industry.

In the printing industry therefore, more than in any other sector, industrial relations form the foundation for a high degree of structure, close involvement by both employers and trades unions in vocational training, and an extensive training infrastructure. These are the institutional pivots influencing the responsiveness of the system of vocational education in the printing industry.

This section briefly describes the general situation in the printing industry from an economic point of view and as regards size, composition and labour market situation. It then discusses industrial relations in the context of the labour market and qualifications and the system of vocational training for the sector. Finally, it provides a description of the institutional basis for responsiveness within the industry.

Economic situation

The printing industry is that branch of economic activity concerned with the production and finishing of printed materials. The closed-shop provision in the collective labour agreement means that all firms in the industry are supposed to belong to an employers' organisation and all employees involved in technical printing work to be members of a trade union. Organised businesses may appoint only organised employees, and technical workers are allowed to work only for organised employers. The degree of organisation (90 to 100 per cent) is therefore exceptionally high by Dutch standards; this makes the position of the printing industry as a sector fairly easy to identify. The description below is based on the printing industry as such.[2]

As of January 1990, the printing industry comprised over 3 000 firms, employing a total of more than 62 000 people (some 65 to 70 per cent of whom fall under the category of technical printing staff). The industry accounts for around 5 per cent of all employment in the Netherlands. The printing industry is in a vulnerable position due to its dependence on the state of the economy as a whole. It is thus difficult to make an accurate prediction concerning its economic development. The majority of printing firms work to order on a piecework basis. One consequence of this is that production planning is difficult in the longer term, as is the identification of staffing needs. A particularly important source of income for the printing industry is advertising expenditure by trade and industry as a whole.

The increasing significance of print media in general has produced a gradual employment and turnover growth in the printing industry over the last few years. Despite increasing computerisation of the production process, the number of employees rose between 1986 and 1989 by some 13 per cent and the number of printing firms by 8 per cent.[3] Primarily as a result of increasing advertising expenditure by Dutch industry as a whole, further annual growth in turnover in 1989 and 1990 amounted to some 5 per cent, despite the emergence of competing audio-visual media. Paper consumption increased by some 10 per cent over these two years, and the estimated increase in the volume of production in 1990 was 3 per cent. A broader information and media industry is beginning to emerge, and the printing industry is increasingly aiming to present itself as part of this printed medium within this wider communications industry.

Size, composition and labour market

Table B1 shows the trends between 1980-1990 in numbers of printing firms and numbers of employees by company size.

Table B1. Composition of the printing industry by size of company workforce, 1980 and 1990*

Size of workforce	1980		1990	
	% firms	% employees	% firms	% employees
0 - 4	43	6	43	4
5 - 9	22	8	22	7
10 - 19	16	12	15	10
20 - 49	12	19	3	19
50 - 99	4	14	4	12
100 - 199	2	13	2	13
200 and over	1	28	1	36
Total abs.	2 513	45 746	3 009	62 455

* The figures are taken from KVGO annual reports.

A distinctive feature of the printing industry is the large number of very small businesses it includes: 65 per cent of all printing firms employ fewer than ten people. The contribution of such small businesses to total employment in the industry is, however, only 11 per cent. In all, small- and medium-sized businesses (that is, firms with up to 100 employees) account for 52 per cent of total employment in the industry. The remaining 32 large firms (one per cent) with over 200 employees, employ over a third of the total workforce in the industry. Between 1980 and 1990 the proportion of jobs in small- and medium-sized firms fell by over 7 per cent, in part the result of concentration in the industry.

The production process in the printing industry can be broken down into three broad phases: pre-press (preparation and production of the forme), press (the actual printing) and

122

post-press (finishing of printed matter). The pre-press phase (preparation and production of the forme) involves setting the text and processing the illustrations so that, once the two have been combined (the make-up), a forme can be made. This forme can then be used to apply the right amount of ink to the paper in the right place. In the press phase there are three printing procedures which account for almost all printing production: relief (or letterpress), planographic (or offset) and gravure printing. Gravure printing is used for very large runs of high quality products. Post-press finishing involves the cutting, folding, collating, binding, stapling, etc. of the printed matter. However, the scope of the production process in individual printing firms varies. By far, the majority of firms are equipped to carry out a number of different phases in the production process, but a small proportion (around 300 firms) specialise in the preparation and another small proportion (around 400 firms) in the finishing of printed matter. In terms of distribution of jobs and occupations, aside from managerial and administrative staff, the "pre-press" category of occupations accounts for around 36 per cent of staff in the printing industry, the "press" category for around 24 per cent, the "post-press" category for around 14 per cent and the "other staff" category (primarily auxiliaries) for around 26 per cent (survey year 1989). Within these four occupational categories, some 70 per cent of staff possess relevant technical qualifications. Table B2 gives a detailed breakdown of the distribution of the total number of employees between the main occupational categories in 1986 and 1989.

Table B2. **Percentage of persons employed by main occupational category in 1986 and 1989**

	1986	1989
Main occupational category:		
Preparation	4	3
Typesetting	10	9
Image/mounting/production of form	15	16
Proof printing	–	–
Processing of forme (printing)	20	30
Finishing	12	11
General technical duties	5	5
Auxiliary duties	17	17
Management	3	3
Administration	14	16
Total (= 100%)	45 990	51 890

Source: Employment Surveys 1986-1989 (taken from BOGI 1990-1995).

Unemployment among skilled print workers is very low (2.1 per cent in late 1989) and can largely be attributed to frictional unemployment. Total unemployment in the industry fell from 4.9 per cent in late 1988 to 3.8 per cent in late 1989: at the end of 1989, over 2 000 people were registered both as seeking employment in printing firms and having been employed by printing firms prior to being unemployed. Workers without technical printing skills (including administrative staff) are over-represented among the total number of unemployed, while skilled staff (including auxiliaries) and managers are under-represented. There is currently a staff shortage in certain categories of skilled print workers, especially in the pre-press and post-press areas. In particularly, there is a demand for colour compositors, scanner operators, offset operators, folders and cutters.

Industrial relations, the labour market and qualifications

Industrial relations in the printing industry are unique within the Dutch industrial world. The actors in this system and the agreements they have made, have to a great extent determined the development of vocational training. One of the corner-stones of this system is the commitment of employers' organisations and trade unions alike to external control over and internal management of the labour market in the printing industry.

As early as the beginning of this century, employers and trade unions – recognising their mutual interests in the matter – opted for a policy of protecting and regulating the printing market, including the labour market. Employers had an interest in establishing uniform prices and wage rates in order to safeguard the printing business against "cowboy" companies who would perpetually force down prices and create the risk of chronic under-exploitation of production capacity in the industry. The best way to achieve this was a coalition with powerful trade unions, who themselves had an interest in protecting the printing labour market against unqualified workers.

For this reason, the "constitution" of industrial relations within the industry, the collective labour agreement of 1914, established the closed-shop system. In 1917, a second collective labour agreement included, at the request of the trade unions, a provision regulating entry to skilled work in the printing industry. Since then, the only route to gain professional competence and the status of skilled print worker has been via training in the workplace and the acquisition of an "industrial diploma". These agreements have provided the basis for an extensive system of joint institutions that regulate the relationship between the two sides of industry and cover all important matters affecting the industry. The closed-shop system has been a prime factor in determining the climate within the industry. It creates a mutual dependence between employees and employers and this has led to intensive co-operation between the two sides of industry in a variety of areas.[4] Vocational training is one of these.

Since, even today, skilled printing work can only be performed by people with relevant professional training recognised by the industry, or by people undergoing such training, vocational training continues to constitute one of the key regulatory mechanisms in the industry. Not only is entry from the external labour market to skilled printing work in the sector determined by the possession of recognised professional qualifications, but access to the various subsidiary occupational markets within the printing industry (the internal labour market) is also regulated via recognised trade qualifications. A skilled worker may only exercise a different trade within the industry if he has acquired the requisite qualification. This means that existing staff switching to different or new procedures have to be retrained before they are allowed to work in new occupations or jobs.[5]

These are not the only regulations safeguarding the position of experienced professionals in the industry. Firstly, the composition of the workforce in terms of different categories (craftsmen, junior craftsmen, apprentices and auxiliaries) is regulated by means of numerical ratios, and the extent and nature of the duties which may be performed by unskilled workers (auxiliaries) are carefully defined. Secondly, workers in the industry are safeguarded against the adverse effects on employment of reorganisations and new investments (the industry has its own regulations on dismissal and jurisdiction and arbitration arrangements).

Since the 1960s, the industry's traditional labour market has come under pressure from technological innovations and changes in the organisation of production, while relations with other industries have also been subject to change. Key words are heterogeneity, company-specific considerations and the blurring of the dividing lines between industries. Negotiations between the two sides of industry have produced modifications and relaxations of the rules, while emphatically retaining the institutional structure of the labour market. Collective labour agreements have included new jobs, the potential for using non-printing staff has been expanded and during the 1980s vocational training programmes began to differentiate between different jobs and job levels. A professional diploma is still, however, a necessary entry requirement. This means that a key component of labour market policy remains in the hands of the Printing Industry Training Centre.

Development of vocational training

The industry's first two collective labour agreements (those of 1914 and 1917) constitute, therefore, the basis for the development of vocational training in the printing industry, with apprenticeship training as the dominant type. The printing industry was the first sector in the Netherlands to institutionalise the principle of on-the-job training, with the apprenticeship scheme for the industry being established in 1925. This has traditionally been, and still is, the predominant form of vocational training in the printing industry. In addition, there is the KMBO (short senior secondary vocational education) programme in printing technology and the MTO (senior secondary technical education) printing programme (geared to middle-management jobs). The apprenticeship scheme and the MTO programme were, however – at least until recently – two completely separate worlds, which for various reasons had nothing to do with each other.[6] With the recent trend towards a single school of printing, this is beginning to change (see Section 3).

In recent years, a more important role in the system of vocational training for the industry has been reserved for the body of retraining and refresher courses, which has been gradually expanding and becoming more elaborate. The Association for the Advancement of Vocational Training in the printing industry (VBGI) and the Special Courses Organisation (SBO) are the only institutions allowed to award diplomas or certificates recognised by the industry, the VBGI with regard to apprenticeship training and the SBO in connection with retraining and refresher courses. Both are represented in the Printing Industry Training Centre.

Until the early 1970s, the printing industry was characterised by a relatively stable structure of subsidiary occupational or trade markets. This occupational structure also

125

formed the basis for vocational training. The occupations for which people were trained were based on the position in a particular segment of the production process and the type of firm for which the apprentice was being trained. Elementary apprenticeship training was broken down into 16 occupational areas and advanced training into 37 occupational specialisations (each of which had not only its own training programme but also its own wage structure).

Traditional vocational training was for a long time subject to little if any change: between and within subsidiary occupational markets, changes occurred only very gradually, there were substantial similarities between firms with regard to technology and organisation, and there were wide opportunities for a more or less casual process of on-the-job training. There was an almost perfect match between the actual content of jobs and the occupations for which people were trained.

In the late 1960s it became clear that the existing structure of training was no longer working efficiently. Technological innovation and changes in the organisation of production were producing a growing heterogeneity in the industry, so that production processes were becoming much more company-specific as regards both technology and organisation. The developments can be classified on the basis of the emergence of three new trends.

The first of these emerged in the 1970s and can be described as "the new pattern". According to this pattern, the key objective of vocational training was to produce flexible professionals; that is, skilled workers capable of both horizontal and vertical mobility. The result was a broad initial professional training with a system of retraining and refresher courses explicitly geared to it. The second trend appeared in the first half of the 1980s and centred on efforts to increase the flexibility of training provision itself. The training objectives were scarcely modified, but there were changes in particular in the organisation of the training courses, allowing a closer match to be achieved between training and the needs and resources of firms. The key concepts were flexibility, differentiation and a more market-oriented approach. The late 1980s saw the emergence of a third trend, the establishment of printing schools in which day-release programmes for apprentices (BBO) and the KMBO and MBO programmes would be integrated to form a single structure geared to the needs of both the industry and trainees. Section 3 explores in more detail these various new trends or phases in the development of the system of vocational education.

Institutionalisation and responsiveness

The development of vocational education in the printing industry has to a large extent been controlled by the institutional framework dominated by the two sides of industry. The Central Bureau, the top body within the sector, is comprised of employers' organisations and trade unions who together determine policy with regard to all matters of interest to the sector, including those affecting vocational training. The Central Bureau operates through committees and working parties, the membership of which includes specialists in the field. The central employers' organisation is the Royal Federation of Printing Businesses (KVGO), and the key trade unions are the FNV union for the printing and paper industries and the CNV print union.

126

Training policy development and implementation are in the hands of the Printing Industry Training Centre (GOC). The innovations introduced in the early 1980s had the effect of strengthening the position of the GOC and it became the industry's training centre par excellence. The GOC office has increased rapidly in size over the last few years and now has a staff of over 100.

In the 1970s, the Special Courses Organisation (SBO) was set up to deal with retraining and refresher courses, and various apprenticeship schemes were also merged with the Association for the Advancement of Vocational Training in the Printing Industry (VBGI). Since 1973, both these organisations have come under the umbrella of the GOC.

As already mentioned, the GOC has its own training institute (in Veenendaal). During the 1970s the number of colleges providing day-release programmes in printing was reduced from thirteen to four (in Amsterdam, Rotterdam, Eindhoven and Utrecht). A fifth was later added. The sector formation and innovation operation in senior secondary vocational education has since led to the integration of the three MTS printing colleges with the day-release colleges to form grafische lycea (schools of printing). The GOC provides a secretariat for the consultative structure (BOOB) which exists between the industry and education, the Industry/Education Consultative Committee (OBO), which advises the Minister of Education and Science with regard to innovations in printing education.

The printing industry's ability to respond to change is ultimately determined by the scope of the Central Bureau to take action. In practice, however, its responsiveness greatly depends on the way in which the GOC performs its tasks. These may be summarised as follows:
- to inform the industry of labour market trends in relation to training needs;
- to assist training institutions with curriculum development and professional development of staff;
- to safeguard the quality of practical training;
- to provide training (i.e. retraining and refresher courses at its training centre, as well as correspondence courses;
- to maintain training standards;
- to inform companies about new technologies;
- to provide a central training facility (to transfer new printing techniques into public-sector vocational education);
- to take measures to train particular target groups;
- to undertake public relations activities on behalf of the printing industry.

2. Developments in the Workplace

Technological innovations are rapidly changing the production process of the printing industry, but economic and organisational developments are also having an effect. This case study focuses on the most relevant elements affecting vocational education in the printing industry, those of direct interest in relation to the question of responsiveness.

The changes taking place can be broken down into three categories: quantitative, qualitative and inter-sectoral. First, economic and technological developments will be examined where relevant to employment in the printing industry and in particular to shifts in employment between different occupational categories. This culminates in an assessment of future staffing needs in quantitative terms. Second, qualitative changes are considered in the printing industry itself as a result of technological and organisational innovations in the production process, with a special focus on the qualifications required for skilled print workers in the industry. Finally, the section examines changes in the relations between the printing industry and other sectors, particularly as a result of the diffusion of skilled print work and the blurring of the industry's boundaries. This latter term refers explicitly to the increasing opening-up of the printing industry, which was until recently a relatively closed world.

Economic trends and the labour market

While the printing industry has seen strong growth and high employment in the past, more recently the growth in the volume of annual production has lagged behind that of Dutch industry as a whole Central Bureau of Statistics (CABS) forecasts expect the rate of growth to slow in the future. Major underlying factors may be the increase in national and international competition, the fact that large publishing houses are increasingly shedding their printing shops and the rapid development of desktop publishing (DTP) systems, which is leading non-printing firms (i.e. clients) to have work at the pre-press stage done in-house.

It is not clear what the impact of all these factors will be, notably for employment in the printing industry. The GOC commissioned a study of the likely trends in workforce composition and training needs in the printing industry in the period between 1990 and 1995.[7] The "BOGI" study, as it is known, concluded that it is impossible to predict accurately economic trends in the printing industry, primarily because of its heavy dependence on general developments in the Dutch economy and the Netherlands' dependence on the rest of the world. It also points to negative and positive factors which affect the industry. Among the negative effects it cites, for instance: declining economic growth in the United States, the recent rise in and expansion of commercial TV advertising, and the appearance on the market of advanced photocopy machines with facilities for colour, large formats, binding, etc. On the other hand, positive effects might flow from, for example, a further segmentation of target groups, a boost in advertising expenditure resulting from the unification of Europe, improved export prospects as a result of German unification, increasing demand for colour printing, etc. Briefly, the study forecasted continued growth in the next few years.

Technological developments and the labour market

The BOGI study also estimated the impact of technological innovations in staffing needs in the printing industry. Its principal findings for each phase of production or occupational category are set out below. The next section gives an overall picture of expected staffing needs, taking into account the effect of both economic and technological factors.

Pre-press

The pre-press area in particular is likely to undergo major changes over the next few years due to rapid improvements in desktop publishing (DTP). Facilities to make up pages in colour are now available, reasonably user-friendly and inexpensive. Black and white pages can already be produced using DTP to perfect finished quality. These developments mean that clients themselves can now make up pages completely. Only the final high-end phase (i.e. scanning of illustrations, proof production and colour corrections) now needs to be done by a reproduction firm.

It is clear that specialised typesetters will eventually disappear, that many of the traditional micro make-up workers will have to be retrained to work as DTP operators and do on-screen make-up, that retouches will tend to become systems operators and that repro staff will in general become "electronically skilled" workers. In addition, there will be a greater need for systems managers and database management. Scanner operators will, for the time being, still be required.

Given constant production volumes, it is estimated that between 1990 and 1994 the number of people involved in the pre-press phase within the printing firms will decline by 25 to 35 per cent. This decrease will be largely due to an extremely marked decline in the number of typesetters and also of monochrome make-up staff and monochrome film processors.

Printing

Printing will remain a mechanical process. Increased production per employee will be achieved by increasing the turn-round speed when changing rollers, reducing set-up times and breakdowns and introducing more efficient peripheral equipment. The increase in productivity is not, however, expected to be any higher between 1990 and 1994 than in the preceding years.

Finishing

The main developments in the finishing field are associated with changes in processes. As periodicals and magazines become more sophisticated and expensive, there will be an increase in the proportion of binding work, with or without stitching, as compared with stapling. New binding and drying techniques will emerge, though these have virtually no impact on the demand for staff. Over the next few years, the setting up of finishing equipment will be further automated and simplified and registration, control and error warning devices will appear. This will somewhat improve process management and consequently productivity, due to a higher level of capacity utilisation. In addition, the next few years will see considerable investments in new machinery with a substantially increased output. This will lead to higher production, particularly in the large firms.

Quantitative demand for staff and training

On the basis of the estimated economic and technological trends, the demand for staff in the printing industry will, according to the BOGI report, on balance decline by a minimum of 2 per cent and a maximum of 11 per cent in the period between 1990 and 1994. The middle scenario is a decrease of around 6.5 per cent as compared with the 1990 staff total (that is, excluding managers and administrative staff), or 1.3 per cent per year. In other words, there will be a contraction of demand resulting from the combination of a positive trend in demand consequent on increased production volume plus a rise in productivity, i.e. declining demand for staff due to technological developments. Table B3 summarises these trends. This shows once again that the decline in demand for staff will be substantially influenced by a considerable net decrease in non-colour dependent occupations in the pre-press phase (greatest amongst typesetters, monochrome film processors and monochrome make-up staff).

Table B3. **Trends in staffing needs as a result of both technological and economic developments**

Occupational categories	Estimated number 1990	changes in staffing needs 1990-1994 due to:		Per mutations:	
		volume of demand	technological trends	%	actual
Pre-press – non-color dependent	12 212	+ 9 to 15 %	− 30 to − 34%	− 15 to − 25%	−1832 to −3 053
– colour-dependent	3 198	+ 12 to 18 %	− 16 to − 20 %	− 2 to − 8 %	− 64 to − 256
web-fed planographic minders*	1 038	+ 5 to 8 %	− 10 to − 13 %	− 2 to − 8 %	− 21 to − 83
– sheet-fed planographic minders*	5 977	+ 10 to 17 %	− 11 to − 16 %	+ 6 to − 6 %	+ 359 to − 359
web-fed relief minders*	346	+ 4 to 8 %	0 %	+ 8 to + 4 %	+ 28 to + 14
gravure minders	405	+ 2 to 3 %	− 22 to − 27 %	− 19 to − 25 %	− 77 to −101
other forme processing	2 521	+ 11 to 19 %	− 6% to − 9 %	+ 13 to + 2 %	+ 328 to + 50
finishers	5 907	+ 10 to 15 %	− 10 to − 15 %	+ 5 to − 5 %	+ 295 to − 295
auxiliaries	5 086	+ 9 to 13 %	− 10 to − 15 %	+ 3 to − 6 %	+ 153 to − 305
other staff	6 077	+ 9 to 13 %	− 12 to − 16 %	+ 1 to − 7 %	61 to − 425
Total	42 767	+ 10 to 15 %	− 17 to 21 %	− 2 to − 11 %	− 770 to − 4 813

* No account has been taken of the effects of substitution between these sectors. It is assumed that the effect of substitution on the total number of minders will be modest.
Source: BOGI 1990-1995 (draft).

Around half of all skilled print workers are in the pre-press area. The demand for retraining and further training over the next few years will be greater in this area than in the printing and finishing fields. Typesetters, make-up staff and web-fed relief minders in particular will need to be retrained because of job shortages in these fields. The increasing use of DTP and the associated input/output hardware will create a demand for further training courses. On the assumption that around 25 per cent of all skilled print workers will require retraining or further training in the 1990-1994 period due to the introduction of new technologies, this demand will amount to a total of between 5 000 and 6 000 over the period, or between 1 000 and 1 200 per year.

Developments in the production process

Until the late 1960s, all printing firms were using the same kind of equipment. Thereafter, the situation changed quickly. In each of the various phases of the production process different technological developments are occurring, while changes are also taking place in the organisation of production. These include:

- The introduction of new equipment of varying quality and technical level.
- Radical changes in the processing of text and images as a result of changing procedures (from hot metal to filmsetting), replacement of the process camera by the scanner, and flexible automation; these have brought major changes in production organisation and qualification requirements, particularly in the pre-press phase.
- Changes in the printing phase from relief to planographic procedures, and the phased automation of equipment and machinery. These changes in the press and after-press phases were the least dramatic for the staff.
- Changes in the organisation of production with increasing emphasis on preparatory tasks and product-oriented specialisation, and the introduction of different forms of work organisation in order to use staff more effectively (job rotation, expansion and enrichment); firms have acquired greater freedom of choice in the design of jobs and production organisation, so that production processes have become more individualised from company to company.
- The switch to a style of management that responds rapidly to change, with larger firms in particular leading the way.

Particularly in the pre-press area, the emphasis is again being placed on genuine professional typographical skills, the shift from manual to procedural skills (primarily cognitive and communications skills) is continuing and (as a result of increasing user-friendliness) there is a decline in the importance being attached to the capacity for abstract thought.

In general, the developments taking place in the production process are resulting in major changes in the occupational structure of the industry: certain occupations have disappeared, new ones have been created and yet others have been greatly changed. The organisation of printing work is increasingly being dominated by changes in production organisation and equipment, which are making printing work ever more dynamic, heterogeneous and specific to a particular company or type of equipment. Given the increasing diversity in skilled printing jobs, it is difficult to talk about any real occupational structure (however dynamic in character). The actual content of various occupations is beginning to differ ever more widely from the customary definitions.

Firstly, the rapid pace of technological change is leading to major differences between printing firms, with an obvious distinction to be drawn between large and small businesses. Major technological innovations exceed the absorption capacities of small businesses. This can be illustrated by the following quotation from a newspaper interview with a small businessman: "We don't have the money to buy something like a page-maker system. That can easily cost a million guilders. Anyway, we don't need one. In the odd case where we do, we just contract out that advanced sort of work. Also, with that kind of expensive equipment, you couldn't react so fast to rush jobs. And that flexibility is precisely the strength of small businesses" (*Volkskrant,* 22.07.1991).

Secondly, there is the tendency towards an increasing diversity in products and markets. This not only places higher demands on the flexibility of the technical staff, in connection with the variety of assignments and the more frequent and faster resetting of the printing equipment, it is also the decisive factor in determining the technology brought in, which is often highly specialised. The diversity of products and machinery is so great that skilled workers are no longer necessarily interchangeable. Both types of product and the techniques geared to products vary widely. Moreover, at least where non-printing firms doing printing work are concerned, printing often takes place within a wider framework, as an integral part of an automated total process.

Thirdly, there is a growing tendency towards integration in the production process. Where in the past firms specialised in particular parts of the production process or in special printing processes firms are now, by contrast, increasingly offering a complete product and undertaking all the stages in the production process. There is also, at the level of the individual firm, a growing integration of various jobs. The traditional boundaries between writing, typesetting and printing are being eroded; image and text are becoming much easier to integrate. One activity runs into another, and one operation blends with the next. Where in the past it was clear that a typesetter was a typesetter and a lithographer a lithographer, the effect of technological developments is to make their spheres of work blend more closely together. Experts believe that further computerisation will in the near future, albeit earlier for some technologies than for others, create a direct link between DTP systems and printing machines.

Phases in production are, therefore, being integrated and new ways of storing, handling and transferring information are gradually eroding the boundaries between different occupations (and industries, see below). This process of restructuring also involves media which used to belong to entirely different kinds of organisation.

The tendencies described above are bringing about considerable changes in the qualifications demanded of print workers, The impact on the training process is significant. The apprenticeship system has always been regarded as the lifeblood of the printing industry. The advanced equipment now used in firms is, however, not only increasingly costly but also in more intensive use. This often gives rise to organisational problems with regard to on-the-job training. Not only is the risk of damage relatively high, but heavy demands are also imposed on the flexible deployment of workers, including trainees.

Diffusion of printing work: relations with other industries

Printing activities are not confined to the printing industry. They have long been carried out in the in-house print shops and binderies of major companies, engineering offices, insurance companies etc. This work falls outside the sphere of influence of the printing industry.

Technological innovations, however, are leading to an erosion of the boundaries between the printing industry and the outside world. These boundaries had traditionally been drawn by the production process, the nature of the processed and processable materials, the professional skills involved and the traditions of the trade. External clients are increasingly using wordprocessors and DTP systems to intervene in the production process, and "outsiders" are encroaching ever further upon the traditional sphere of activity of the printing industry: designers using design systems as much as secretaries using wordprocessors and DTP configurations.

The developments in the pre-press area in particular are leading clients to undertake more make-up work in-house. This trend means the loss of printing work for the industry, but not its disappearance. While it reduces the control which the printing industry is able to exercise, printing techniques and therefore print workers will increasingly be employed outside the industry, and the demand for training will extend to areas outside the industry. It will, for example, become increasingly important for publishers to possess a large measure of expertise in order to be able to offer clients certain services.

Furthermore, increasing numbers of firms are finding that they need printing knowledge as part of their own production process. Printing is also emerging as an integrated part of the production process in other industries where there is call for highly specialised printing techniques. Examples are the packaging industry and the breweries. This development is relevant not only to the labour market for print workers (there is a growing trend for experienced print workers to be offered financial inducements to tempt them away from the printing industry), but also to education and training policies in the industry. Not only are new markets opening up for retraining and refresher courses (already being targeted by the GOC, particularly in its company-oriented training projects), but the development also offers – at least in theory – an increased supply of host companies willing to take on apprentices.

No exact figures are available concerning the extent of printing activities generally as compared with the size of the printing industry. However, estimates indicate that the areas in which printing work is being carried out is over twice the size of the industry itself. In addition, production chains are becoming more integrated, with the result not only that jobs and occupations are increasingly overlapping, but also that industries are becoming more closely involved with each other: there is an evolution in the direction of a media industry characterised by an absence of clear dividing lines and in which relations between organisations are of growing importance.[8]

The external "management problems" which this entails for the printing industry seems to be exacerbated by the unrest among its own rank and file, where a conflict has recently arisen between large and small businesses.[9] The erosion of the boundaries between both occupations/jobs and industries undermines the traditional mechanisms for regulating the industry. Obligations flowing from the collective labour agreements for the printing industry are often evaded in practice, and there is an attempt on the part of employers to reduce the scope of the regulations contained in collective labour agreements.

3. Developments in Education

This Section looks at the main developments in vocational education with regard to the printing industry. The present training structure for the printing industry will be outlined, along with the patterns of participation in vocational education to determine the extent to which vocational education is meeting the quantitative demand for skilled staff. The emphasis here is on the most recent policy development but as an aid to understanding we also outline the developments which have occurred since the traditional occupational structure and the traditional form of vocational training grafted upon it first became subject to erosion as a result of technological innovations.

Current structure of training and patterns of participation

Training programmes for the printing industry

The apprenticeship system focuses on teaching practical printing skills. Elementary training consists of three blocks: an orientation block (identical for all apprentices), a vocationally-oriented block (3 streams: preparation, printing and finishing: identical for all apprentices within each stream) and vocational modules (optional subjects, mainly in the final part of the programme). The advanced training programme provides for further specialisation. In 1989, over 3 600 apprentices were involved in the elementary and advanced programmes together. This figure includes special target groups (such as the long-term unemployed and women returning to the workforce) taking part in training projects via co-operative schemes between the industry and employment offices (at the end of 1989 this amounted to almost 100 persons, 60 per cent of whom were long-term unemployed, 35 per cent women returning to work and 5 per cent disabled persons).

For over 15 years, a basic one-year training programme in printing, has served as a bridge to elementary apprenticeship training (in 1989, around 100 participants), and some years ago a tertiary apprenticeship training programme was also set up for instructors and production managers/foremen (in 1989, around 200 apprentices). The basic training or bridging programme is intended for apprentices lacking the B-level LBO diploma or proof of graduation from the third to the fourth year of junior general secondary education (MAVO). The syllabus of the bridging programme emphasizes arithmetic, Dutch language, mathematics and physics, while also imparting a general knowledge of printing. The tertiary training is directed primarily at the acquisition of those social skills which are needed to work as an instructor or foreman but cannot be learned purely on the job.

Alongside initial vocational training for new staff entering the printing industry, retraining and refresher courses for existing staff occupy a major place within the structure of vocational training. In 1973, a separate organisation was set up to provide such courses, the Special Courses Organisation (SBO), which now (like the VBGI) comes under the umbrella of the GOC. In 1976 a separate training centre was set up in Deventer (later transferred to Veenendaal), which gave the printing industry its own centre for retraining and refresher courses (in 1989 there were almost 40 different programmes and over 120 courses on offer). Of particular interest in this context are, for example, the individual company training projects, whereby the GOC provides training specially tailored to the needs of companies both in the industry itself and in the outside world.[10]

Aside from courses offered by the training centre, there are two alternative sorts of training leading to a professional qualification recognised by the industry and comparable with that of the elementary and advanced apprenticeship system: on-the-job training combined with distance learning and the "elementary combined programme" (PCO). The

134

programme is composed of a theoretical element consisting of correspondence courses and one-day practical sessions at the training centre or a printing college. For the practical training in Veenendaal, a complete replica of the plant in a small printing business has been set up. With its emphasis on producing versatile and flexible staff and its relatively short duration (18 months), the programme is specially designed for the small business sector.

Table B4 provides an overview of the present structure of training within the printing industry, (initial training, retraining and refresher programmes).

Table B4. **Structure of training in the printing industry**

	Initial training*				Retraining and updating		
	Apprenticeships (under Act)	Corresp. courses	Elementary combined	Retraining course Veenendaal	Company projects	Introductory course	Refresher course
elementary training	content: prep. print. finish.	content: prep. print. finish	content: basic vocat. course + options	content: wordproc.	content: all occup.	content: prep. print. finish.	content: prep. print.
	length: 2-3 yrs	length: 1 1/2-2 yrs	length: 18 mths	length: 22 days	length: as agreed	length: 5 days	length: variable
advanced training	content: prep. print. finish.	content: prep. print. finish.		content: prep. print. finish.	content: all occup.		
	length: 1 year	length: 1 year		length: variable	length: as agreed		
tertiary training	content: instructor, foreman						
	length: 1 year						

* Apprenticeships or equivalent.

In addition to the training structure outlined above, printing programmes are also available in full-time public-sector education. The KMBO (short senior secondary vocational education) offers a printing technology programme (some 370 students in 1989/1990), and the MTO (senior secondary technical education) printing programme trains students for jobs in middle management (over 1 550 students in 1989/1990). Until recently, co-operation and consultation between the apprenticeship system and the MTO printing programme was minimal. The two formed separate worlds, which for various reasons had (and wished to have) nothing to do with each other. The recent creation of schools of printing have changed this (see below). Finally, there also exists a management programme in printing at higher vocational level (HBO) and the junior secondary vocational education (LBO) printing programme, which is a preparation for further education leading to a vocational qualification.

135

Patterns of participation: trainees and companies

Table B5 summarises the trends over the last few years in the numbers of trainees and companies providing training, with respect to training courses run by the industry itself (GOC courses).

Table B5. **Numbers of trainees for each type of GOC course and numbers of GOC companies providing training (as at mid-October)**

	1987	1988	1989	1990
Total trainees in initial training programmes including	3 462	3 796	4 270	4 454
Elementary apprenticeship*	2 332	2 459	2 628	2 699
Advanced apprenticeship	557	600	658	644
Tertiary apprenticeship	76	125	236	329
Elementary Combined (PCO)	–	–	–	–
Correspondence (elem. + adv.)	497	612	675	654
Total trainees on retraining and refresher courses including:	1 009	1 280	1 094	1 163
Company projects	445	649	552	537
Veenendaal retraining courses	564	631	542	626
Total trainees	4 471	5 076	5 364	5 617
Total no. of companies providing training	1 335	1 414	1 570	1 654

* Including adult elementary vocational education (PBVE).
Source: Internal GOC documentation.

• *Training by the industry itself*

Table B6 provides a summary of the trends in participation in the full-time printing programmes in public-sector education, i.e. MTO and KMBO.

Table B6. **Participation in MTO and KMBO printing programmes**

	1985-1986			1986-1987			1988-1989			1989-1990		
	m.	f.	tot.	m.	f.	tot.	m.	f.	tot.	m.	f.	tot.
full-MTO	1 079	306	*1 385*	1 084	337	*1 421*	1 079	438	*1 517*	1 081	474	*1 555*
KMBO	229	47	*276*	244	69	*313*	236	95	*231*	252	117	*369*

Source: CBS, *Statistiek van het middelbaar beroepsonderwijs* (Senior Secondary Vocational Education Statistics), The Hague 1988 and 1990.

• *Training provision in printing firms*

Of the total number of GOC firms, 49 per cent provide no training at all. Of those firms which do provide training, over 80 per cent make use of the apprenticeship system; 45 per cent do this in combination with correspondence courses and/or courses at the training centre in Veenendaal. Between 1987 and 1990, there was a growth of over 300 in the number of firms providing training – from 1 335 in 1987 to 1 654 in 1990. In 1990, these firms were training a total of 5 617 people.

Meeting the quantitative need for staff

The above gives a quantitative impression of training efforts. But how far do these efforts go towards meeting the need for skilled staff in the printing industry? The 1991 BOGI study showed that the "market share" of the GOC courses in the apprenticeship system was not far in excess of 50 per cent in terms of meeting the real demand for skilled staff entering the printing industry between 1986 and 1989. Disregarding those who drop out of elementary apprenticeship courses without qualifying but nevertheless continue to work in the printing industry, this market share was only 37 per cent. Between 1986 and 1989, total demand in the printing industry for new staff with vocational qualifications at elementary level was 5 900 people, while the number of skilled workers delivered by the apprenticeship system at elementary level was less than 2 200.

The BOGI report indicates that elementary or equivalent training programmes in the apprenticeship system are at any rate failing to meet the expected 70 to 80 per cent of demand. They suggest that the remaining demand for qualified staff is therefore being met in some other way: through in-house company training programmes, through suppliers or through other training institutions.

Returning to the estimated demand for newly trained staff in the 1990-1994 period, the annual total is 1 200 to 1 750. Given the premature drop-out rate, this net demand needs to be multiplied by a factor of 1.4 in order to arrive at the number of enrolments necessary to meet the demand for newly trained people. This means that between 1990 and 1994, apprenticeship or other training agreements must be concluded for an average of 1 680 to 2 450 people a year. In 1989, the number of enrolments for elementary GOC training courses came to over 1 900. If this level is maintained in subsequent years, the GOC will be able to meet 80 to 100 per cent of demand for newly trained people. It is, however, doubtful whether this can be achieved. The number of new apprenticeship agreements fell between 1989 and 1990 from 1 543 to 1 374. Demographic trends and the declining supply of school leavers are giving rise in the printing industry (as elsewhere) to anxiety about the future state of the labour market. The correspondence and PCO programmes would appear to have a role to play here in meeting shortages. In 1990, the number of people taking correspondence courses (elementary and advanced together) fell from 675 to 654 as compared with 1989, while participation in the PCO programmes increased from 73 to 130.

More generally, it would appear that over the next few years increasing demands will be made on the ability of the printing industry to increase further its attractiveness to school leavers and the willingness of its firms to provide training. Efforts have been made in the industry to develop a model training plan which for firms needing it can provide help with future staffing and recruitment policies. The GOC has undertaken a campaign – with advisers specially taken on for the job – which aims to persuade businesses to hire young print workers.

Vocational training in the 1970s and 1980s

The preceding sections have focused attention on the quantitative dimension. Below, the qualitative developments in the structure of vocational training in the printing industry are examined. An essential factor here has been the role of the two sides of industry, the agreements they have made in relation to external control and internal management of the labour market, and the institutions set up by them, chief of which is the GOC. It is primarily this set-up that has determined the way in which the industry has responded to developments in the outside world since the late 1960s.

Up to that date, apprentices were trained for an occupation involving specific equipment, procedures and positions within the production process. There was an almost perfect match between the actual content of jobs and the occupations for which people were trained. The collective labour agreement included the obligation to pursue the advanced training after the successful completion of the elementary programme (four years of vocational training). The occupations for which people were trained (the elementary training distinguished 16 occupational fields and the advanced one 37 occupational specialisations) were based on the place in a particular segment of the production process and the type of firm in which the apprentice was being trained. Until the end of the 1960s, this structure was fairly stable.

The new pattern

Changes in the printing production process in the late 1960s put considerable pressure on traditional vocational training. In response to the growing heterogeneity in the industry, and with production processes becoming far more specific to individual companies as regards both technology and organisation, it was decided in 1973 to adopt the "New Pattern". At the heart of this new structure of training was the idea of broad-based basic training with supplementary retraining and refresher courses. Initial vocational training and retraining and refresher courses were all seen as part of a single structure, within which retraining and refresher courses were to dovetail with the initial training as regards both content and teaching methods. There was to be a coherent system of training courses, directed at producing flexible craftsmen capable of keeping pace with technological innovation and changes in the workplace.

It was decided to make broad-based basic training the starting point of initial vocational training. This was supposed to prepare trainees to work in a number of different jobs within a particular segment of the production process. It was also supposed to lay the foundations for vertical mobility, eventual promotion to higher-level jobs and the retraining and updating required in the case of job changes. This objective, to provide a broad-based

138

training for a wide horizontal and vertical range of jobs, was supported by all the parties concerned. The GOC laid down the following principles of training:

- emphasis on understanding the rudiments, directly applicable knowledge and skills to be taught in job-oriented training courses;
- training to be geared to non-polarised, integrated jobs, in other words a commitment to jobs of an attractive nature;
- trainees to be prepared for greater flexibility and mobility, for example rotating between several jobs, departments or even firms;
- both theoretical and practical attention to socio-instrumental and socio-normative aspects of the occupation (company and workplace orientation, participation in progress meetings, etc.).

The same principles were adopted with regard to retraining and refresher courses. These were to be more than simply equipment or job-oriented training, and they were also to pay more attention to the socio-psychological aspects of the work. The new courses marked a break with the established traditions of training in several ways:

- Training was no longer given for a particular type of job, but for an occupational field, with the choice of the nature and level of the basic training also relying on normative elements (stipulated by the partners to the collective labour agreements). The original 16 streams in the elementary training programme were reduced to four, corresponding to the segments in the production process: reproduction techniques, forme production, printing processes and binding/finishing technology.
- Similarly, the number of specialisations in the advanced training programme was reduced, from 37 to 24.
- Differentiation in levels of training was introduced by eliminating from the collective labour agreement the obligation to pursue the advanced training. This raised the status of the elementary training certificate, since it was no longer an intermediate step but regarded as a terminal qualification in its own right.[11]
- It was made possible for several different firms to enter into a single apprenticeship agreement with a trainee and to provide the training collectively. The reason for this was that some firms did not have all the relevant equipment available or that it was dispersed between different firms.[12]
- In individual company retraining projects – a new development – it became possible for firms to contribute knowledge and skills specific to their own company (around 40 per cent of the course), while the rest was put together by the SBO (Special Courses Organisation), building upon the apprenticeship training courses.
- Both the initial training and retraining and refresher courses paid considerable attention to the social aspects of work: organisational and communications insights and skills, a flexible attitude with regard to changes in the workplace, and a greater awareness of the role of the employee.

Entry restrictions were also substantially eased: in addition to the traditional intake from the LTO printing programme, school leavers with MAVO and HAVO qualifications could now pursue vocational training in the printing industry.

139

Increasing the flexibility of training provision

In general, the trade unions have been pleased with the results of the restructuring under the new pattern. On the employers' side, however, there have been objections. For example, over the perceived discrepancies between training provision and the firms' available resources and needs (for tailor-made solutions). Employers called for:
  – a more differentiated and flexible training structure;
  – a relaxation of the policies on access to retraining and refresher courses;
  – efficient use of financial resources and the distribution of costs between government, the printing industry and individual companies.

The employers' criticisms eventually led to a review of the new pattern of vocational training and in 1983, the trade unions agreed to modify the structure of training. In subsequent years, however, they have frequently intervened in the further implementation of this new structure, particularly in order to safeguard the aim of producing a skilled worker with a broad-based vertical and horizontal training.

This development has been described as "increasing the flexibility of training provision itself". During the 1980s, changes were made in the organisation of the training courses and related matters in order to create a closer match between training and the needs and resources of companies. The catchword "flexibility" refers in this context not so much to the (future) skilled worker, but rather to training provision itself. The reform of vocational training has focused on two points: *i)* the development of a structure of training permitting a closer match between training provision and the needs of employers; and *ii)* reinforcing the position and improving the procedures of the GOC. The objectives of the "new-pattern" training courses have hardly changed, but they are being interpreted in a different and tighter way.

The present structure of vocational training is for a large part the result of the process of increasing the flexibility of training provision itself. Programmes continue to be based on occupational fields. Processing of images and text is (in connection with the extensive technical and organisational integration) accommodated within a single occupational field – "preparation" – so that there are now three occupational fields or streams within the elementary training. These occupational fields are subdivided into specialisations – occupations – with each occupational field including between nine and twelve different specialisations.

A major difference as compared with the "new pattern" is the division of the programmes into different levels. Three levels are now distinguished: the skilled print worker *a)*, the printing technician *b)*, the process supervisor *c)*, corresponding to the elementary, advanced and tertiary programmes within the apprenticeship system. Each level culminates in specialisations. This contrasts sharply with the previous situation, where the elementary training provided for virtually no specialisation. The elementary and advanced types of training were then regarded as a single entity leading from broad to specialised. Presently, each level leads the trainee from broad to specialised (since even the advanced and tertiary training programmes begin with a basic element). The range of training on offer is thus considerably more differentiated as regards both nature and level.

Each level includes *orientation modules*, allowing the trainee to choose between large and small companies. At A-level, these are the workplace and company orientation modules; at B-level, business organisation; and at C-level, production and process organisation. Following the orientation modules, trainees each select one of the *basic modules* in their occupational field. These basic modules lead on to several *occupational modules* (specialising in particular occupations). This same structure is repeated at each level.

Vocational training in the 1980s offers far more choice with regard to routes and (with an exception for the elementary training) length of training. A wider choice of training routes is referred to as *increased flexibility*, while differences in length of training are known as *differentiation*. In order to make this greater flexibility and differentiation possible, the training programmes are divided up into modules. The modular concept was already being applied in vocational training in the 1970s. The difference is that now the whole system of training is based on modules.

An interesting feature is the newly introduced tertiary level of process supervisor (practical instructor or foreman). Here, the GOC has expanded its scope upwards, creating a programme that may well become a formidable competitor of the MTS printing programme. A simplified programme for printing assistants has also been created (i.e. "downward expansion"). The existing possibility of on-the-job training combined with distance learning is retained. All this has made the vocational training courses of the 1980s more flexible and differentiated. While firms cannot choose any level at will, they do have a wider range of choice from the differentiated package of training routes.

The issue of gearing training provision to meet the needs of the industry is even more important in the area of retraining and updating than in initial training. A decision has been taken to run the training centre in Veenendaal on a more commercial basis. Here too, the principles being pursued are flexibility, differentiation and market/company orientation. It is particularly interesting that, as compared with "the new pattern", companies are being given more scope to contribute job-specific knowledge and skills, that courses will, to a greater extent, cover their own costs and also that the training centre is to make use of the same modules used in initial training. Access to retraining and refresher courses is being widened: unqualified people (both inside and outside the printing business) are also being admitted and training can be organised for individual companies if so required (company training projects).

Finally, the structural basis of the training policy outlined here has also been made more explicit and strengthened in the course of the 1980s: agreements concerning the number of apprentices are now made in the context of the collective labour agreement (and no longer only within the Central Bureau); active labour market research is being developed (cf. the BOGI study and the employment surveys); and participation in both initial vocational training and retraining and refresher courses is now financed collectively (via an equalisation fund).

Vocational training in the 1990s: towards the establishment of schools of printing

A major development in vocational education in the printing field has been the establishment of *grafisch lycea* or schools of printing. This operation has two main objectives: *a)* the linking up of different types of educational establishment (i.e. MBO,

KMBO and BBO) to form a single institution or *lyceum*, allowing a coherent structure of education to emerge; and *b)* the educational harmonization and reform of the range of programmes on offer. This is expected to take a number of years but the new system is expected to be in operation by 1994/1995. There are five schools of printing in the Netherlands, in Amsterdam, Rotterdam, Eindhoven, Utrecht and Zwolle.

The decision to create these schools is based on the assumption that occupational practice, i.e. the actual content of occupations in industry, should form the basis for the restructured system of vocational education in the printing field. The system of qualifications and the harmonization between different types of institution will stem primarily from the needs of industry, this being the key point of reference. The establishment of the schools of printing accordingly demands that attention be paid to four key elements, of which the content and structure of education is the most important. This, after all, is primarily where the relationship with the industry needs to be created. To quote from the 1988 OBO memorandum on the establishment of the schools of printing: "If the new schools of printing are to make a useful contribution to the successful operation of the printing industry and at the same time offer their students good prospects in their future careers, they will have to be extremely well informed both as to nation-wide and regional needs within the industry and as to the individual needs of (future) trainees. This is because the differences in needs affect not only the content of programmes but also the kind of training that needs to be pursued. This demands an unusual degree of flexibility in the range of courses on offer in the schools of printing."

The content and structure of programmes is therefore the main element of the reform operation. The other elements are modification of the organisation of educational institutions, of teaching materials/equipment and of staff expertise. These changes will be based on the desired content and structure of education. The question of feasibility comes second. A brief outline follows of the principal changes to be made.

Alignment of education and the actual content of occupations in the workplace

The changes in curriculum content are prompted by changes in the content and organisation of work. The Research and Development Department (GOC), together with the Printing Industry Economic Advice Centre (GEA), carried out a study of current occupational profiles in the printing industry. The study concluded that the printing industry (or rather, printing activities) can be subdivided into six occupational fields: artwork/design, preparation, printing, finishing, management and packaging.

It is interesting that two of these, artwork/design and packaging, are not a traditional part of the printing industry. Within each occupational field there are different occupations, and within them different specialisations. These occupational profiles are being used to draw up definitions of requisite skills and knowledge for each occupation, as well as attainment targets (see Annex). This information will to a great extent determine the content of the courses. The occupational profiles are the starting point for the changes in vocational education in the printing field.

Gearing the structure of courses to their content

The structure of vocational education in the printing field will no longer follow the present pattern (duration of training, trend towards a dual system combining working and learning, etc.), but will instead depend upon the content of training as determined on the basis of the occupational profiles. The length of the programme and whether the most appropriate form is full-time study with a work experience placement or in fact a dual system of training are issues which are being determined for each individual programme on the basis of content. The criterion will be "how best to teach the trade" and a totally new structure of training will be created. All the courses will include set basic elements. A minimum of eight certificates (credits) will be required to obtain an initial qualification, after which further courses can be taken to qualify as a manager, etc.

A coherent range of programmes

The differences in structure between MBO, KMBO and BBO/apprenticeship training are set to disappear. Geared to the content of training within the six occupational fields, programmes will be designed with clearly identified overlaps (i.e. the areas which are the same for each programme). This will enable horizontal and/or internal vertical transfers to take place. The traditional terms to designate the different levels (MBO, BBO, etc.) will be eliminated and programmes will be organised by occupational field instead of by level. An important point is that the training will be recognised as senior secondary vocational training.

Modular qualifications or certificates

The new schools of printing will provide three kinds of qualifications: social, occupational and transfer qualifications. The social qualifications will relate to communications skills, preparation for work and scientific knowledge. The occupational qualifications will relate to printing, technology, the occupational field, the occupation and the specialisation. The transfer qualifications will relate to both internal and external transfers (to HBO). The vocational qualification, will be composed of modules, which apart or in combination with each other lead to a certificate. These certificates will in turn count as credits towards a nationally recognised vocational qualification. The aim is to create a route through the training system tailored both to the individual and to the situation in a specific company. It will, moreover, be possible swiftly to adapt course components in the form of modules in line with changing job content.

Relationship with pre-vocational education/LBO

The LBO printing programme will offer recognisable elements of several of the printing school programmes which lead to vocational qualifications. LBO students transferring to any of these programmes will then be exempted from these course components. The vocationally-oriented part of the LBO printing programme will therefore be based on the current content of occupations. For students coming from MAVO and HAVO there will likewise be consideration on a case-by-case basis to see where exemptions may be granted.

Relationship with retraining and refresher courses

The Veenendaal courses, correspondence courses and contract courses at the schools of printing are all being integrated into the new structure of education. The new range of courses at the schools of printing will become a coherent whole comprising both initial vocational training in the printing field and continuing training courses.

Implementation

Clearly, the present restructuring is a vast operation. As already mentioned, this operation is expected to be completed by 1994-1995. The OBO and the principals of the new printing schools will bear final responsibility, with the GOC playing a co-ordinating role. The whole operation demands a major change in thinking on the part of those involved. Educational attitudes are very different in MBO and BBO establishments. In particular, the MTO printing programme will have to become a genuine vocational training programme and will have to be harmonized with what is already being done in the apprenticeship system. The problems lie not so much with the school management and boards as with the teachers, in the area of staffing and legal status.

Funding

The costs of the entire system of training in the printing industry, including infrastructure, amount on an annual basis to over 16 million guilders (1989 figures: 7.5 millions US dollars). There are three sources of funding: the Ministry of Education and Science (about 29 per cent), the industry itself, i.e. the collective labour agreement levy (about 27 per cent) and income from the provision of services (around 44 per cent). It has been agreed in the collective labour agreements that a certain percentage of average earnings (presently around 1 per cent) be put into an equalisation fund: the collective labour agreement levy (in the latest agreement the levy is 1 per cent, 0.7 per cent more than in the previous one).[13]

Under the collective labour agreement, companies able to demonstrate that they are providing adequate training under the apprenticeship system receive substantial subsidies, which – under the latest agreement – can amount to NLG 25 000 per trainee (1989: 11 800 dollars). Training/employing women and ethnic minorities attracts extra subsidies. Companies that draw up training plans together with other companies and provide training courses for new entrants by means of a GOA (joint training activities) receive an additional subsidy to cover the organisational costs involved.

The fees companies pay for the GOC programmes attended depend on membership of the KVGO (Royal Federation of Printing Businesses) and contributions to the Equalisation Fund.[14] Taking PCO programmes as an example, the actual costs of the basic programme, the vocational training programme and one optional programme amount to NLG 8 750 (4 125 dollars). Companies belonging to the KVGO pay NLG 7 000 (3 300 dollars). Employers contributing to the Equalisation Fund (the collective labour agreement levy) receive a subsidy of NLG 5 000 (2 358 dollars) and therefore in effect pay NLG 2 000 (943 dollars).

4. The Interaction between Education and Work

The key issue in this sector study is the responsiveness of the system of vocational education in the printing industry. Responsiveness means the way in which vocational education responds to relevant developments in the world around it and the effectiveness of its response. Responsiveness has, in other words, to do with the relationship between the system of vocational education and its environment, and refers primarily to its ability to react or its flexibility vis-à-vis developments in the outside world. This study chooses the broader perspective of responsiveness, meaning the entire conceivable range of ways of reacting, from the purely adaptive (reactive) through to and including the purely creative (proactive).

Previous sections have outlined the historical development of the system of vocational education in the printing industry and the changes in the world around it. This section takes stock of the situation, and discusses aspects of relevance to the question of responsiveness. This section looks at: the main regulatory factors in the printing industry, the main instruments used as part of responsiveness strategies in the sector, the main actors involved and the scope for controlling responsiveness.

Regulatory factors

The previous sections have made it clear that there are currently three regulatory factors in the printing industry which dominate the relationship between vocational education and the world around it: problems concerning the supply of manpower, absorption and the content of qualifications. These factors give rise to responsiveness strategies aimed at achieving the best possible relationship between vocational education and the world around it. The next section outlines the main ways in which these factors manifest themselves in the printing industry.

One of the regulatory factors clearly dominating the printing industry is the *supply of manpower*. Shortages are expected and already to some extent being felt among experienced print workers in specific occupational or job categories, including that of managerial staff. Related to this is the practice of poaching staff from other firms or the general mobility in the printing industry labour market (particularly as a result of the blurring of the industry's boundaries) or the relative attractiveness of the printing industry to school leavers. In connection with these issues, attention needs to focus on the tendency towards increasing openness in the printing industry, including the growing problems that this implies for the control and management of the labour market for print workers (sectoral versus intersectoral). Another aspect of manpower supply is the significance of expected surpluses in other areas (especially the pre-press area).

Absorption problems due to the predicted surpluses of staff (in certain segments in particular) are another regulatory factor. As already indicated, this can largely be dealt with by retraining. Absorption problems are, however, felt to be more serious where they affect the market for apprenticeship training places. The problem is being fuelled on both the supply and demand sides of the market. On the demand side (i.e. the intake of new apprentices) the problems are primarily the consequence of demographic trends and the image of the printing industry in the minds of school leavers. Occupations or jobs in the pre-press area seem relatively attractive – precisely because of the widespread computerisation of the production process – while occupations in the press and post-press area are much less so. Future staffing requirements in the printing industry are evolving in precisely the opposite direction.

On the supply side of the market, absorption problems are being fuelled by the limited willingness or capacity of printing companies to provide training. Moreover, opportunities to train for a printing occupation are also declining because of the increasing complexity of the production process and companies' desire to maximise the use of equipment.[15]

A third regulatory factor of crucial importance to the printing industry relates to the *content of qualifications*. Problems stem from the conflict between occupation-oriented and job-oriented training. On the one hand it is clear that the core of traditional printing qualifications will need to remain intact, even though there is a shift away from manual and towards cognitive and communications skills. Accordingly, the parties in the printing industry are agreed on the desirability of preserving printing craft skills as the basis for initial vocational education. On the other hand, developments in the production process are increasing the demand for qualifications of an extremely heterogeneous and diverse character, and direct employability and relevant training are ever more important considerations for printing companies.

The ever growing conflict between occupation and job exists in other sectors as well (supplementing the accepted categorisation by Lutz and Sengenberger of different kinds of sub-markets)[16] termed a trend in the direction of complex sub-markets or market segments. Complex sub-markets demand qualifications consisting of typical combinations of occupational and company-specific elements (Hövels, 1990). While traditional printing skills remain a major basis for qualification, their application and use in particular settings is becoming ever more company- and equipment-specific. This is focusing policy interest in the printing industry not only on retraining and refresher courses, but also on the content and structure of the initial training itself.

Finally, directly connected with the problem of qualifications, the institutional regulatory mechanisms rooted in the system of industrial relations within the printing industry are increasingly being undermined. Not only are printing activities spreading far beyond the bounds of the industry but, in recent years, increasing numbers of workers without a printing qualification have been entering the industry. Training is in practice not infrequently confined to the acquisition of the skills required to work a particular system, and the transfer of knowledge is in this case frequently determined by the supplier of the equipment. This highlights a regulatory factor facing the industry which is of a different order from that outlined above, where the problems related directly to supply or demand: that is, a *problem of management or control*.

Instruments

A fairly wide range of instruments is employed within the industry to achieve the best possible relationship with the outside world. Some instruments are directed at particular problems, while others are broader in nature. All, however, relate clearly to one or more of the regulatory factors outlined above. Accordingly, these instruments have been categorised in terms of sets of instruments corresponding to each particular regulatory factor. The principal instruments are used to identify developments in the quantitative need for staff and training; to identify developments in the qualitative need for qualifications; to stimulate the operation of the apprenticeship training market.

The quantitative demand for staff and training

The main instrument used to identify policies to be pursued by the printing industry in relation to the labour market and training is a regular survey of the composition of the workforce and of training requirements in the printing industry.[17] The BOGI study looks at major changes in the printing industry, their significance for the future size and composition of the industry's workforce and their effect on training demand in the industry.

The BOGI study is carried out periodically (once every three to four years) on the initiative of the Central Bureau and under contract to the GOC. The BOGI study provides the basis for the annual labour market plans for the industry. It is also needed in order to establish target group policy (in connection, for example, with the declining numbers of school leavers).

Forecasting future developments is no easy task. This is recognised by both the industry and the research teams, who stress, therefore, that it is important not to regard the results of the BOGI study as a dogmatic basis for future policy, but rather as "quantified development guidelines".

The BOGI study is itself subject to change: the most recent version (1990-95) predicts developments in terms of main categories of occupations rather than, as in the past, for each individual occupation. The reason for this is that, in view of the major changes in occupational practice (especially in the pre-press area), meaningful prognoses at the level of individual occupations are now impossible. In addition, and at the special request of the industry, the latest BOGI study has been expanded in two respects: it now also looks at non-technical jobs in the industry and at possible regional differences.

Following the recently completed BOGI study for 1990-95, it has also been concluded that it is not enough to conduct such a study once every three to four years, that the mass of relevant factors makes the study extremely complex and wide-ranging, and that to obtain the necessary statistical material the researchers are dependent on a large number of organisations whose data is moreover in no way harmonized. For these reasons, the researchers recommend that the study be conducted annually and adopt a different and more approximative approach. It would seem that the methodology has become so refined that it is beginning to overextend itself. There is a proposal to develop a model involving a manageable number of variables which would be calculated and lead to new prognoses each year. To this end, use would be made of existing information or of information specially updated for the study. Opinions concerning expected developments could, for example, be collected via written questionnaires. It is not yet clear to what extent these recommendations will be adopted by the industry.

Demand for qualifications, training profiles and innovation

The GOC (i.e. the industry's Research and Development Department) has worked jointly with the Printing Industry Economics Advisory Centre to investigate current occupational profiles in the sector. This was done on the basis of a conscious prior decision to use a group of six occupational fields. Their study investigated the processes involved in each of the main occupations and specialisations in each area, and the practical and theoretical knowledge required in relation to these processes. This was done using qualitative methods, by defining (via observation and interviews within companies) what was expected of staff in the workplace (occupational profiles). The GOC has designed a model to catalogue and refine the required skills (on the basis of categories such as preparation, execution, control, management, organisation, etc.).

The key aspects of this regulatory instrument are the fact that it involves a pragmatic approach which awards a central role to experts in the field, that it has been developed and implemented by the industry itself. There is a distinction but not a rigid divorce between the drafting of the occupational profiles and that of the training profiles. The industry's own involvement means that it can make for itself the fundamental choices necessary to structure the reality of work in relation to education.

In the future, the relevant information concerning substantive developments in occupational practice will increasingly have to be obtained through the industry's own networks of experts, who have their feelers out among companies, equipment manufacturers, etc. To ensure a good input, i.e. satisfactory identification of trends, large numbers of people will have to be involved in that network and work together with educational experts to organise the implementation of reforms in education and training. The GOC will act in this context as a kind of permanent development centre, serving as the "seed bed" for substantive reform: continually picking up changes through sound analyses of the labour market and occupational practice, suggesting modifications, and channelling them through to schools and teachers in the form of new curricula, teaching materials and initial and in-service training. The GOC will continue to play an important part within the network of companies, but will mainly be active at a national level, as an umbrella organisation. In the end, it will be up to the schools themselves to develop the capacity for change in the content of education.

The GOC is currently working on a number of experimental training courses in Veenendaal which aim to teach occupational theory in a more system-independent way, i.e. to unlink theory from specific equipment. Another example of an interesting new development is the attempt to channel technological innovations covered in GOC courses through to initial training programmes wherever it is clear that such innovations are beginning to acquire a broader and more general significance within the industry. This is giving the GOC a role not only as a pioneer in training in new printing techniques but also as a point of transfer to initial vocational training.

The market for training places: supply and demand

Broadly speaking, three kinds of instruments are currently being employed to tap the existing supply of potential new workers for the printing industry, i.e. to stimulate the intake into initial vocational training:

- General reference may be made to the efforts to make training provision more flexible (i.e. geared not only to the needs of the industry but also to the needs and opportunities of potential trainees) and, of course, to the recent restructuring operation which has led to schools of printing (resulting in a substantial broadening in the range of potential routes to qualification and a significant expansion in recruitment potential).

- The printing industry is placing greater emphasis on public relations and a collective approach by training institutions and companies. For example, campaigns have been undertaken to promote public knowledge about the industry and to recruit trainees.

- A target group policy has been implemented under which – in consultation with, for example, employment offices – specific educational and training opportunities are being developed for target groups. Examples are the basic training or bridging class and also various training projects for adults (PBVE). Another aspect of target group policy is the financial incentives available for training women[18] and ethnic minorities. The aim is to train particular target groups for occupational categories where there is a shortage of skilled labour, i.e. in particular, offset operators, folders and cutters.

A key, and increasingly important, regulatory factor concerns the demand side of the market for training places, i.e. the supply of training places by companies. In this connection, the elementary combined training programme, with its modified content and duration, is especially geared to the needs of small printing businesses. The more established on-the-job training programme combined with distance learning can also be included in this category. Some within the industry have called for efforts to achieve greater flexibility with regard to the organisation of training, in order to make it easier for companies to plan courses into their schedules and cover for absences due to training. One concrete possibility being considered is, for example, to organise vocational training within the apprenticeship system in such a way that an apprentice would attend classes one week in five, instead of one day a week. In order to encourage apprentices to go on to advanced training (about 65 per cent now do so), consideration is also being given, for example, to the possibilities of providing training in the evenings or on Saturdays. In addition to modifications in the organisational design of dual training, other measures of support include the equalisation fund, and the possibilities for companies to provide training collectively via GOA schemes.

Printing activities outside the industry

It is difficult to evaluate the extent of printing activities outside the industry and therefore the size of the potential training market. Nevertheless, the relationship between the printing industry and printing activities in other sectors is a question which goes right to the heart of the industry's vocational training policies. There are two – rather paradoxical – responses to this on the part of the printing industry.

On the one hand, the industry is pursuing a strategy directed at maintaining its traditional control over the printing market by entering into coalitions with other sectors and deliberately presenting itself as a part of the wider "communications industry". Efforts are also being made to broaden the training scope of the printing industry with the six occupational fields which are to form the basis of the new structure of qualifications in the schools of printing.

On the other hand, training policy is explicitly committed to an active client-oriented attitude specifically including non-printing companies among the industry's clients. Obvious examples are the GOC company training projects and its development of specific courses for the packaging industry as part of marketing strategy. While there are co-operative agreements with the packaging industry, there are no direct relations at industry level, for example, with the metal and electrical industries other than individual company contacts. The GOC takes an extremely client-oriented attitude: a company, whether inside or outside the industry, has a knowledge problem, to which the GOC claims it can to provide a solution. This can be done either via the standard pattern of apprenticeship training or on a purely commercial basis. The only difference is that the bill for services provided is lower for companies within the printing industry or allied sectors.

In other words, there are both elements pointing to a strategy of retaining the closest possible control over the printing industry labour market and elements pointing to an active market strategy likely to result in a further opening up of the traditionally closed world of the printing industry. There is clearly a conflict between internal and external control over the labour market. So far, the choice has been to favour development as an integral part of a broad media industry without clear dividing lines. It remains to be seen what the consequences will be for the traditional regulatory mechanisms of the printing industry.

Actors and the scope for control

Actors: central and local

The main actors in the printing industry are the trade unions and employers' organisations. Through the Central Bureau, they determine policy with regard to such matters as the labour market and vocational education for the industry. This is done in general consultation, using the collective labour agreements to record committments[19] and the institutional framework created by them over time. The closed-shop provision and the requirements set for entry to and promotion within the industry's labour market still constitute one of the corner-stones of industrial relations within the printing industry and therefore of the system of vocational training. It has been noted that this corner-stone has, however, over the last few years begun to show unmistakable cracks not only as a result of the rift between large companies and small- and medium-sized businesses within the printing industry, but more particularly due to the drift in the direction of a less clearly defined industry.

The Printing Industry Training Centre (GOC) has a not insignificant position within an extensive network of contacts with companies – both inside and outside the printing industry – and with educational institutions. These features guarantee the GOC a relatively large potential for development. The initial impetus for the recent reforms formally came from the OBO, but it is clear that there are major institutional and staff links with the GOC.

150

Within the context of the restructuring operation aimed at the establishment of the new schools of printing, the GOC will over the next few years – at least as far as initial vocational training is concerned, withdraw to a greater extent into its role as a centre for ongoing reform and development. Other actors will come into the picture more than they have done in the past, particularly where the implementation of training policy is concerned, but also with regard to content. The schools themselves will need to emerge more clearly into the limelight, both because they will have final responsibility for their own capacity for substantive change and because about a quarter of the curricula will be elaborated at regional level. During the restructuring operation, the GOC plays a co-ordinating role but remains the guiding body at national level. National qualifications will remain the norm (with approximately 75 per cent to 80 per cent of curricula being determined at national level).

The implementation of the recent restructuring operation has seen few problems at management level within the schools involved; this is likely due to their systematic involvement in the implementation process. There are problems among teachers, however, primarily as a result of differences in educational attitudes between different types of school and due to complications regarding the legal status of staff.

The two sides of industry are happy with the details of the plans for the new schools, which in fact originated in part from the GOC and the Central Bureau itself. Despite some differences between large and small businesses, employers see particular advantages in the opportunities provided by the new structure for reasonably job-specific training. The unions are particularly pleased to see things like consultative and analytical skills included in the new structure.

The government too has played a major role in triggering the recent restructuring operation, notably because of the opportunities provided by changes in the regulations governing senior secondary vocational education and part-time vocational programmes. The industry has promptly and decisively seized these opportunities. The Ministry of Education and Science has given the industry a fair amount of scope to decide exactly how the new schools will look, and has imposed few specific requirements. This, doubtless because the printing industry is playing a pioneering role in putting into practice the framework outlined by the government. The printing industry is seen by the government to be a test case.

The scope for control: reactive and innovative

Particularly in the context of the demand for responsiveness in the system of vocational training, it is important to recognise that control can in principle be a two-way process: control of education or the system of vocational training itself, or control of external developments, i.e. developments in the workplace. In the relationship between education and work in the printing industry, control is at the moment being exercised mainly over education: generally developments in the labour market and in occupational practice are the dominant points of reference for changes in vocational education. The workplace has indeed traditionally been subject to control, certainly insofar as the workplace and the labour market had, via the rules agreed within the sector, to gear themselves towards vocational training.[20] In practice, these rules were in the past often flouted and are themselves now coming under pressure. In the development of the vocational training system over the last few years, the relationship between vocational education and the workplace, which was at least reciprocal, has changed into a one-way street.

In this light, the scope for control in the printing industry is increasingly acquiring a mainly reactive character. Insofar as there is now any scope for control over the workplace, this really relates only to the capacity and willingness of printing companies to make training places available: financial incentives, the encouragement of GOA joint training schemes and – recently – active attempts to systematise training policies (by means of training plans) are being used in an attempt to induce companies to make (more) places available for on-the-job training. Moreover, the institutional structure guarantees strong legal protection against dismissal, in part through the existing system of opportunities for staff threatened with dismissal to retrain for other occupational or job categories within the printing industry. There is, however, no possibility of controlling the quality of on-the-job training places or the structure of employment itself within companies.

The reactive character of the training system's relationship with the workplace is reflected primarily in the current policy of basing the design of vocational education in the schools of printing mainly on the requirements of occupational practice, i.e. the qualification profiles demanded by industry. To describe the dominant relationship as "reactive" is not, however, to deny the innovative powers of the system of vocational training in the printing industry. Innovation refers here, however, to its relative capacity to anticipate and adapt to developments in the world around it, i.e. the world of work.

Firstly, a deliberate course is being steered towards the creation of an efficient system for the transfer of technological developments within the industry to initial vocational training, particularly via the identification and development activities of the GOC. Secondly, the policy-making bodies in the industry are themselves also making choices with regard to the design of the training system structure, for example via the choice of particular occupational fields as the basis for structuring the content of initial training programmes and in their direct involvement in the elaboration of training profiles. The latter in particular implies a conscious decision not to attempt to mirror the reality of work in all its diversity in the vocational training syllabuses. A more or less "transcendent" approach is being adopted as the basis for strategic choices by the printing industry, encouraged among other things by the need to broaden the scope of training to embrace fields beyond the traditional printing industry and by the need to preserve the core of traditional skills (the basic skills or key qualifications required). For the printing industry these constitute two essential commitments with regard to the further development of the system of vocational training.

Within the general picture outlined here, there are other, more specific means of control, including:
- retention of national qualifications as the norm, with the possibility of regional additions and specialisations,
- differentiation of course content, while guaranteeing a sufficiently broad core of skills (minimum number of certificates, with structured options);
- greater flexibility in the organisation of vocational training, achieved by means of a modular structure, optimum combinations of classroom-based and on-the-job learning, and courses of varying length;

152

- formation of co-operative networks with other more or less related industries and efforts to make the printing industry part of a wider communications industry;
- modification of training routes and use of resources directed both at new target groups in the external labour market and at existing personnel;
- active market orientation and tailoring of refresher courses to companies' needs, and wider access to retraining and refresher training courses;
- strengthening the identification, development and transfer functions of the GOC (by, for example, further strengthening its position within networks of companies, educational institutions and experts);
- optimising instruments to keep pace with developments in the labour market and in occupational practice.

5.   Responsiveness: Between Adapting and Changing the System

Preceding sections revealed the "state of the game" in the printing industry, identified the major players and explained the rules by which the game is being played. It has been shown that the printing industry is in the midst of turbulent external and internal developments, which are having a major influence both on the playing field (i.e. the system of vocational education) and on the players (i.e. the role of the various actors). The main responses or strategies in relation to developments in the internal and external environment have also been reviewed. This final section, taking a global view, attempts an answer to the question of the responsiveness of the vocational education system in the printing sector.

Responsiveness is understood as meaning the ability of the system of vocational education to react to developments in the world around it, while still preserving the basic features of the system itself. This ability to respond can in principle relate to the whole range of adaptive and creative (i.e. proactive) mechanisms available to the sub-system in relation to the world around it (i.e. other sub-systems). The answer to the question of responsiveness can be analysed in terms of a number of interdependent components.

Between occupation and job

A central dilemma faced by the vocational education system in the printing field over the last few years is how to achieve a compromise between two different commitments: to preserve the core of traditional printing skills and to provide training tailored to the specific needs of companies (i.e. company-oriented qualification profiles). The response of the system to this dilemma has emerged in the various phases it has experienced over the last few years. The solutions chosen enjoy the broad support of the principal actors, i.e. the trade unions and employers' organisations in the industry.

The direction of the solutions selected has to a great extent been determined by pressure from developments in the workplace, and influenced by preferences articulated by one or other of the actors. When the traditional type of vocational training was abandoned in the early 1970s, the initial choice was for a system of vocational education involving a broader initial training and a range of retraining and refresher training courses building on the initial programmes. Since then, there has been a change of track and differentiation has become the key concept. The range of programmes on offer has been further differentiated in accordance with demand from the industry, the needs of individual trainee-workers and training opportunities within companies. Initially, this differentiation in the range of programmes lay mainly in their content and design (modular structure) and recently it has also been occurring in the character and length of routes to qualification (varying combinations of dual and school-based). This differentiation response by the vocational education system in the area of initial vocational training is matched in the area of retraining and refresher courses with an increasing emphasis on client- or market-orientation, (such that the original commitment to harmonization of initial vocational training and retraining and refresher courses is increasingly being abandoned). With its retraining and refresher courses the GOC has begun to enter the open market for training, and in doing so is also deliberately abandoning entry requirements for this form of training.

Existing balances of power between the two sides of industry (and between them and the education world), together with their interdependence, seem for the time being to provide reasonable guarantees for the maintenance of the core of traditional printing skills within initial vocational training. An immediate threat to the vocational training system is posed by the potential attractiveness to companies of the range of part-time programmes on offer at the new printing schools and the GOC.

Margins of flexibility at different levels

Traditionally, both sides of the printing industry, employers and unions, have largely determined the frameworks for the relationship between the vocational training system and the world around it. In this respect, the printing industry has always occupied a unique position within the Dutch system of vocational education as a whole and was able at the same time to act relatively autonomously within the framework of legislation laid down by the government. In other words, within the system of vocational education for the printing industry there has always been a major role for what may be termed the intermediary level: the level of the industry, i.e. the unions and employers' organisations, and – via the principle of delegation – increasingly the GOC. The relatively wide degree of freedom at this intermediary level is highly relevant to the ability of the education system to adapt. This can be ascribed not least to the fact that the actors at this intermediary level for many years determined their strategies on the basis of the principle of consensus, and to a great extent still do so.

Recent developments indicate three points of importance for future margins of flexibility in the vocational training system in the printing sector. First, the "ground rules" of the system of industrial relations in the industry are beginning to reveal cracks: the consensus principle on which the two sides of industry base their strategies would seem to be being undermined and their traditional position of control is starting to crumble. So far, it would seem that the industry's "machinery", i.e. the GOC, is compensating for this by presenting itself as a co-ordinating and controlling body, legitimated by its expertise and staff capacity and by deliberately adopting a strategic position in the "open print workers' training market".

A second striking point is the alertness with which actors at the intermediary level – principally thanks to the powerful position of the GOC – are exploiting developments in government legislation. It is interesting, for example, to see how the industry is making use of new government legislation and regulations to come as close as possible to achieving its own aims based on clear commitments (for instance, to a single industry). Examples are the opportunities the SVM regulations offer for expanding the training capacity of the industry by explicitly taking on board full-time education (KMBO and MBO programmes), for resolving the middle management problems in the printing industry through the scope for linking up MBO and tertiary BBO programmes[21], and also – in the face of declining numbers of school leavers – for increasing its share of young people leaving the first stage of secondary education. In addition, increasing scope is being created for channelling the traditional proportion of drop outs into other occupations within the printing industry.

The third and final point – which follows on from the previous one – is the intended development in the direction of greater room for manoeuvre on the part of the new merged schools of printing. The idea is that the GOC, as the controlling body at the intermediary level, should take a back seat in favour of the individual actors (schools). Following on from the intentions of the present SVM (restructuring operation) legislation, this means that greater demands will be made on the capacity for change of the individual schools. This fact is of importance in relation to the responsiveness of the vocational training system in the printing industry, particularly insofar as the change will make it possible to tackle differential developments at regional level. In order to answer the question of effectiveness, however, it is particularly important to know to what extent schools will in practice be capable of fulfilling this task, as well as exactly how the GOC will set about interpreting its more low-key role. The co-ordinating and innovative role of the GOC would seem to hold out good prospects in relation to the system's ability to respond. The potential for responsiveness at individual school level, the co-ordinating and innovative capacity of the GOC and, last but not least, harmonization between schools and the intermediary level are what will in all probability determine the future responsiveness of the system of vocational training in the printing sector.

The printing industry: autonomous or part of the communications industry

The previous sections have shown the printing industry less and less a single, clearly delineated sector. The dividing lines which separate it from other sectors are being eroded and what was a relatively closed industry is increasingly opening up. This has major consequences, as this report has shown. At the moment the industry is in the paradoxical situation of striving to maintain the traditional, external and internal control mechanisms which however are proving steadily less effective in practice while openly fighting for recognition as an integral part of the "communications industry". Indications of this can be found in the GOC's attempt to secure a strong position for itself in the open market for training in printing activities, the expansion of the scope of initial vocational training in the new schools of printing, and the establishment of co-operative links with other related industries.

The printing industry cannot ignore its links with other sectors and the changes taking place within society. The key question with regard to the system of vocational education is therefore not whether existing intra-industry structures will remain intact, but to what extent the printing world will be able to continue to maintain its own separate vocational training system directed at traditional printing skills.

Conclusion

This report has drawn particular attention to elements of long-term structural importance in examining the level of responsiveness of the vocational training system in the printing industry. Nevertheless, mechanisms relevant to the responsiveness of vocational training in the shorter term should not be ignored. These can and should be sought in the extent to which the GOC in particular is capable of fulfilling a number of important roles regarding:
- the continual availability of adequate information on developments in the printing industry;
- flexible and rapid techniques of adaptation with regard to both quantitative and qualitative developments in the workplace;
- sufficient flexibility in the range of programmes on offer and in the structure of training;
- steady participation of industry in initial and further training;
- sufficient appeal of industry to potential new workers;
- finding satisfactory solutions to the present conflict – especially in small- and medium-sized businesses – between production and training for vocational qualifications.

This report has outlined the strategies the GOC is pursuing on these points. To what extent these will prove effective will be made clear in the near future. For the time being, the level of activity is high and there seems to be a strong inclination to adapt present strategies to changing conditions.

Annex

1. Overview of occupational fields

Vocational education for the printing industry recognises six occupational fields, each of which consists of a number of closely related occupations. These occupational fields are to a large degree isolated from each other within the system of education. Together they embrace the greater part of all printing activity within the printing industry, as well as covering a proportion of the communications industry. Some activities in the packaging industry are also covered by these occupational fields.

Artwork/design

This occupational field includes those printing occupations which link the printing industry and the broader communications industry, in particular the worlds of design and advertising. It includes marketing, communications, conceptualising, creating, visualising, presenting and writing slogans. In addition to these creative skills, craftsmanship and technical skills such as draughtsmanship are also important. Computers are of course occupying an increasingly important place.

Preparation

Preparation comprises those occupations which follow the design stage and extend up to and including the production of the form and the proof stage. For many of these occupations there are two variants: the conventional and the electronic. The latter is sometimes termed EPP (Electronic Pre-Press). Functions or specialisations which have traditionally been separate are sometimes integrated, but sometimes continue to exist in isolation from each other. Computer-related knowledge and skills, such as file management, are becoming increasingly important, but craftsmanship – typesetting (typography), reproduction (lithography), making up and exposure (developing, contacts, plotting) – remain highly relevant. The growth area specialisation of technical planning is becoming important.

Printing

Printing is a clearly delineated entity. Each occupation has its own specialisations. Offset printing is particularly varied. This occupational field also includes proof printing, even though this activity frequently takes place not in the print shop but in the preparation stage. A knowledge of equipment, quality control, and environmental and safety considerations is something which every printer needs to have. The printing of packaging also falls into this occupational field, since it has more to do with knowledge and skills from the world of printing than from the packaging industry. Particular attention is paid to small businesses. Printers in small businesses need to acquire techniques not only for printing but also, for example, for finishing materials. Relief, screen and offset printers may all require these skills.

Finishing

The area of finishing is difficult to chart due to the great diversity of equipment. There is a broad distinction between work done by hand, work with single machines and work in large-scale production lines. Categorisation by semi-manufacture or final product is also possible. The job profiles are subdivided into four types of company: publishing bindery, paper-cover bindery, print shop bindery and craft book binders. In this occupational field a link is drawn between these different types of company and the complexity of the aids employed. The specialisations vary from operating the machines in a large-scale production line including a number of "units" to, for instance, the growth specialisation of binding restoration. In the finishing field, a proportion of the occupations require a feel for materials, traditional printing know-how and product knowledge, while elsewhere it is becoming increasingly important to be able to deal with machines and computers.

Packaging

Packaging is a new offshoot in vocational education and has not yet been clearly delineated. Many of the packaging occupations originally came under finishing. Printing of packaging comes under printing. The preparation of packaging work is to a great extent covered in the preparation field. The design of packaging comes under artwork/design. However, the preparation and manufacture of stamping dies is not traditional printing work. Packaging demands a knowledge of machines and products different from the usual ones. This justifies the existence of a separate occupational field for die stampers through to and including envelope-makers.

2. Attainment targets for modular occupational qualifications

Every occupation and its various specialisations consists of a number of different categories of processes. These processes have a logical or chronological sequence, determined by the way in which people act and deal with problems (work). The three occupational fields of Preparation, Printing and Finishing are subdivided into the following groups:

- preparing/setting up;
- operating/executing;
- monitoring;
- maintenance;
- management;
- organisation;
- quality control;
- experimenting.

Some processes are common to all specialisations within an occupation (general), while others are job-specific or common to only some of the specialisations. It is precisely this communality and overlap which is important, and which will emerge in the structure of attainment targets for each occupation. The structure of attainment targets for each occupation shows which attainment targets are general within the occupation and which are specific.

Notes

1. The principal sources of information for this section are: Kayzel (1985), Ramondt and Scholten (1985), Leisink (1989), Van de Vee (1990), Annual Reports from the KVGO and GOC, and interviews with key figures in the industry.

2. Printing work or closely related tasks are also performed outside the "industry", where they fall outside the sphere of influence of the collective labour agreement for the printing industry. No exact figures are available on the extent of such work. Section 2 explores this question further.

3. This rise was, however, due in part to the effect of introducing a shorter working week, first agreed in the collective labour agreement of 1984 (initially cut to 38 hours and later to 36 hours), and the artificial effect of the merger in 1989 of the Organization of Manufacturers of Printed End Products, a related sectoral organization, with the employers' organization for the printing industry, the KVGO.

4. Relations between the two sides of industry have for many years been a model of harmony. Since World War II, for instance, there have been only two occasions when industrial disputes have led to strikes: in 1974 and 1989.

5. The Printing Industry Employment Bureau acts as an internal employment office for the industry.

6. There is also an HTS (institute of technology) printing course and printing at LBO (junior secondary vocational) level.

7. The GOC is using the findings of this study to formulate and review its multi-year policy plans. The results of the study are also regarded as highly important by other bodies, including the Committee on Labour Market Policy. Section 4 looks at the significance of the BOGI study as one of the key instruments employed by the printing industry to keep abreast of developments in training needs.

8. Within the publishing world, for example, sharper international competition is increasingly leading to concentrations and restructuring by way of mergers and consortia. The corporate policies of publishing houses are in some cases directed at concentrating on core activities, while in other instances companies are moving in precisely the opposite direction, towards a balanced spread of production activities across a number of different segments of the market. Another important point is the ever-clearer emergence of networks within which firms operate and to which firms outside the industry also belong (publishers, the audio-video industry, and even the electronics industry). Corporate strategic policies are increasingly being geared to this (see Veersma, 1991).

9. Notably in connection with the arrangements reached in the collective labour agreement concerning a 36-hour working week.

10. Specific courses have, for example, been developed for the packaging industry.

11. The collective labour agreement preserves the right of the trainee to take the advanced training course. However, the employer cannot oblige him to do so.

12. A more general point is that the informality of the traditional type of training is rapidly disappearing and host companies are having to make special arrangements for training in the Organization of production. This is increasing the tension between production and the training of staff.

13. The aim of the Equalization Fund is not to build up a fund, but (as expressly laid down in the agreement) to distribute the available resources each year.

14. Offset and screen printing businesses in particular belong to the KVGO but have separate collective labour agreements.

15. It is interesting, however, that a barrier identified elsewhere in relation to opportunities for on-the-job training in advanced production processes – viz. the increasing lack of transparency of the production process – (see Kayzel, 1985) is growing less rapidly in the printing industry than previously predicted. In particular, the greater user-friendliness of technological innovations (see DTP systems) means that less substantial demands have to be made on the ability of trainees/skilled workers to think in abstract terms.

16. Lutz and Sengenberger distinguished professional or occupational sub-markets, company-specific sub-markets and non-specific sub-markets (Lutz and Sengenberger, 1976).

17. Other instruments are: the KVGO printing industry Employment Survey, statistics from BWGI records on supply and demand (broken down by occupational group and region), GOC figures on apprentice numbers, and general statistics relating to the labour market in the Netherlands (Ministry of Social Affairs and Employment, Central Manpower Services Board).

18. It is also interesting to note the decision taken as part of the collective labour agreement to institute a Childcare Fund to subsidize the costs of childcare and increase the number available in day care centres. The aim of this is to attract and retain staff with family commitments.

19. Commitments with regard to a number of the regulatory instruments mentioned earlier have therefore been explicitly recorded in the collective labour agreements.

20. In the 1970s, the "new pattern" of vocational training was used as a conscious attempt to "control" the organization of work within printing companies by encouraging the creation of integrated jobs.

21. Middle management posts are increasingly disappearing and/or moving closer to posts at shop-floor level. There is, moreover, a certain rivalry between MBO and tertiary apprenticeship training.

Bibliography

Central Bureau for the Printing Industry in the Netherlands (1989), *Arbeidsmarktplan grafische industrie 1989-1990* (Labour market plan for the printing industry 1989-1990), Amstelveen.

DAALDEROP, J.H., de BEEST, H. and HUBREGTSE, L. (1991), *De beroepssamenstelling en opleidingsbehoefte in de grafische industrie 1990-1995* (Labour force composition and training needs in the printing industry 1990-1995), draft, Amsterdam,Tilburg.

DAALDEROP, J.H., de BEEST, H., JANSSENS, J. and PHILIPOOM, J. (1987), *De beroepssamenstelling en opleidingsbehoefte in de grafische industrie 1986-1991* (Labour force composition and training needs in the printing industry 1986-1991), Diemen.

ELTEN, J. (1989), *Innovatiestrategie bij de realisatie van het grafisch lyceum* (Innovation strategy for the establishment of the new schools of printing).

"Gemoderniseerde grafische sector zit te springen om oude rotten" (Modernized printing industry keen on old hands), newspaper article, *Volkskrant,* 22 July 1991.

GOC (1989), *Projectplan Ontwikkeling beroepsprofielen, Ontwikkeling beroeps- opleidingsprofielen* (Plan for development of occupational profiles and vocational training profiles).

GOC Annual reports 1988, 1989 and 1990.

GOC (1991), *Grafische lycea Nederland* (Schools of printing in the Netherlands) and SLO, *Leerplan voor het grafisch beroepsonderwijs. Structuur van het leerplan.* (Curriculum for vocational education for the printing industry; structure of the curriculum) Part O, Structure of qualifications and attainment targets, Compiled for the OBO.

HÖVELS, B. (1990), "Bringing the professional back in, paper presented at the international experts conference on vocational education and training", Boekelô, 16-19 October.

KAYZEL, R. (1985), *Opleidingsbeleid in de grafische industrie* (Training policy in the printing industry, preliminary study for the Organization for Strategic Labour Market Studies), The Hague.

KVGO, Annual reports 1989 and 1990, Amstelveen.

KVGO (1990a), *Kerngegevens grafische industrie Nederland* (Key figures on the Dutch printing industry), Amstelveen.

KVGO (1990b), *Feiten en cijfers over de grafische industrie* (Facts and figures on the printing industry), Amstelveen.

LEISINK, P. (1989), *Structurering van arbeidsverhoudingen. Een vergelijkende studie van medezeggenschap in de grafische industrie en in het streekvervoer* (The structuring of labour relations. A comparative study of employee participation in the printing industry and regional transport business), Utrecht.

LUTZ, B. and SENGENBERGER (1974), *Arbeitsmarktstrukturen und öffentliche Arbeitsmarktpolitik* (Labour market structures and public labour market policy), Göttingen.

NEDERMEYER, J. and van ELTEN, J. (1989), *Masterplan voor de realisatie van het grafisch lyceum* (Master plan for the establishment of the new schools of printing).

OBO (1988), Industry/Education Consultative Committee for the printing and communications/ information industries, "Realisatie Grafisch Lyceum" (The establishment of the new schools of printing).

OBO, Annual report 1988.

OBO (1989), *Voorlopige Opleidingsstructuur Grafisch Lyceum* (Provisional structure of training in the new schools of printing), 's-Hertogenbosch, October.

RAMONDT, J. and SCHOLTEN, G. (1985), *De stille voorhoede. De grafische bedrijfstak te midden van economische en technische turbulentie* (The silent vanguard, The printing industry amid turbulent economic and technological change), Leiden, Antwerp.

van EYCK, A., HARTEVELD, J. and KORPEL, J. (1991), *Inventarisatie nuldejaar- en voorschakelprogramma's leerlingwezen* (Inventory of zero year and bridging programmes in the apprenticeship system), draft report, Leiden.

van den BERG, A. and van den MAGERE (1991), "Jaren Voor de Grafici" (Lean years for print workers), *Intermediair,* 29 March.

van der VEE, M. (1990), *Berufsausbildung in der niederländischen graphischen Industrie* (Vocational training in the Dutch printing industry), Druckforum, Stuttgart, 27 January.

VEERSMA, V. (1991), *Technologische veranderingen bij uitgeven en grafische produktie: nieuwe sectoren en beroepen* (Technological changes in publishing and printing production: new sectors and occupations), paper for the WESWA seminar, 14 November, University of Nijmegen.

Working party on the new schools of printing, *Uitgangspunten vernieuwing grafisch beroepsonderwijs* (Principles for the reform of vocational education for the printing industry), December 1990.

List of Abbreviations

BBO	Beroepsbegeleidend onderwijs Day-release programmes for apprentices
BOGI	Beroepssamenstelling en opleidingsbehoefte in de grafische industrie Trends in workforce composition and training needs in the printing industry
BOOB	Bedrijfstakgewijze Overleg Onderwijs Bedrijfsleven Sector-wide Education and Industry Forum
BWGI	Bureau Werkgelegenheid Grafische Industrie Printing Industry Employment Bureau
CBS	Centraal bureau voor de statistiek Central Bureau of Statistics
CIBB	Centrum voor de innovatie van beroepsonderwijs bedrijfsleven Centre for Innovation in Training for Trade and Industry
CNV	Christelijk nationaal vakverbond National Federation of Protestant Trade Unions in the Netherlands
DTP	Desktop publishing
EPP	Electronic pre-press
FNV	Federatie Nederlandse vakbeweging Federation of Netherlands Trade Unions
GOA	Gemeenschappelijke opleidingsactiviteiten Joint training activities scheme
GOC	Grafische opleidingscentrum Printing industry training centre
HAVO	Hoger algemeen voortgezet onderwijs Senior general secondary education
HTO	Hoger technisch onderwijs Higher technical education
HTS	Hogere technische school Institute of technology (higher vocational level) packagings
KMBO	Kort middelbaar beroepsonderwijs Short senior secondary vocational programmes
KVGO	Koninklijke verbond van grafische ondernemingen Royal Federation of Printing Businesses
LEAO	Lager economisch en administratief onderwijs Junior secondary commercial education

164

LBO	Lager beroepsonderwijs Junior secondary vocational education
LHNO	Lager huishoud- en nijverheidsonderwijs Junior secondary home economics education
LTO	Lager technisch onderwijs Junior secondary technical education
MAVO	Middelbaar algemeen voortgezet onderwijs Junior general secondary education
MBO	Middelbaar beroepsonderwijs Senior secondary vocational education
MTS	Middelbare technische school Senior technical school
OBO	Overleg bedrijfsleven onderwijs Industry/Education Consultative Committee
PBVE	Primair beroepsgerichte volwassenen educatie Adult elementary vocational education
PCO	Primaire combinatie opleiding Elementary combined programme
SBO	Stichting bijzondere opleidingen Special Courses Organization
SVM	Sectorvorming en vernieuwing van het middelbaar beroepsonderwijs Sector formation and innovation in MBO
VBGI	Vereniging bevordering beroepsopleiding grafische industrie Association for the Advancement of Vocational Training in the Printing Industry
VBO	Voorbereidend beroepsonderwijs Pre-vocational education (new name for LBO)

C. Installation Technology

A.F.M. Nieuwenhuis and J.R.L. Steijers
Rotterdam Institute for Social and Policy Research,
Erasmus University of Rotterdam

1.   Background and History

Description of the market

Installation technology, part of the metal industry, consists of seven branches in the small- and medium-sized business sector, including the metalworking, electrical engineering, motor mechanics, processing and gold and silversmithing industries. These branches operate under a common collective labour agreement.

Although some 6 000 companies are registered in the Netherlands as "authorised installation engineers", not all of them belong to the installation sector. For many companies, installation is not their main activity. The installation sector includes all those companies providing consultancy, design, costing, repair, alteration, maintenance and management services for roofing and central heating, ventilation, air conditioning, refrigeration, greenhouse, domestic sewerage, drainage, gas and water, fire prevention (sprinklers) and sanitary installations (Braaksma and Overweel, 1990). About 80 per cent of installation companies, more than 3 500, belong to the Association of Dutch Installation Companies (VNI).

Installation technology companies can roughly be divided into two main categories: those involved in central heating and mechanical engineering, and those involved in plumbing (gas fitters, water fitters and sanitation engineers). Engineering activities include those relating to gas, water and sanitation facilities, roofing and central heating and air conditioning installations. These companies depend on developments in the building industry for their sales. They are active in new building, and in the restoration, rebuilding and maintenance of existing houses and utilities. New housing includes that commissioned by housing associations and local government for later rental, and subsidised and other housing to rent or for sale and commissioned by investment companies, builders and private customers (Coenegracht, 1990). Utilities include all buildings which are not used for housing. Some utilities are private, others are public. Private utilities are those used by industry, agriculture, business, traffic and services. Public utilities include buildings for health care and education and special buildings such as old people's homes.

These market areas can be further classified in terms of scale: the small-scale market and the building project market. Small-scale plumbing businesses concentrate on maintenance, i.e. installing water and gas pipes, repairing and replacing internal drainage and sewage pipes, gutters and roof tiles and renovating sanitation facilities, particularly bathrooms. Small-scale central heating and ventilation businesses are mostly engaged in replacing and maintaining central heating boilers. Plumbing businesses operate mainly in the large-scale project market in new building and public sector restoration and reconstruction work. The central heating and ventilation companies operate in house building projects in new building, restoration and reconstruction work. Plumbing businesses supply the sanitation facilities in utilities. The mechanical engineering installation sector has the largest share in the utilities project market. Their main activity is supplying heating, refrigeration and air conditioning installations. They also supply specific production process installations in the field of energy technology, dust extraction, water purification etc.

Vocational education

For the most part, installation companies recruit their personnel among certified and non-certified leavers from vocational education schools. This education is trade-specific since LBO (junior secondary vocational education), KMBO (short senior secondary vocational education) and the apprenticeship system all offer training in installation technology. There are also some specialised part-time programmes at MBO (senior secondary vocational education) and HBO (higher vocational education) level.

The departments of installation technology in LBO schools have a long history. Training in these schools used to prepare students for careers as plumbers. At present, some 70 LBO schools offer programmes in installation technology. The apprenticeship training system was introduced just after the Second World War. Just as in LBO, young people were trained for jobs as gas fitters, water fitters and plumbers. The SOG (Plumbers' Training Foundation), the national training body for the plumbing sector operated an apprenticeship scheme. The SMO (Mechanics' Training Foundation) the national training body for the central heating sector, was set up after the discovery of natural gas in Slochteren in the early 1960s. This apprenticeship system provided training on a small scale for central heating fitters. Business activities continued to overlap so that these two national bodies had increasingly more in common. In 1986 they merged into the present national organisation, the SOI (Training Foundation for Installation Technology).

Three MTS (senior secondary technical) schools (Zwolle, The Hague and Eindhoven) introduced programmes in installation technology in 1983. Installation technology may be chosen in the second year by those studying mechanical engineering, after they have completed the general first year. It was no coincidence that the programmes were introduced in three MBO institutes which already had MBO part-time programmes. In 1988 three more locations were added (Beverwijk, Amersfoort and Sneek) so that there are now six MBO schools in the Netherlands offering programmes in installation technology.

The KMBO (short MBO) programme in installation technology was set up at 16 institutes. The KMBO, which was introduced in 1980, is an experimental form of education. Day courses at primary apprenticeship level have been set up in 52 trial locations. After a rather difficult start, this experiment is considered a success: the social partners accept KMBO programmes as a preparation for secondary installation technology apprenticeship programmes and the government has therefore decided to establish KMBO programmes on a regular basis.

The part-time programmes at MBO and HBO level originated in the central heating sector and were set up by the industry itself via the national body, the SMO. The part-time MBO programme has two levels: W1 and W2. The intake for the W2 course consists largely of the output from W1 while the intake for the W1 programme comes mainly from MTS students with a general education in mechanical engineering. Students entering the part-time HBO programme have mainly taken mechanical engineering at HTS (higher technical education) level. These part-time programmes meet the growing demand for managers with specialised training. As they feared for their competitive position, firms initially attempted to meet this demand by setting up their own internal training programmes in conjunction with five MBO colleges. They provided the lecturers while the schools provided classrooms and administrative support. This situation changed soon after the SOI was set up and the part-time programmes are now completely in the hands of the schools.

Institutionalisation

The organisations in this trade have their roots in the medieval guild system. The guild system was eventually replaced by associations. One of the first associations for the plumbing trade was set up in Rozendaal, some 150 years ago. Around the year 1900, plumbers/sheet metal workers were organised in various national confessional bodies. This remained so until the Second World War. Excessive shortages of materials arose as a result of the war and the period of reconstruction that followed. A national council was set up for plumbers' and fitters' businesses to assign and distribute materials and tools regionally. Partly as a result of this, the plumbers later came to a cartel arrangement with the wholesalers whereby only authorised plumbers could obtain materials. This protection was withdrawn in 1972 following a Common Market ruling, and "do-it-yourself" businesses later took over a large share of this market.

A governing council covered the three confessional organisations of gas fitters, water fitters, plumbers and roofers. The installation of central heating in houses became more widespread, particularly in the 1970s. From 1972 plumbers were also permitted to install central heating. Although company activities increasingly overlapped, the business associations remained separate in this period. In 1969 the AVOL (the general association of contractors in the plumbing sector) was set up as a merger of the Catholic fitters' organisation, the general fitters' organisation and the council mentioned above. The ACI (the general association of central heating installation engineers) was then set up. In addition to this general association of central heating installation engineers, there was also an association of Protestant fitters.

With the establishment of the OLC (Education and Development fund for plumbers, fitters and central heating engineers) in 1981, institutionalisation developed quickly. The OLC was set up on the initiative of the AVOL to harmonize the training costs of the separate companies. Employers' and employees' associations from the various sectors were brought together in this fund. When, in 1983, the government introduced a compulsory contribution to young people's vocational training, the OLC became the body responsible for collecting and administering it.

In 1986 the social partners in the OLC, excluding the directors of the SMO/SOK and SOG, finally merged into the new Training Foundation for Installation Technology, SOI. With one organisation responsible for training and one education and development fund for the various branches, the amalgamation of the business associations was merely a question of time. The results of a study into its structure (IKON, 1984) showed that the installation technology sector could only survive if it adapted to the economic developments that had taken place since 1960. On the basis of the study the different business associations merged into the present-day VNI, Association of Dutch Installation Companies. The 95 AVOL and 7 ACI departments merged in the wake of this national movement into 55 VNI departments.

With the amalgamation in January 1991 of the examination committees for entrepreneur gas and water fitters, the plumbers and the central heating branch put their integration problems behind them. This new institute sets examinations for entrepreneurs' programmes in gas, mechanical and water technology installation engineering, pattern making, plumbing and central heating and air conditioning installation, and tests tradesmanship and business knowledge as prescribed by the government. The board of the institute consists of representatives of the VNI and of the public utilities, associated in the VEGIN and VEWIN (the Associations of Gas and Water Suppliers in the Netherlands). The VNI, together with the trade unions and the organisation responsible for training, established the examinations institute in order to ensure that training standards throughout the industry are maintained. The public utilities have a statutory responsibility for safeguarding public health and safety; it is therefore in their interest to ensure that installation engineers are properly trained.

2. Economic Developments

Developments in the sales market

New building, the need for renovation and the money supply determine the demand for installation work. Three factors influence economic developments in installation. First, the new European regulations; second, the higher demand for quality and comfort by customers and users; and third, the environmental regulations incorporated in the National Environmental Policy Plan.

In the early 1980s, the building industry suffered as a result of the economic recession. According to Coenegracht (1990), drawing on figures from the EIB (Institute for Small- and medium-sized Business) and the CBS (Central Bureau for Statistics), 1981 was the turning point. In all sectors – new housing, renovation, utilities and maintenance – there was a significant fall in building activity until 1984. Thereafter, building production began to pick up, with recovery continuing into the second half of the 1980s. Activities in the building utilities, and in renovation and restoration work increased considerably. Maintenance work increased slightly. The building of new housing reached a peak in 1988, but the period as a whole was considered unsettled. In 1988 production levels were back to those of 1980. More recently, production has stagnated. The downturn observed in the building industry in 1981 was reflected in the large drop in production (16.5 per cent) in the installation technology sector. The central heating sector was particularly hard hit. In the following few years, production recovered slightly; but in 1986 it fell once again.

For the period 1984-1988, the EIM noted a strong increase in production for the total installation sector with an average yearly growth of 8 per cent (Braaksma and Overweel, 1990). The growth could even be said to be explosive in the housing renovation and rebuilding sector, with the fitters' businesses benefiting the most. There was however a heavy drop in the utilities maintenance work. In this period the growth in production in the fitters' businesses amounted to 5.2 per cent, while the total growth of turnover in central heating and mechanical engineering came to 6.3 per cent. This was largely realised in house building and maintenance and particularly in the new building, renovation and rebuilding of utilities.

The plumbing sector must also be on its guard. The market position of the installation engineer depends increasingly on the distinctive quality of what he has to offer. Competition from the "'do it yourself'" market and from the "informal circuit" is steadily increasing. According to the EIM, better quality can be achieved in the small-scale sector through specialisation in depth, thus by offering services in electrotechnology, heating, central heating and building.

Prospects in the middle term are not unfavourable in spite of the downturn in large housing projects and of increasing competition. Turnover in restoration work should develop favourably in the short term as a result of greater concern for preserving the present supply of housing, and in the middle to long term it should at least stabilise, since renovation and rebuilding are installation intensive. The maintenance market should also produce above average growth in installation turnover through the expanding market in the replacement of central heating boilers and the relatively strong market growth in luxury sanitary equipment. Prospects for central heating and climate control installations in the utilities market sector are favourable since investment in the service sector is soon translated into building production. Buildings become outdated more quickly as a result of changing production techniques and of the demands made by consumers regarding, for example, air conditioning installations. The EIM predicts a growing turnover in installation work in the horticulture under glass sector. The demand for greenhouse heating, climate control and independent energy production installations should grow. More investments are anticipated in the cattle farming sector in the replacement and renovation of stalls.

Environmental policy should also stimulate economic opportunities. Environmental planning provides business opportunities in, for example, the treatment of waste and manure, gas purification and energy technology in the utilities project market. High efficiency techniques are attracting attention in the central heating market and all sorts of subsidy regulations will stimulate their use. The introduction of both large and small high-efficiency boilers is anticipated on a large scale. Within the context of energy conservation, computer applications in the mechanical engineering sector are under development to allow designers to calculate optimum combinations of options on the basis of the energy-relevant characteristics of a building and of the available installations. A computerised energy management system is also under development. It is a system that relates the energy-relevant characteristics of the indoor and outdoor climate to the behaviour of people and installations and their energy use. A 10 to 15 per cent reduction in energy is anticipated.

Developments in technology

Installation companies will be confronted with many interesting innovations in the next few years, in particular with respect to products, work methods, and to some extent work processes. Modernisation of production by installing new machines will be less pronounced since the sector is concerned with consultancy, design and implementation rather than with the delivery of goods. The "invisible product" of the installation sector comprises the performance of installation activities by means of the tools, apparatus and products provided by industry (Coenegracht, 1990, p. 40).

Only a few large installation technology companies will use new computer-assisted technologies such as CAM, CAD and CAP in production, design, product planning and stock control.

Product innovation in installation technology is evident in terms of new or improved products and materials. Specific mention can be made of the use of plastic piping, and of micro electronics in the fitting of heating equipment etc. Many changes are taking place in activities and working methods as a result of changes in building methods and variations in building forms. Setting up complete installations will involve less on-site assembly and incorporate audio-visual and computer-assisted apparatus.

Employment opportunities

The labour market has followed economic developments. The economic recession at the beginning of the 1980s led to the collapse of many companies and a gradual decrease in the number of installation technology workers. Economic growth in the later 1980s brought a resurgence in demand.

In 1990, the RISBO (Rotterdam Institute for Sociology and Public Administration Research) was commissioned by the OLC to investigate future supply and demand in the installation trade labour market (Coenegracht, 1990). In view of the existing personnel problems, the VNI (Association of Dutch Installation Companies) sought an overview of future personnel developments.

Table C1 shows estimated average yearly supply and demand up to 1994. Trends in the different levels of skill are shown. A distinction is made between external and internal supply. External supply refers to certified school leavers arriving on the labour market until 1994. The A-level is comprised of LBO and MAVO (junior general secondary education) school leavers entering the apprenticeship system each year, approximately 2 270 people. Levels B and C are the KMBO and MBO students who took installation technology programmes, some 240 people per year. The internal supply consists of the people already

171

working in the trade who obtained the primary apprenticeship diploma and became trainee tradesmen, level B. This, as the table indicates, amounts to approximately 1 050 people per year. They become general and specialised tradesmen on attaining the secondary and tertiary apprenticeship levels. In total, some 1 000 people per year were expected here. This includes those from the part-time MBO and HBO programmes. The total supply, internal and external together, comes to 4 560 people per year.

Table C1. **Supply and demand of installation personnel 1990-1994**

Level	External supply	Internal supply	Demand
A. unskilled	2 270	–	220
B. trainee tradesman	150	1 050	615
C. general tradesman	90	700	1 010
D. specialised tradesman	–	300	350

Total demand until 1994 is however only about 2 200 people on average per year. Supply is more than double the demand. At some skill levels there will be a labour shortage, as comparison of supply and demand figures shows. For the higher levels of general tradesman and specialised tradesman, supply does not meet demand, while for the lower skill levels supply far exceeds demand.

Developments in qualitative aspects

In 1989 a professional analysis was carried out by the CIBB (Centre for Innovation in Training for Trade and Industry) regarding middle- and higher-level personnel in installation technology. A clear structure can be seen in the professional practice of middle and higher management. This structure can be divided into five main groups; 16 profiles can be distinguished based on the nature of the work or the context in which work is done. The work activities of the middle and higher management personnel can be grouped into 12 activity clusters. These clusters generate the following profiles:

- four profiles in the management group: technical manager, project leader, site/branch manager, and business manager;
- three profiles in the planning engineer group: central heating technician/planning engineer central heating, buyer/planning engineer and planning engineer/technician;
- five profiles in the design group: department head, chief technician, central heating technician, gas/water/sanitary technician, and measurement and control engineer;
- two profiles in technical drawing: draughtsman and technician/draughtsman.
- two profiles in technical management: maintenance manager and head of technical services.

An overview of future prospects also accompanied this professional analysis. Present developments indicated more demands for middle- and higher-level positions.

172

The issuing of rules and regulations shows the influence of both national and international developments. At national level, companies are confronted with a shift from conditions specifying means to performance standards, and higher environmental and energy standards. At international level European regulations are increasingly pervasive, although European requirements are often less rigorous than Dutch minimum standards.

Technological developments require attention to product innovation in energy-saving systems, building management systems, open buildings (open choices in the layout of buildings) and computerisation as process innovation.

The future is expected to bring a reduction in specialised businesses. Companies will offer a broader package with services and internal quality control playing an increasing role. Three enterprise types will evolve: consultancy bureaus, installation companies and maintenance companies. Separate process control companies are likely to disappear. Business management developments will lead to the integration of work processes and knowledge. As a result of these developments, professionals in the field will need:

- a greater knowledge of related subjects such as structural engineering and physics, electronics, electrical engineering, process control;
- more fundamental knowledge of thermodynamics, heat transfer and systems engineering;
- higher level skills in design and calculation in view of increasing process integration and complexity;
- higher level skills in design and calculation for the control of the indoor climate;
- more knowledge of environmental and energy-related aspects;
- better quality control to meet the stricter demands of clients;
- greater social and commercial skills in addition to subject;
- planning and planning management as a result of the increased demands of project management.

3. Developments in Education

Students taking installation technology programmes

The CIBB (Centre for Innovation in training for Trade and Industry) was commissioned by the BOTO-I, the consultative body for vocational education/the trade and industry sector for installation technology, to investigate the numbers of students graduating with certificates in installation technology (Van der Hout and Ouwens, 1989). These authors have categorised the numbers of certified school leavers for the period 1985-89.

From the first column of Table C2 it can be seen that the number of certified school leavers from the junior technical schools fell by an average of 5 per cent each year. This decrease is for the most part a result of the reduced intake into junior secondary technical education. The number of certified school leavers from the elementary and advanced apprenticeship programmes rose. For the elementary programmes more than doubled. This increase is in line with the aims of the Bijdrageregeling Vakopleiding Jeugdigen (Grants

Scheme for Youth Vocational Training) which was drawn up at the beginning of the 1980s in order to double the number of apprenticeship places and thereby improve the work prospects of young people. In contrast with the growing number of certified school leavers from senior secondary technical education (MTO), the number of certified school leavers from the KMBO (short secondary vocational education) programmes in installation technology fell. While the figures for MTO-I denote a rise of 200 per cent, in the KMBO there was a corresponding fall of 19 per cent.

Table C2. **Total numbers of school leavers with certificates in installation technology for the period 1985-1989**

	LTO-1	LLW-SOI		KMBO-I	MTO-I	pt-MBO		pt-HBO
		elementary	advanced			WI	W2	
1985	1 410	401	475	233	28	101	88	14
1986	1 265	432	480	194	54	87	66	22
1987	1 162	589	636	169	54	100	65	17
1988	1 208	766	575	199	70	169	76	17
1989	1 107	885	625	189	88	171	72	18

LTO   Junior Secondary Technical Education
LLW-SOI   Junior Apprenticeship Training LW-SOI (Training Foundation for Installation Technology)
KMBO   Short Senior Secondary Vocational Education
MTO   Senior Secondary Technical Education
pt-MBO   Part-time Senior Secondary Vocational Education
pt-HBO   Part-time Higher Vocational Education

The part-time MBO programme (W1 level) has shown an increase, particularly since 1987. The graduates from this programme rose by 69 per cent over the period 1985-1989, an average of 17 per cent per year. In the same period, the number of graduates from the W2 level programme fell by an average of 4.5 per cent per year. The numbers from the part-time HBO programme has been fairly consistent over the last few years.

Shifts in the structure of educational provision

Traditionally, qualifications in the installation technology trade or sector have been obtained largely through internal training. Most new employees are recruited from the lower rungs of the training ladder i.e. from LBO and MAVO, and are then trained to the level of skilled worker within the business. The apprenticeship system plays a particularly important role in the plumbing sector. In the central heating sector the role of the apprenticeship system is less prominent; the reason for this can be found in the more polarised labour distribution in this sector, which was industrialised from the outset. In the central heating sector an internal training scheme of part-time MBO and HBO programmes has provided the necessary advanced courses for the trade for a long time.

Important shifts have taken place in the training structure in the last decade and two trends can be distinguished: the trade has made further use of the external provision of education and training, and there has gradually been a more extensive, structured provision of in-service and further training courses.

On-the-job training in installation technology has also suffered a reduction in training places, a result of the recession in the early 1980s (see also Hövels and Verrijdt, 1987). Increased competition and technological developments have led some available vacancies to be classified at the intermediate level. Dissatisfaction with the increasing autonomy of the national apprenticeship training bodies has also led the trade and industry sector to rely increasingly on external provision of training. As a result, the external supply of training programmes has also evolved at various levels during the last decade. In full-time KMBO education, a department of installation technology was set up at most experimental locations at the outset. A national development group brought out the first programme units structure in 1984 (PCBB, 1984). KMBO has established its place in the provision of programmes in installation technology, even if that place is a small one. In 1983, in addition to KMBO, day programmes in installation technology were set up at three MTS schools, despite opposition from the national bodies. The initiative came from the schools already offering part-time MBO programmes who wished in this manner to make better use of the expertise they had accumulated. The trade and industry sector has fully supported the initiative and in 1988 the number of training locations was doubled. MTO-I became a specialisation in the mechanical engineering department.

The introduction of optional courses in installation technology in HBO is of very recent date. For this, at the initiative of the VNI, the foundation for HIT (Higher Installation Technology Education) has been created, in which the social partners can participate, together with the gas company and a number of engineering organisations. In the spring of 1991, the HIT foundation and two HBO colleges entered into a contract to offer installation technology as a degree programme within the faculties of mechanical engineering and operational technology. The OLC (the Education and Development Fund for Plumbers, Fitters and Central Heating Engineers) and the gas company have provided a substantial initial subsidy for the colleges concerned. These programmes began in the academic year 1991-92. Meanwhile, the trade has also established contacts with the technical universities in order to create or buy external educational courses. The trade hopes not only to meet the need for highly educated personnel but also improve the sector's image.

Although the trade and industry branch is trying to put more emphasis on external educational provision at the various levels, the apprenticeship system nevertheless remains the most important way of becoming qualified in installation technology. The sector has also co-operated enthusiastically in the operation designed to double the number of apprentice places, such as those set up at the instigation of the Wagner committee (see Part I). Hövels and Verrijdt (1987) have described the policy lines along which installation technology attempts to meet this objective: firstly, via compensation for educational costs and transfer of government contributions from youth industrial training provision and via the industrial sector contribution of 0.6 per cent from collective labour agreements (the OLC was set up in 1981 for this purpose); and secondly by the double-track sandwich system, in which one student place is occupied by two students, supplemented by a prgoramme at a practical training centre.

The practical training centres were set up in order to give the practical programme more variety than would be possible within one company/work situation, and in order to increase educational capacity. These practical training centres have in fact never really got off the ground. Two reasons can be put forward for this: the OLC has not arranged any structural financing by earmarking part of the trade and industry sector's contribution, but has always resorted to incidental funding; and the start signal for the double track system was given at the very moment that the labour market began to recover, thus reducing the importance of the initiative. The trade and industry sector has also had great difficulty in realising the CAO collective labour agreement to offer training to the long-term unemployed within such a system.

In addition to the provision of internal and external programmes for the initial qualification in installation technology, the provision of secondary qualification opportunities for refresher and further training has been extended. In 1987, a training leave regulation was incorporated by the social partners in the CAO collective labour agreement. The right to training leave is thereby established and translated into a compensation regulation per company; each company can obtain compensation for a number of training days equal to the number of employees, on condition that a training plan has been agreed with the employees. In order to facilitate this, 2 per cent of the wages of every employee are transferred to the OLC. The regulation has not as yet been greatly utilised: only 20 per cent of the funds reserved have been paid out, and only about 10 per cent of employees have benefitted. This is likely due to the absence, in many cases, of a company training policy and unawareness among employees of the training leave regulation.

Renewal and development

Content renewal and course development in installation technology are concentrated on apprenticeship training and the LBO programme. The development of MBO and HBO programmes derive from the apprenticeship scheme; as the apprenticeship programmes form the foundation of the education system in installation technology, externally organised programmes are identified in relation to this reference point. The most important aspects of renewal are the implementation of the results of professional analyses, modularisation of programmes, quality control of the practical study places and the transfer of technological innovations. For each of these aspects the main development trends will now be outlined.

Professional analysis and enrichment procedures

The benefit to date of the professional analyses carried out is that the structure of functions in installation technology has been completely charted, both for tradesman functions and for middle and higher executive levels (see Section 2). For the apprenticeship programmes the consequence is that the separate educational routes of the old national bodies have been integrated into a new educational structure with six primary, six secondary and seven tertiary programmes. This structure is recognised by the social partners. The levels to be attained and the variations are for the most part associated with the professional profiles in installation and distribution technology. In order to improve articulation even further the SOI has set about making educational programmes more flexible by implementing a modular structure.

176

This educational structure for the apprenticeship scheme will form the core of initial professional programmes in installation technology. The curriculum for LBO-I now follow this design, so that the preparation for the apprenticeship will be dealt with as the starting point. The OLC supports this curriculum development project and gives financial support for the production of learning materials and course books. For LBO students the attraction of choosing installation technology is enhanced by being exempted from one year in the primary apprenticeship programme in exchange for the completion of a renewed LBO-I programme. This is an attempt to promote the choice of installation technology as a profession at an early stage in the school career.

The professional analyses, and the professional profiles to which they lead, also constituted the starting point for negotiations to set up the MBO options for installation technology. The benefit gained from the professional analysis also plays an important part in the proposals for an HBO-I variant.

Modularisation

De Bruijn and her colleagues (1991) have described in detail how the curriculum can be structured in a modular form for four sectors in the apprenticeship system. One of De Bruijn's cases is the installation technology sector. She describes a highly differentiated module structure designed to bring about cohesion between the different educational pathways. The creation of this cohesion is realised by intermediate transfer possibilities and through streams. The basic criterion for the construction of modularised educational paths depends on the complexity of the professional activities; fundamental treatments are put in sequence from simple basic skills to more complex professional skills, and integration modules which permit the acquisition of integrated treatment patterns are only thereafter added to the programme. An example of such a sequence is: metal working skills (basic skills such as cutting and slicing), pipe laying (professional skill) and the installation of a piece of sanitary equipment (integrated treatment pattern).

For primary apprenticeship the development programme was finished in 1990-1991, but its realisation is still at an early stage. The introduction of the new programmes makes heavy demands on the schools and the companies providing practical experience, not only with regard to the organisation (timetables, inventories, learning time), but also with regard to the expertise of the teachers and practical tutors. The new educational structure requires extensive retraining of teachers while an even greater demand is made on the educational environment in the companies. For a successful innovation process, support at branch level is indispensable.

From the SOI's viewpoint, curricula modularisation must be flexible enough for three types of adjustment process to operate more smoothly:
- adjustment to developments in the professional field can take place more easily, since course elements which may need to be changed are more easily identified;
- articulation between theory and practical components is simpler to bring about, since the module structure gives stricter guidance for the assignments students must carry out in the work placement in order to obtain their trade diploma;
- improvement in the possibilities of adjusting the learning path to the individual needs of students can be made, for example by introducing extra remedial modules where necessary.

Modularisation is not intended to assemble separate packages for individual students or companies. On the one hand, the examination structure has been set up so that the possibility for this is minimised, and on the other hand, the SOI has negotiated contracts with the implementing schools whereby modules in the apprenticeship programme may not be offered as separate courses in the context of contract education. The SOI (supported by the VNI and the trade organisations) endeavours to ensure that students complete as many course packages as possible so that the national recognition of the qualifications and certificates is not endangered. The branch organisations recognise that this may to some extent affect the flexibility of the educational programme.

Practical learning places

Theme perspectives for LBO: since the 1980s the curriculum for installation technology in LBO has centred on four themes which together form the corner-stones of installation technology: shelter (a roof over one's head), comfort (warmth and air conditioning), hygiene (sanitary provision) and household care (kitchen installation). The curriculum appeals to LBO students as the four themes can be recognised in the practical activities. On the basis of these themes, LBO can maintain a nationally uniform curriculum, one that connects well with the SOI programme. The OLC funds the LBO initiative and the SOI plays an important advisory role in curriculum development.

Accreditation of companies providing practice places: the SOI is seeking to arrange an accreditation system that registers companies providing practical instruction in order to facilitate quality control of the training placements. The modularisation of the curriculum makes the necessity of good training placements even more apparent.

The practice of providing regional places for practical learning in installation technology has developed in a piecemeal fashion. In the early 1980s, the idea of regional practice places arose in several companies in order to counteract the shortage of apprenticeship places resulting from the economic recession. Regional practice places could provide a variety of practical experience which an individual company could not provide due to, e.g. a limited range of activities. This policy did not get very far either because of the increasing lack of capacity in the companies. Towards the end of the 1980s the regional practice again received attention through the CAO collective labour agreements designed to help the long term unemployed to return to work. The trade associations in particular have striven for an introduction back to work via regional practice places with a job guarantee at the end of the link course. This policy has only been implemented in a few regions, with quite different budgetary agreements in each of them. In 1991 the OLC, at the instigation of the trade union, again tried to centralise the developments round the regional practice places and to develop a policy for these places for the usual apprenticeship training and also to facilitate recruitment from non traditional groups. It is not yet clear whether this policy will be successful.

4. The Interaction between Work and Education

In this section, the developments described above will be analysed according to the underlying mechanisms which influence the interaction between work and training. The question is, along which paths and by what means have the different parties tried to optimise qualification provision in installation technology? This analysis proceeds from the coherent system of internal and external training paths (Nieuwenhuis and Steijvers, 1991) (See Figure C1).

Figure C1. **Qualification problems and solution strategies**

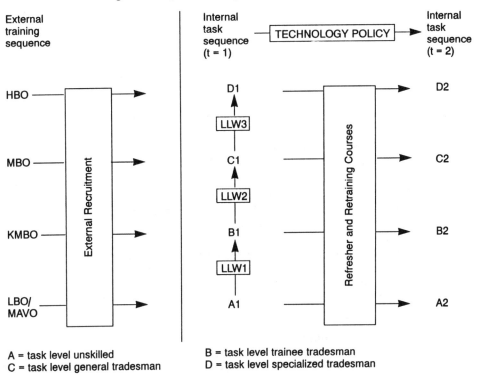

A = task level unskilled
C = task level general tradesman

B = task level trainee tradesman
D = task level specialized tradesman

Training is one policy instrument available to a company or trade to solve skill shortages. Other management options include a recruitment strategy based on the external training sequence, or more extensive computerisation and alteration of the production process so that qualification problems become differently defined. Two types of internal training can be distinguished: horizontal training and vertical training. Horizontal training is concerned with improving skills within a task level via refresher courses and retraining. Vertical training raises the qualifications of existing employees so that they may be promoted to higher positions. The established apprenticeship schemes play an important role here. The external training sequence, the internal training sequence and horizontal training policy together form the basis for the interaction between education and work in installation technology. These three elements will be discussed in turn. The organisational embedding of these innovations is important. A short historical overview is indispensable for a clear exposition.

History

Prior to 1980 there was very little interaction between work and training in installation technology. Little information was exchanged and the system of qualification provision was static. Fitters depended heavily on the internal educational sequence: every employee followed a standard pattern as an apprentice with a position as an independent contracting plumber as the final career prospect. Participation in primary training was the usual pattern in the fitters' sector. In central heating there was a polarised structure resulting in part from the sector's industrial origins. Middle- and higher-level personnel were recruited from the external sequence of MBO and HBO education and were then trained for trade-specific tasks via further part-time MBO and HBO programmes. Workers in the central heating sector frequently lacked initial training and sometimes underwent in-service training in the special apprenticeship system.

This system remained unchanged until the late 1970s, with companies enjoying a favourable sales market, based on the housing programme, the laying of the natural gas distribution network and the installation of central heating that network made possible. The 1960s and 1970s were characterised by large numbers of school leavers so that labour supply was sufficient.

However, the economic recession at the end of the 1970s and beginning of the 1980s resulted in many redundancies and a substantial reduction in in-service training. When the economy recovered in 1982 it was evident that the training system was no longer adequate. The installation technology sector at that time was characterised by:
 – an underrepresentation of young people in the distribution of personnel;
 – a tarnished trade image with fewer people choosing to enter the profession;
 – a shortage of training places and training supervisors in the companies;
 – an out-of-date, rigid training approach which failed to meet market developments.

Towards an innovative organisation of training

The social partners, with the employers' organisations taking the lead, undertook to reform the training system in the first half of the 1980s. Internal training was first reorganised. Following a shift in national politics the social partners were able to obtain control of government funds to finance trade courses. By excluding the national bodies in the re-establishment of the OLC training and development fund, the social partners obtained an important management mechanism. Furthermore, the exclusion of these national bodies from the OLC-commissioned professional and job analyses, which provided the grounds for the reorganisation of training, led the two national bodies to lose their power. Finally, the social partners threatened to hire the services of other national bodies for the trade training courses.

Under this pressure from the social partners, the SOG and the SMO/SOK merged in 1986 into a new education and training institute, the SOI. After a hesitant start the SOI developed into a strongly innovative organisation and in the second half of the 1980s took a leading role in curriculum development for installation technology. The SOI is the innovator in BOTO-I in setting up the external training sequence and advises at LBO level on the development of new curricula. VNI and SOI together developed plans for the innovation centre (the IOC) in which the SOI is now integrated. Since 1991, the new innovation centre has been responsible for distributing information on technological developments to promote the reassessment of professional profiles, the adjustment of curricula and the stimulation and support of in-service refresher and retraining activities. At present the IOC is the focus of the reorganisation of the training structure in installation technology.

Developments in the internal educational sequence

Since 1983, policy concerning the internal training sequence has focused on quantitative and qualitative aspects. Quantitatively, the number of trainee work places in the (primary) apprenticeship system has doubled since 1982. In order to expand the number of apprenticeship places, the social partners, united in the OLC and later in the SOI, agreed that companies would create and fund collective training centres. Apprentices are trained partly in off-the-job situations. In addition to those offered in collective training centres the number of apprenticeship places was further increased by the government grants scheme for youth vocational education. This policy was successful – goal figures were attained – but the collective training centres did not become a permanent feature of educational policy.

At the end of the 1980s the quantitative problem changed and the number of incoming trainees was insufficient to meet the sector's needs. The trade used intensive advertising campaigns to recruit entrants, including non-traditional target groups such as women, immigrants and the long-term unemployed (see Van der Aa and Vlaanderen, 1991).

Qualitative policy on the internal sequence begins by using the profiles from the professional analysis as a starting point for renewal and integration of apprenticeship training. Through the SOI, the results of the different professional analyses were translated into a new educational structure which fits the modern professional structure in installation technology. At the same time the restructuring process was used to reform the programme fundamentally; the new programme structure is totally modular in form, providing flexible training. In 1991 the SOI will be playing the main part and the other social partners will only advise. It is hoped that with the help of a flexible training programme technological developments can be followed more adequately in the future, particularly if the innovation centre goes ahead as planned. The structure of the courses has important consequences for the arrangements for apprentices in the training companies. Since the courses have been carefully designed and specified the apprenticeship contract is now much less open to the employer's interpretation; the training makes demands on the quality of the training supervisors and the nature of the learning tasks.

Developments in the external educational sequence

Policy concerning the external training sequence has two objectives: first the trade, and in particular the employers' association, the VNI, wishes to increase the intake of externally qualified employees at all task levels; second (albeit a hidden goal) an improvement in the image of the trade is looked for. The presence of a complete external educational sequence indicates a well-organised profession (see, for example, Geurts, 1989). In the course of the 1980s, VNI policy was to steadily expand external training. Before 1980 only LBO education had an installation technology option. When the KMBO programme was introduced, installation technology options were made available in 16 of the 52 education centres. Since both forms of education are under threat, LBO and KMBO institutes appreciate the support of the SOI and VNI: the LBO schools may disappear due to demographic trends, while the KMBO programme may merge with other MBO variants. This support has been translated into curriculum content in LBO and KMBO programmes developed on the basis of the professional analyses.

Policy at higher levels has met with only limited success. In MBO education there are only six schools with an installation technology option and the chances of the courses surviving the large-scale merger operation in MBO ending in 1991 are not high: for the new MBO colleges it is not financially attractive to offer too many options in the initial package. As far as HBO is concerned, the industry, via the HIT foundation, has entered into negotiations with two HBO institutes. This has resulted in a contract in which the HIT foundation stands as financial guarantor for development costs while the institutes are required to offer an installation technology option at HBO level. These programmes are scheduled to start in 1991, with the HBO curricula based on the results of the professional analyses.

Refresher and retraining course policy

The SOI and OLC provide support by indicating what is available on the training market and updating courses. Their role in certification is important: courses only benefit from funding and appear in the catalogue of the OLC on approval by the SOI and OLC. This catalogue is updated yearly and distributed throughout the industry.

Public and private training institutes are in this way being challenged to build up and implement a good supply of courses in installation technology. The SOI has gone a step further with the regional schools and MBOs; a co-operative contract is concluded at institution rather than course level. The modules in the apprenticeship scheme which may not be offered as separate courses are specified in the contract.

Coenegracht and colleagues (1991) conclude that this policy is bearing fruit in the installation sector: the smaller companies are beginning to bridge their traditional training gaps as the trade organisations are now responsible for personnel and training provision. The chances that a successful strategic training policy might be developed have improved.

From one-way traffic to interaction?

The economic recession of the early 1980s made evident that these systems had grown apart, and the social partners, under the leadership of the employers' organisations, came to the conclusion that the vocational and training education system required fundamental reform. The period 1980-1990 was one of strongly unidirectional communication:

education came under heavy pressure to renew and restructure. This reorganisation produced a strong training organisation, the SOI, which stimulated further interaction between work and training. The SOI developed in a short time into a professional educational organisation which could negotiate with the employers' organisations and trade unions and could deal with public and private educational establishments. A passive educational policy was becoming active, sending impulses for innovation to the trade organisations.

This innovative educational organisation has become the foundation of a flexible education system with the internal sequence of apprenticeship training as the core. The external training sequence receives proposals for branch-specific options at all levels. Whether those proposals will be implemented depends on the outcome of the current policy debate on vocational education in which apprenticeship systems and the shared responsibility of government and social partners play a central role. Activities geared to the cursory education market take the apprenticeship system as their starting-point: indeed, the results of the professional analyses and their reassessment on the basis of technological developments form important arguments for assessing training needs and developing training policy on the shop floor. The policy makers in installation technology presently assume that training and innovation in the trade are two sides of the same coin.

5. Summary and a Look Ahead

Developments in work and training have been sketched in the preceding section and the relationship between training and the installation technology labour market has been outlined. Two factors characterise the trends which emerged in the latter part of the 1980s, following the economic recession and the resulting government concern about work and training. The desire to manage more effectively in the sector has led to the merging of different policy bodies. In the field of work, this is expressed in the new demarcation and institutionalisation of the sector on the basis of the companies' economic activities. In the field of education, the trend is towards a sector-based structure of internal and external training sequences both in mainstream education and in the refresher and retraining system.

In light of the above processes, this final section looks at the capacity of the vocational education system to react to change and changing demands. A number of trends affecting the future responsiveness of education will be presented in light of present-day developments.

Because of the increasing overlap of the economic activities of the companies in the different installation technology entrepreneurs' associations, it was obvious for a long time that the associations and the separate national bodies would have to merge. The merger was blocked for a number of years by the distribution of power and conflicting individual interests. Economic welfare made the necessity less urgent. However, the economic recession in the early 1980s changed matters entirely. Just as other sectors, installation technology was confronted with a steep fall in production. This led to an increasing loss of work and a decreasing input in sector education. The position of vocational education was weakened as a result of this setback.

With the revival of the economy in the mid-1980s, vocational education came back into the picture. The proposals from the Wagner committee were formulated at just the right moment to lead the government and the social partners towards active vocational education policy. Within the total installation sector, the shrinking labour market and the predicted economic growth led to a major role for vocational education and its quantitative and qualitative links with the labour market in the policy of both the entrepreneurs' organisations and the trade unions. Mutual co-operation increased.

This co-operation had already found an institutional context in the establishment of the OLC (the Education and Development Fund), to collect and transfer payments to the government-initiated Grants Scheme for Youth Vocational Training. This ruling was intended to counter the shortage of apprenticeship places. The joint focus on vocational education and economic developments led to renewed plans to merge the two national bodies.

The CAO agreement of 1986 stipulated that 0.2 per cent of the total wages would be allocated to the OLC to set up and implement further in-service training. The OLC then turned to the task of restructuring the content and organisation of training.

As the economic situation had weakened the position of the national bodies, the social partners, whose power base had grown in the OLC, were able to create a collective apprenticeship system.

To ensure appropriate content, the job profiles study was set up and this generated the educational profiles. This study of job profiles occurred together with the merger requested by the social partners who undertook responsibility for the developments. Initially, the newly formed national education body was excluded. The first job analysis examined tasks at the primary apprenticeship level. Later, profiles were undertaken at all professional levels, including that of entrepreneur. The total professional practice of the installation technology sector could thereby be measured and charted in qualitative terms.

The merger of the various employers' associations occurred at almost the same time as the integration of the separate national bodies. Following the findings of a structure study of the sector, the three entrepreneurs' associations merged into a new association, the VNI, less than a year after the education merger. The new association professionalised education policy by setting up an education secretariat and an advisory committee to prepare policy on educational developments. Both social partners, represented in the OLC, were responsible for adapting developments in education to those in the reorganised trade sector.

A series of studies was carried out. All quantitative and qualitative aspects concerning education and harmonization with the labour market had to be assessed. From the beginning, the resulting policy options were geared by the OLC to the sector. Independent, internal sector management and control of problems was (and is still) the motto. After the internal education sequence had been reorganised, policy focused on the external educational sequence taking developments in the newly formed national body as its basis. The content of the LBO programmes in installation technology needed to be attuned to current professional practice. A new association, which includes an advisory function for the national body, ensures co-operation and harmonization at LBO level. Further provision of the installation technology option at a greater number of MBO and HBO institutes and even at university level is being sought. Centralised examinations and certification ensure that education and training activities are in tune with each other.

The merger in 1986 into one joint apprenticeship system occurred at a time when vocational education was undergoing thorough review. The result was that the new national body could gear reorganisation to the new developments in vocational education. In this way, previously inflexible attitudes towards curricula could be changed. The merger also caused internal instability. Organisational problems prevented the national body from giving its full attention to the content of the renewed curricula. The social partners, under the leadership of the employers' association, were therefore able to exert influence on the vocational education curricula. With financial support from the OLC and in co-operation with the national education body the external educational sequence was then organised to include courses in installation technology at all levels. The content of these courses was worked out on the basis of the professional profile research studies.

The general conclusion is that a sector-based, modular education system (for both internal and external education sequences) improves the scope for responding flexibly to internal labour market demand for trained personnel. The policy strategy implemented has led co-ordination of the training programmes with respect to curriculum development, examination and certification, integration of theory and practice, in both mainstream and cursory education.

On the other hand, reaction to quantitative developments in the internal labour market is expected to be less flexible because of the systematic structure. The specialised sector basis of diplomas and certificates makes mobility patterns rigid. The sector basis of education and training systems also risks decreasing the capacity to react flexibly to the external labour market. Supply and demand of qualifications might become increasingly sector-specific and less frequently formulated in general terms. Further sector-based qualifications will hinder mobility. The result could be reduced responsiveness to the external labour market.

Bibliography

AMENT, A. and RUTTEN (1988), *Economie van de gezondheidszorg* (Economics of the health care sector).

BATENBURG, T.A., LOKMAN, A.H. and NIEUWENHUIS, A.F.M. (1990), *School- en beroepsloopbanen van MBO-leerlingen. Eerste rapport: de aanvang van het onderzoek* (School and professional careers of MBO students. First report: setting up the study), RION, Groningen.

BRAAKSMA, R.M. and OVERWEEL, M.J. (1990), *Installateurs op de markt* (Installation engineers and the market), EIM, Zoetermeer.

BRUIJN, E. de, de JONG, M.W. and MOERKAMP, T. (1991), *Modulering in het leerlingwezen. Vier cases* (Modularization in the apprenticeship system. Four cases), SCO, Amsterdam.

COENEGRACHT, A.M.M.A. (1990), *De toekomstige vraag naar installatietechnici* (The future demand for installation technicians), RISBO, Rotterdam.

COENEGRACHT, A.M.M.A., MEELISSEN, M.R.M., OIRBANS, P.H. and WIGGERS, J.A. (1991*a*), *Scholing van werknemers in de installatie- techniek* (Training of employees in installation technology), RISBO, Rotterdam.

COENEGRACHT, A.M.M.A., MEELISSEN, M.R.M., OIRBANS, P.H. and WIGGERS, J.A. (1991*b*), *Steun voor scholing in de installatie- techniek* (Support for training in installation technology), RISBO, Rotterdam.

GEURTS, J. (1989), *Van niemandsland naar beroepenstructuur. Een studie over de aansluiting tussen onderwijs en arbeid op het niveau van aankomend vakmanschap* (From no-man's-land to a professional structure. A study of the relationship between education and work at the level of trainee tradesman), ITS, Nijmegen.

HOFMAN, W.H.A., NIEUWENHUIS, A.F.M. and in 't VELD, R.J. (1991), "Het cascademodel: scholing als werkbare oplossing voor marktimperfecties tussen vraag en aanbod" (The cascade model: training as a feasible solution for discrepancies between supply and demand on the market), *Tijdschrift voor arbeidsvraagstukken*, vol. 7, No 4.

HÖVELS, B. and VERRIJDT, H. (1987), *Naar een versterking van het leerlingwezen* (Towards improvement in the apprenticeship system), ITS, Nijmegen.

NIEUWENHUIS, A.F.M. and STEIJVERS, J.R.L. (1991), "Scholing: Bedrijfs- of brancheprobleem, (Training: a problem for company or industry?), in Mulder, M. (ed.), *Scholing en opleiding voor het bedrijfsleven*, Swets and Zeitlinger, Lisse.

OIRBANS, P.H. and MEELISSEN, M.R.M. (1990), *Mobiliteit in de installatiebranche: een onderzoek naar de in-, door- en uitstroom van werknemers in de installatiebranche* (Mobility in the installation sector: a study of the intake, throughput and output of employees in the installation sector), RISBO, Rotterdam.

OUWENS, E.J. (1991), *Methode herijking beroepsprofielen en eindtermen* (Method of reassessing professional profiles and goals), CIBB, Den Bosch.

van der AA, R. and VLAANDEREN A. (1991), *Een weg met hindernissen. Een onderzoek naar instroombevordering van niet-reguliere arbeidsmarktgroepen voor de branches metaal- bewerking en installatietechniek* (A path with obstacles. Promoting the intake of non-traditional labour market groups into the metal work and installation sectors), RISBO, Rotterdam.

van der HOUT, G.J. and OUWENS, E.J. (1989), *Eindrapportage BOTO-I- abituri-entenonderzoek* (Final report BOTO-I final examination research), CIBB, Den Bosch.

D. CNC Machining and Flexible Production Automation

J.N. Streumer and A. Feteris
Faculty of Applied Education Science,
Technical University of Twente

Introduction

The present study focuses on developments in CNC machining over the last ten years. Developments in the field of Flexible Production Automation (FPA) followed on logically from these and for this reason FPA is also discussed. The preceding case studies focused on the sector level (tourism, the printing industry and installation technology). The present study looks at the effects of a specific technological innovation, that of CNC (computer numerically controlled) machining.

Section 1 outlines the rise and position of CNC machining in the metal industry in the Netherlands and of national developments in vocational training in relation to CNC machining. In addition to initiatives undertaken by individual schools, a number of national innovation projects which introduce new technologies in education have had a major effect on the position of CNC machining in the school curriculum. Section 2 focuses on developments in industry; Section 3 on developments in education. The final section examines the interaction between education and the labour market.

One final point that needs to be made here concerns the level of the training programmes dealt with in the study. Emphasis is placed on CNC machine operators; the required training for this work is at the level of either the junior technical school (LTS) supplemented by apprenticeship training, or the senior technical school (MTS). Other levels of education and training (junior secondary technical education, LTO; higher vocational education, HBO; university) are therefore dealt with only in passing.

1. CNC Machining in the Dutch Metal Industry

Technological developments

The adaptation of production strategies has been largely determined by technological developments. Since the early 1980s, production automation has been introduced in the metal industry in the Netherlands on the basis of numerically controlled machine tools

(Computer Numerically Controlled machines or CNC machines) in a wide variety of types. Advantages of CNC machines include faster processing and high-quality products as well as flexibility where stocks are minimised. The basis of production automation is the replacement of individual, repetitive programs carried out by skilled workers with programs based on logic and mathematics. The advent of CNC machines has meant that mass production is no longer necessary, because it is now possible to change to small-scale batch production. Once a program has been entered into the memory, it can be implemented whenever required in a short production time.

The development of turning and milling machines has progressed from the initial use of conventional machines operated by skilled workers, to the isolated introduction of CNC machines to their inclusion in a network of an automated production system. Production techniques have undergone changes brought about by the integration into production of automated sub-processes, with logistic planning and control systems on the one hand and computer-controlled design and calculation methods on the other (Computer-Integrated Manufacturing, (CIM) Flexible Production Automation (FPA). As CNC machines play a role in FPA systems, this study will also examine developments in the field of FPA, where relevant).

Thanks to automation, companies are not only able to introduce a greater variety of end products, but they are also able to specialise. The production of semi-manufactured products is more and more frequently contracted out. End products are increasingly the outcome of production in closely linked chains of customers and suppliers, each setting stringent standards for quality and delivery times. The pressure of production deadlines and time scales for product development, and the drive towards customer-oriented production to specification have forced companies to shorten their lines of communication. A consequence of this has been the integration of company departments, such as production and sales.

Labour market trends

The labour market is in a state of flux due to the automation of production. In the development of theories on the subject there was an initial period of optimism about the effect of automation on the quality of work; later, pessimism gained the upper hand. The pessimistic view was exemplified by the degradation theory (Braverman, 1974) and the polarisation theory (Kern and Schumann, 1970). The polarisation theory postulates that automation leads to the removal of the element of skill, leaving a large body of simple and routine tasks with only a very few highly skilled jobs in automation itself. However, research done in the late 1970s showed that the polarisation theory did not apply equally to all companies. It was demonstrated that companies structured their production in all manner of ways in order to achieve their objectives. It became clear that technology was not the sole determining factor: the production structure of companies is based on a combination of technology, organisation and labour.

Kayzel (1986) concluded that it appeared feasible in both technical and economic terms to apply automation techniques on the basis of prior social criteria. In view of continuing far-reaching developments in computer-based technology, this conclusion appears increasingly relevant. It is becoming possible to automate more complex work processes more cheaply and in a technically less complex manner. An ever-increasing flexibility in design and applications has also become possible. The high speed and constant quality with which numerically controlled machines can now be made to operate with the aid of current programs cannot be matched by a conventional machine operated by a skilled worker.

Developments in vocational education and training

Skilled employees in the metal industry have traditionally often had extensive training in a wide variety of subjects. Prior to the introduction of CNC machines, machine operators mainly required professional knowledge and manual skills.

At present, instruction machines are available only to a limited extent in junior secondary vocational education (LBO). A "spearhead" policy was initially pursued whereby a small number of schools would have the use of CNC machines; this was not fully implemented, however. In 1990 the Ministry of Education and Science, initiated a phased introduction of "technical computer science" classrooms at junior technical education (LTO) schools, equipped with CNC machines. All LTO schools will be provided with such facilities in the coming years.

In senior secondary vocational education (MBO) more schools possess CNC machines. All senior secondary technical education (MTO) schools are now equipped with a basic unit consisting of one CNC instruction machine with three external programming locations. The maximum configuration consists of one CNC turning machine, one CNC milling machine and six to eight programming locations.

In higher vocational education (HBO), equipment for the more familiar technologies was initially distributed on request. After 1986, however, there was a change of policy and more advanced equipment was assigned to selected colleges of higher vocational education.

Another important development was the establishment of regional centres. These are equipped with CNC machines and are accessible to students and teachers in senior secondary and higher vocational education (MBO and HBO) and employees in industry who wish to gain experience with them.

The training options currently available to aspiring CNC machine operators is either the junior technical school (LTS) supplemented by apprenticeship training or a programme at a senior technical school (MTS).

It is anticipated that future CNC operators will be LTS-trained personnel with a supplementary programme of training. In order to introduce this group as early as possible to this type of business automation and industrial applications, a start was made in the early 1990s to provide LTO schools with CNC instruction machines. Thus, CNC education begins at the level of junior secondary vocational education (LBO).

In view of the training options available (MTS or LTS plus apprenticeship training), the present case study emphasises senior secondary vocational education (MBO) and apprenticeship training. A large number of innovation projects were instituted at both these levels in the 1980s, following structural changes in vocational education (the Sector Formation and Innovation – SVM – operation).

Programmes at various levels in both MBO and the apprenticeship system have brought the two types of education closer together. An example of this trend is the co-ordination of proposals for the introduction of a Flexible Production Automation curriculum in both systems.

The apprenticeship training programme for the metal industry underwent a large-scale modernisation process after 1981. Apprenticeship training is a full-time programme where learning on the job is supplemented by general and vocationally-oriented education. New training programmes were developed and introduced from 1988 onwards by means of three projects (Restructuring, Modular Training and Occupational Analysis). Prior to 1982 there were three apprenticeship training bodies for the metal industry, all operating independently. Their amalgamation to form the Metal Industry Training Organisation (SOM), led to harmonization and modernisation of existing programmes. Training programmes were divided into occupational groups and rearranged in modules. Modules in the new technologies such as CNC turning and CNC techniques were added. CNC machining modules fall into the general occupational group of machining. The SOM determines which courses and programmes are needed in the apprenticeship system. The Organisation provides training in 128 occupations to more than 12 000 apprentices each year. Approximately 74 per cent of all apprentices followed elementary training and 26 per cent an advanced programme (1990 figures). There were 307 female apprentices in 1990.

Following the restructuring process begun in 1987 in senior secondary vocational education (MBO), which led to the creating of four sectors, training courses in CNC machining fall within the technical sector the Mechanical Engineering department. Within this department, General Mechanical Engineering and, in some schools, Production Technology are relevant to CNC machining. Production Technology was developed as a subject in the early 1980s; currently its subject matter is being transferred to General Mechanical Engineering.

In April 1990, the Association of Senior Technical Schools (VMTS) published a plan to introduce Flexible Production Automation (FPA) in senior secondary technical education (MTO). This programme is intended not only for the Mechanical Engineering department but also for Electrical Engineering and, to a lesser extent, Building.

Responsiveness and institutionalisation

In response to the advisory report by the Wagner Committee (1984) (see Part I), the government, education and industry began to view vocational education as a joint responsibility. One of the measures taken to this end was the establishment of the Secondary Education Consultative Committee. This committee recommended that a consultative framework be set up for each branch of industry involving the two sides of industry and the education unions; these were set up under the aegis of BOOBs (sector-wide education and industry fora). For the metal industry, the Technical Education-Metal Industry

Consultative Forum (BOTO-M) was set up. This body has the task of identifying new shop-floor developments and is primarily concerned with short senior secondary vocational programmes (KMBO) as well as MBO, but is also interested in the apprenticeship scheme. The first task of BOTO-M was the preparation of attainment targets for students of mechanical engineering at the MTS level. Initially, these were established on the basis of current curricula (the so-called "first generation attainment targets"). In a later phase the final attainment targets will be based on occupational profiles. These second generation attainment targets are due to be ready for use in the second half of 1991. Schools are free to arrange their own programmes around the attainment targets.

In addition to the establishment of consultative bodies such as BOTO-M, co-operation also takes place between educational institutions and industry on an individual and regional basis, in the form of contract teaching, for instance.

National innovation projects

In 1984 a national innovation project, the Information Technology Promotion Plan (INSP), was launched; it was evaluated in 1988 by the INSP Evaluation Committee. One of the topics evaluated was production automation, which was defined in fairly broad terms and therefore included CNC machining. The conclusion was that Dutch industry is lagging somewhat behind other industrialised countries and that education and training in turn is lagging behind industry. Standard industry equipment, such as CNC machines, too often proves to be unfamiliar to school leavers. However, education is making every effort to catch up, despite limited resources. The evaluation of the INSP project concluded that the creation of "human capital" was lagging behind in the long term, partly because "spearhead" projects were receiving more attention than basic applications. It recommended that education be brought back into phase by emphasising standard applications over specialised fields and that greater funding be attracted from industry. The committee also recommended intensive co-operation between industry and education through the establishment of regional centres. In order to forge effective links between public-sector education and industry, the time lag was set at a maximum of 5 years. This was a departure from the situation at the time of the 1988 evaluation when the time lag was greater for standard applications and smaller for specialised fields.

The INSP was considered to be a useful start to the promotion of information technology (IT). The Evaluation Committee advised the decentralisation of the implementation of IT policy to the education support structure and schools. This was put into effect in 1989 by continuing INSP projects under the Introduction of New Technologies Project (PRINT), in addition to introducing new projects. PRINT focuses principally on courseware development and professional development. Production technology is one of the ten areas of technology distinguished in the PRINT project; it is subdivided further and both CNC machining and Flexible Production Automation (FPA) are included in the category of production process automation of discrete processes. PRINT places most emphasis on FPA. It has opted for one FPA project, giving a clear role to regional centres. In addition, PRINT also includes a project on CNC operators/work planners.

The PRINT project produced a number of findings over the first year which indicated the differences of opinion in the late 1980s regarding the introduction of new technologies in school curricula. The findings concern the following: provision of equipment in regional centres, the focus on basic skills and the division of roles in the innovation process (who is responsible for development?; who determines the direction of development?; who is responsible for management?). First, it would seem that in the technical sector of MBO schools there were reservations about the provision of equipment in regional centres and therefore the schools did not co-operate readily in the implementation of such projects. Secondly, PRINT emphasises basic skills. However, MTO schools work in a tradition of translating new applications into a specific technological form with the appropriate body of equipment. Thirdly, MTO schools tend to see themselves in the role of applicants that request subsidies for projects to develop teaching material. The latter does not fit with the nature of PRINT. Fourthly, the distribution of roles between government, schools and the PRINT management was not clearly set out. With regard to the development of courseware, an agreement was drawn up between the Association of Senior Technical Schools (VMTS) and PRINT in which it was agreed that choices would be based mainly on the demand side.

The Coltof Committee concluded, following an evaluation of the PRINT project in April 1990, that the education support organisations had not been successful in promoting the use of new technologies (Advisory Committee on the Promotion of New Technologies in Education, May 1991). The PRINT project was directed too much towards the supply side and was insufficiently based on what was wanted by the schools themselves. A different approach was therefore advocated, within which the wishes of schools could be accommodated and the support organisations could operate as contracting parties. This led to the advent of a new type of project management as of 1 January 1991: Project Management for the Effective Promotion of Technology in Education (PRESTO). This project, which will run until the end of 1993, places the initiative with schools providing vocational education, particularly MBO schools. They are able to draw up their own plans for the future and submit these in the form of a "Technological Innovation Programme" to PRESTO, thus becoming eligible for subsidisation of their plans. Subsidies will be granted on condition that a contribution will also be made by industry, in the form of funds or equipment.

The project entitled Refresher Training in New Technologies (NaBoNT), initiated in 1987, aims to improve the quality of education in public-sector technical schools by providing refresher training for teachers in senior secondary vocational education (MBO) and higher vocational education (HBO). In the second year of the NaBoNT project, production technology was designated one of five priority areas. The production technology refresher training courses focus on new automated production techniques, on automation aids in process management and process control, and on strategic concepts needed for the creation of an automated factory. Work placements for teachers were also introduced as part of NaBoNT, usually organised on a regional basis. One example is the practical training scheme in "flexible production automation" at the Northern Centre for Technological Innovation (NCTI). This is a period of three to five days spent in the centre's workshop.

Co-operation between education and industry

In 1984, the Wagner Committee recommended that junior secondary vocational education (LBO) and senior secondary vocational education (MBO) be oriented more to practical work and seek contacts with industry. The evaluation of the INSP project (1988) also recommended intensive co-operation between industry and education. Such co-operation is now increasing. Research shows that approximately half of all LBO and MBO schools have co-operative arrangements with companies in such areas as:

- the compilation of teaching programmes (20 per cent); .
- provision or renting of equipment and facilities to each other (40 per cent);
- work placements for teachers, and visiting lecturers (40 per cent);
- contract teaching and contract research (20 per cent).

(Committee on the Development Problems of Companies, Socio-Economic Council, COB/SER, 1988; 1989).

In addition, efforts have been made since 1985 to involve the trade unions more fully in developments in vocational education, for example, through the establishment of the Technical Education-Metal Industry Consultative Forum (BOTO-M) referred to earlier. In addition to co-operation between education and industry, public-sector institutions are making efforts to co-operate more with each other. One example of this is the joint provision of practical training by sectoral organisations within particular branches of industry, schools and commercial educational institutions.

Regionalisation

In the 1980s the regional level was viewed as important in the promotion of co-operation between schools and industry and in the introduction of new technologies in school curricula. In 1984, a national plan for innovation in the Mechanical Engineering (MTO) departments of senior secondary technical schools recommended that regional centres should be set up to provide experience in practical work situations with a shop-floor production group, for instance in basic operations like turning and milling and digital measurement for quality control purposes (Bakkenist, Spits and Co., 1984).

A few years later, in 1990, the Temporary Advisory Committee on Education-Industry Liaison (also known, after its chairman, as the Rauwenhoff Committee) likewise recommended that emphasis be placed on the regional level. The Committee's recommendations aim to combat compartmentalisation and fragmentation in vocational education. In order for vocational education to adapt to the specific situation in the regional labour markets, the Committee proposed a dual system of training for the entire field. In exchange for greater influence on the school curriculum, industry would make a larger financial contribution to education and training, for example, by offering more apprenticeship places. The Committee also proposed that schools be given autonomy to determine their own attainment targets and to provide all students, including early school leavers and the unemployed, with the right to attain minimum starting qualifications. The government was in broad agreement with the Rauwenhoff Committee's proposals, and responded by allocating an additional 30 million guilders (16.5 million dollars) for the training of 10 000 young adults. Its aim is to provide greater freedom for educational establishments and industry.

The PRINT project also advocates a major role for regional centres in vocational training, including training in Flexible Production Automation (FPA). Given new technologies, in-school and out-of-school training (work placements) are, according to PRINT, inadequate during initial training. This third element is therefore essential. In the view of PRINT, the arguments in support of regional centres are to be found in: the capital-intensive nature of a flexible production environment, the cost of maintenance and updating, and the low capacity utilisation for individual schools.

In the second half of the 1980s, six regional practical centres for mechanical engineering were established; in the early 1990s three additional centres were set up. The trend towards regional practical training centres for advanced technology is an important one for CNC machining and FPA. For instance, the Twente Technical Training and Service Centre (STODT), the regional centre in Twente where curriculum development for new technologies takes place, has been working on an FPA curriculum and developing courses since 1989. Two major high-tech companies in the region, a senior technical school (MTS) and since 1991, a senior secondary vocational college (MBO) with several MTS schools) and the University of Twente are involved in this initiative. Task analyses for the purpose of curriculum development have been carried out for four jobs: operator (SOM/MTS level); work planner [MTS/HTS (institute of technology) level]; logistics assistant (planning and stock control, MBO/HBO level) and system manager (HBO level).

There has been a debate over the role of such centres. The existing centres are intended for use by industry and education for refresher training in advanced technologies. The target groups are: teachers and students in secondary vocational education and the apprenticeship system; post-MBO students; the employed, employers and entrepreneurs.

Most schools are satisfied with what is offered by the regional centres. The technical guidance provided is considered to be of a very high quality. However, there has been criticism of the costs, with what is taught in the schools and co-ordination of teaching (timetabling and use of teachers).

2. Developments in Industry

Man and machine

Over the years, the tasks of employees engaged in production using CNC machines have changed. These changes have not been due solely to technological advances. The issues confronting companies in introducing production automation relate to the degree to which, and the way in which, programmable automation alters the division of labour between men and machines, the way in which clusters of tasks are distributed across various departments, and the way in which tasks are integrated into jobs, if at all. Alders, Christis and Bilderbeek (1988) refer to these three issues as production technology, the organisation of production and work organisation. Production technology is playing a steadily diminishing role in innovation. Changes in the manner of thinking about the organisation of production and work organisation have become increasingly important.

In the case of CNC machining the question to be asked is what is the most desirable level of training (LTS supplemented by additional training, or MTS). and which skills should be taught in these forms of vocational training. In order to answer these questions it is important to have an understanding of production technology, but also of the organisation of production and work. These may differ among individual companies. In the metal industry a distinction must be made between large and small companies: production technology, the organisation of production and work organisation vary depending on the size of the company. There are also substantial regional differences.

Production technology

Companies are becoming increasingly convinced of the need for product and process innovation using new technologies such as CNC, FPA, CAD/CAM and CIM. Advanced production technologies are employed as a means of reacting to developments and of meeting requirements with regard to quality, variety and delivery time. Production automation has been taking place in many shapes and forms since the beginning of the 1980s.

According to Poutsma and Zwaard (1987) there were approximately 1 000 computer controlled machines in the Netherlands in 1979; in 1985 there were an estimated 12 500 or more CNC machines in use in 6 000 companies (based on figures produced by Bilderbeek and Kalff, 1985). In 1984, 1 650 of 12 000 companies surveyed by the Central Bureau of Statistics (CBS) were using CNC machines (Fruytier, 1988).

Specification of occupational profiles

The Metal Industry Training Organisation (SOM) commissioned the Centre for Innovation in Training for Trade and Industry (CIBB) to conduct an occupational analysis of the metal industry for the purposes of apprenticeship training. Some 900 employees were involved; 1 061 activities were classified in 44 job groups. Occupational profiles were distinguished by creating clusters of activities. Initially a distinction was made between machining and non-machining occupations. The machining occupations included both machining and fitting/toolmaking. A total of 20 occupational profiles were identified, spread over 4 occupational groups (see Table D1).

Table D1. **Occupational groups in the metal industry**

Occupational group	No. of profiles
Machining	6
Fitting/toolmaking	5
Construction/machine construction	5
Assembly/maintenance	4

Source: SOM/CIBB (1987).

A total of 16 activity clusters were distinguished; one of these was "CNC machining". This cluster contains 16 activities and is described as "turning and milling on numerically controlled machine tools".

The CNC machining cluster plays a more or less important role in two of the occupational profiles which were drawn up, i.e. those to whom the profile applies carry out

195

a large number of tasks from this cluster with a high frequency. These two occupational profiles are:

- mechanical machining: a combination of turning and milling with a large number of activities relating to machine grinding;
- CNC machining: a combination of activities in the field of turning, milling and grinding, including CNC machining.

Research for Policy carried out a survey for the Technical Education-Metal Industry Consultative Forum (BOTO-M) of the work of mechanical engineers at MTS level (De Vries and Heere, 1990). The study was able to cluster occupational groups on the basis of interviews with more than 1 000 employees. A total of nine clusters was identified: machining; non-machining metalworking techniques; assembly; technical preparation; pre-production activities and control; process and production supervision; commercial and administrative support; management; trainers and other occupations. Machining accounts for 7.4 per cent of the employees with MTS training in mechanical engineering. Table D2 gives the distribution for this cluster.

Table D2. **Cluster for machining at MTS mechanical engineering level**
(per cent of the total group of employees)

Workers in:	1980 n=393	1985 n=580	Total n=973
1. Machining	2.3	1.9	2.1
2. CNC mach./tool./progr.	1.3	3.1	2.4
3. Bench fitters	0.5	0.7	0.6
4. Toolmakers	0.8	0.9	0.8
5. Instrument makers	0.8	0.2	0.4
6. Supervisory, metalworking	1.5	0.9	1.1
Machining (metal)	7.2	7.7	7.4

Source: De Vries and Heere (1990).

Changes in production organisation on the introduction of CNC machines

The introduction of CNC machines means additional tasks for the operator of the machines. Fruytier (1988) distinguished direct and indirect CNC tasks in their study. The direct tasks are shown in Figure D1.

The traditional craftsmanship required for machining, according to Fruytier et al., is in the case of CNC machining transferred to the task of programming. Various forms of division of labour may be associated with the use of a CNC machine. Fruytier (1988, p. 28) distinguishes five different types (see Figure D2).

The indirect types involve support, preparation and control tasks, i.e.:

- determining the order of production;
- determining the order of machining or processing;
- collecting the raw materials from the storeroom;
- supplying products to the next workstation;
- recording production data;
- selecting and introducing employees, planning and days off.

196

Figure D1. **Direct CNC tasks**

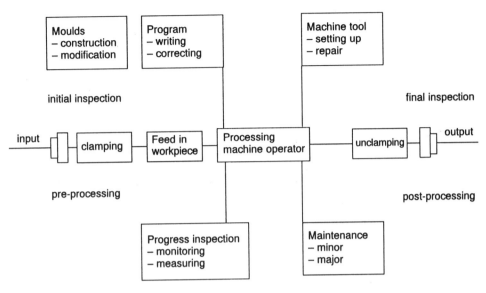

Source: Fruytier (1988, p. 27).

Figure D2. **Five types of division of labour for the CNC machine**

Tasks	I			II			III			IV			V		
Jobs	a	b	c	a	b	c	a	b	c	a	b	c	a	b	c
Programming	•			•			•				•				
Optimise Program		•			—	—	•								•
Set up machine		•				•			•		•				•
Operate/control machine			•			•			•			•			•
Load and unload			•			•			•			•			•

Key :
a = programmer
b = manager, working foreman, machine tool setter
c = machine operator

Source: Fruytier (1988, p. 28).

The total package of direct and indirect tasks for CNC machine operators may be divided into "office" and "factory" components. These tasks may or may not be distributed over different departments. In the 1960s, production organisation was characterised by functional specialisation. Departments were set up according to the particular function performed (e.g. pre-processing, machining, assembly). Actual production occupied a central position; however, the pre-processing departments of large companies increasingly directed their activities towards production control. In the functional production organisation model, programming was organised centrally. This links up with one of the first industrial developments, that of the separation of the pre-processing and production tasks. Under this option it is not the CNC operators who do the programming, but separate programmers *in separate departments*. This creates two problems: first, the tasks of the traditional skilled operator are substantially reduced, and second, the expert knowledge and skill to make the new techniques effective is lacking in the pre-processing stage. The separation of tasks in this way can lead to a shortage of skilled workers and conflicts may arise between pre-processing and production. Pre-processing will be geared to controlling production, but the skilled operators will endeavour to maintain their autonomy. Solutions to these problems have been sought in decentralised shop-floor programming, whereby skilled workers can be called in to perform qualified tasks. In shop-floor programming, however, the working conditions under which programming takes place are poor. In the 1980s, some companies adopted modified forms of shop-floor programming, with the actual programming being carried out in separate office-type spaces in the production areas.

The labour market

The specific effects of technology on work are difficult to separate from other factors such as economic aspects and the decisions taken by the entrepreneur. The type of automation selected is partly determined by the competitive position of the company and the availability of equipment. Micro-electronics provides the option of decentralisation, but in the introduction of CNC machines it seems that the effect on the work performed is dependent on the way in which work with the new equipment has been organised. If the new tasks engendered by the machines are added to existing individual tasks, the level of skill is maintained and jobs can even be upgraded. But if the new tasks are introduced as new specialisations, operators' jobs are classified at a lower level of qualification. Sorge (in Poutsma and Zwaard, 1987) found that qualification development for jobs using CNC machines is dependent on production batch size and the size of the company. It is also heavily influenced by the way in which programming and setting work is allocated.

The introduction of CNC machines and changes in work organisation

Automation often means the introduction of a different type of work organisation in many companies. Existing jobs change (narrowing/widening of scope); a re-orientation of jobs caused by the inclusion or exclusion of control tasks and the building-in of safeguards to ensure that professional skill is maintained is a consequence of this. During such periods of re-orientation, problems of over- and under-qualification may arise. For the operator of a conventional machine, training at the level of junior secondary vocational education

(LBO) or LBO plus a supplementary course was sufficient. This was the view of 90 per cent of the 180 companies participating in a study of technological developments and changes in the employment structure, as opposed to 9 per cent who considered the higher MTS level to be necessary (Alders et al., 1988).

The perceived training requirements for CNC machine operators of the 180 companies studied who were involved in machine building are higher than those for the operation of conventional machines. The study showed that 45 per cent of the companies believed that training at senior secondary vocational education (MBO) level was necessary, while 53 per cent were satisfied with LBO or LBO with supplementary training. The authors, Alders et al., make no distinction between those with junior technical school (LTS) training just entering the workforce and those with experience. They believe that these figures are based on a degree of inflation of the level of training required. For instance, if one looks at the work organisation it can be seen that in cases where the operator does no programming or testing and correcting, 25 per cent of the companies still require training at the MBO level. Although in comparison with the operators of conventional machines there is more likely to be a scaling down of tasks than a scaling up, the perceived level of training necessary in the new situation was set higher by a considerable percentage of companies.

This form of inflation of the qualifications required makes it difficult to determine what the real requirements are, especially if one takes into account the fact that it is related to the question of technological innovation. Fruytier (1988) mentions four causes of inflation of the level of training required:

- the element of uncertainty: since companies familiarise themselves with new technology step by step, the training requirements are often overestimated;
- the "running-in" effect: because of a temporary need for control engineering to get the new system working, a higher level of training is required;
- the anticipation effect: companies expect to require more highly qualified personnel in the future;
- the "image" effect: higher training requirements enhance the image of quality.

The labour market and technological developments

The rate of development of both hardware and software is such that the operation of machines is becoming more and more user-friendly (and thus requires a lower level of training). Initially automation expertise was the preserve of those with a senior secondary or higher technical education. Now automation techniques can be handled by an experienced skilled worker. For this reason a shift is taking place in the training requirement: from MTS level initially to LTS plus supplementary training today. Fruytier (1988) concludes that in all cases the operation of CNC machines by those with junior technical school (LTS) training is feasible, provided the company is prepared to arrange the necessary supplementary training.

Nor will it be easy in the future to recruit MTS personnel for jobs involving the operation of CNC machines. The skills shortage is especially acute in this category of personnel with senior technical training. On the basis of a prognosis of supply and demand for manpower in the year 2000, the Central Planning Office (CPB) (in Van Terwisga and Van Sluijs, 1990, pp. 22-23) has concluded that a critical situation will arise in the technical sector at the senior secondary vocational level as a result of increased demand for this type of personnel.

From a quantitative point of view, a number of developments will have important consequences for the labour supply. Firstly, as the Dutch population ages, companies will find it increasingly difficult to acquire new technological know-how and skills by recruiting school leavers; this means that there will be an increasing need to train existing workers. Secondly, there is very little participation by women in the Netherlands in mathematics and science programmes and the technical professions, a phenomenon known as "wasted intelligence".

It was suggested above that the demand for CNC machine operators at senior secondary vocational level (MBO), i.e. those with MTS training, was in fact a form of inflated demand. However, this hypothesis is open to question. An experienced worker with a junior technical school (LTS) background is not accustomed to having an "office" component in his work package, which involves programming activities. Problems may also arise in the area of the requisite social skills and ability to organise the work. Many companies complain that there are difficulties of a qualitative nature in deploying new personnel; they believe that the level of training is deteriorating and is not sufficiently oriented to practical work. In addition, they say that school leavers are not adequately equipped to apply new technologies and that skills are not up to standard (Van Terwisga and Van Sluijs, 1990). The other side of the coin is that companies require increasingly high standards of their existing and new employees. They must be capable of deployment in a wide range of jobs and must receive regular refresher training, since knowledge and skills rapidly become out of date. These higher standards are required of both existing and new employees because, partly through technological advances, the nature of the work is shifting from labour-intensive to knowledge-intensive, and the organisation is changing from process and function-based to product and market-oriented.

In order to be able to employ workers with a junior technical school (LTS) background as CNC machine operators, solutions are being sought in the form of different training requirements. This development means that demand is shifting in the direction of basic skills. Nijhof (1991) states that the demand in the Netherlands for basic skills to be taught in vocational education is distinctly related to the introduction of new technologies and the resulting need for new levels of competence. There is a concern with increasing the general level of skills. As part of a project on Basic Skills in Vocational Education (Nijhof and Mulder, 1986), 68 basic skills were formulated for mechanical engineering at the senior technical school (MTS) level. For this purpose, basic skills were defined as qualifications with a transfer value for related occupational situations. The emphasis was placed on the transfer value so that employees will gain the potential to adapt flexibly as the demands of technological innovation require. With regard to attitude, the study looked at very general behavioural aspects indicative of cognitive behaviour: precision, accuracy, perseverance, a systematic approach, and communicative and co-operative ability. New-style machine operators are required to possess "learning ability" and a "sense of responsibility". It is estimated that training at the MTS level is necessary to guarantee this (Thijsen, 1988).

It may be concluded that the level of professional skill required of a CNC machine operator lies between junior technical school (LTS) with supplementary training and senior technical school (MTS) level.

Small- and medium-sized businesses vs. large companies

The organisation of work in small- and medium-sized businesses in the metal industry differs from that in large companies. Small firms require experienced personnel who can be put to work without additional training and who have a wide range of qualifications. In the more innovative, technologically advanced companies there is, however, a requirement for personnel with highly specialised training. Small- and medium-sized businesses often lack the facilities and equipment to provide their employees with internal training.

In the metal, machine-making and instrument-making industry there is a difference in the type of work performed in large and small companies. Work is often farmed out to others, the size of production batches varies and more traditional craftsmanship as well as industrial work is done.

In 1986 more than 263 000 persons were employed in this sector, of whom 45 per cent worked in small and medium-sized businesses (Poutsma and Zwaard, 1987). Table D3 shows the distribution of metal workers involved in machining by size of company, as revealed by the study of the work of MTS personnel (De Vries *et al.*, 1989).

Table D3. **Machinists (7.2 per cent of the total number of MTS-trained mechanical engineers) and size of company workforce**

Size of company	Per cent of total number of metal workers involved in machining (n=72)
1-9	9.7
10-49	26.4
50-99	12.5
100-249	22.2
250-999	15.3
More than 1000	13.9

Source: De Vries, Weening and Heere (1989).

The degree of mechanical automation in this sector increases gradually with the size of the company. The use of computer-controlled automation techniques is relatively limited in small companies compared with mechanical automation. This is surprising since a great deal of work is contracted out, and small-scale, varying batch production occurs most frequently. It would seem logical that smaller companies such as these would wish to make their production capacity more flexible by the use of machines which can be programmed and rapidly re-programmed. The cost aspect is undoubtedly an obstacle to small- and medium-sized companies considering the acquisition of advanced technological equipment. In 1986, however, large numbers of these companies were planning to purchase computer-controlled equipment in the near future. Because hardware prices are dropping and applications packages are becoming increasingly user-friendly, this will become a viable option for many smaller companies (Table D4).

The smaller the company, the greater the number of tasks performed by the operator of the numerically controlled machine and the degree of responsibility accorded him. Companies with fewer than 20 employees mentioned tasks such as: monitoring/operating machines, quality control, setting, correction, optimisation and programming. In medium-sized companies operators are required to do less programming and quality control, although optimisation and correction are given as major tasks. In large companies the operator's task is largely restricted to monitoring, operating, clamping the workpiece and setting up the machine. It is principally in discrete production processes that operators do the programming themselves.

Table D4. **Degree of automation in the metalworking and machine and instrument-making industry** (in per cent, by size of company)

No. of employees	1-19	20-49	50 and over
Mechanical	40	60	70
Computer	14	7	50
Clerical	18	28	62

Source: Poutsma and Zwaard (1987, p. 19).

Study of the work of MTS-trained mechanical engineers (De Vries and Heere, 1990) shows that 88 per cent of employees in the "machinists" category are employed in industry. The study also shows that practical activities concerning machining requiring a high degree of accuracy are only performed by the "machinist" group (7 per cent of mechanical engineers with an MTS background). However, the group of MTS-trained employees which has some contact with machining is much larger. One quarter of all employees with senior secondary vocational qualifications (MBO) is involved in machining requiring a lower degree of accuracy ("assembly") and a further quarter of those with senior technical training (MTS) are required to have a good understanding of machining (technical draughtsmen and work planners). The other employees do not perform this type of work and they have no knowledge of machining techniques (De Vries and Heere, 1990). In 1990 half of the machinists were using CNC equipment, and those not yet doing so would be transferring to CNC in the near future. For this group, working with CNC equipment involves carrying out all the procedures at the workbench, including programming. A part of the task of the "technical work planners" group may also consist of programming CNC machines.

Structural shifts due to technological developments in CNC/FPA

The development of the scale of CNC machines in Dutch companies must be viewed in the light of a large number of recent and anticipated technological advances. The most important of these concern the integration of areas of technical expertise and an interdisciplinary approach, at present to be seen in Flexible Production Automation (FPA) activities.

In the 1987 study by the Centre for Innovation in Training for Trade and Industry (CIBB) for the Metal Industry Training Organisation (SOM), experts estimated that by 1995, CNC and other automated production systems would make up approximately 50 per cent of the total production process and/or machinery in small companies in the Netherlands and about 70 per cent in medium-sized and large companies. These developments would take place predominantly in the machining and sheet metal-working production areas. It is anticipated that by 1995 CNC machines will make up about 75 per cent of all machining equipment.

It is thought that in the future there will be both centralised and decentralised programming; centralised programming in mass production and/or a large-scale limited production process, and decentralised programming in small-scale infrequent product batches and/or complex products.

Future CNC/FPA developments should be seen in the broader perspective of general technological advances. Van Terwisga and Van Sluijs (1990) mention the following as some of the major technical developments of the 1980s.

- New possibilities in electronics. Through a combination of electronic and precision engineering components, new possibilities are opening up in the overlapping area between electronics and mechanical engineering, for instance in the automotive industry and consumer articles.
- New materials with applications in, among other things, the aerospace industry, sports equipment and communications technology.
- The integration of various disciplines. Innovation is taking place principally in the overlapping areas of disciplines and this leads to integration.

Krins (1991) confirms this when he mentions the following as the major basic technologies for technological advancement in the field of FPA:

- information technology;
- types of drive, and measurement;
- new materials and machining, joining and design techniques.

Technical integration

Even though he may not work directly with them, the mechanical engineer with MTS training will in the near future increasingly come into contact with related work areas such as electronics, hydraulics and pneumatics, and control systems. In addition to the technical field, integration is also apparent in other areas such as technology, sociology, business administration and commerce. Here too, there has been a shift from labour-intensive to knowledge-intensive work. The introduction of advanced technologies is an interdisciplinary activity which requires an integrated approach: technical change must be accompanied by organisational modifications and the analysis of these has to include personnel aspects.

Flexible Production Automation (FPA)

Technical integration and an interdisciplinary approach can be seen in the field of flexible production automation. The concept of Flexible Production Automation (FPA) refers to the computerisation of activities such as design, work planning, general planning and production, with the aim of rapidly introducing changes and concerns organisation, methods, procedures, production systems and data processing. Various types of flexibility may be distinguished: flexibility in conversion and in setting up machines; flexibility in running in and volume; flexibility in the manpower mix and personnel numbers; and substitution and routing flexibility. FPA is the automation of the entire production process with a view to economical production with minimum conversion times and the processing of small batch production in random order. FPA is in fact an integrated method of dealing with information and material flows. A Flexible Manufacturing System consists of a number of complex CNC processing machines where the loading and unloading of the machines, the movement of the workpiece within the system and the supply of the workpieces to the machine are controlled by a computer. Using a Flexible Manufacturing System it is possible to manufacture economically very small batches of different types of products within a product family. The use of FPA technology is not very widespread and it is difficult to evaluate its importance in Dutch industry.

Conclusions concerning the effects of developments in technology on skill requirements

Machining is undergoing a shift from labour-intensive to knowledge-intensive work. This means that requirements for particular types of work and for quality products are being upgraded and that higher standards of education and training are expected of present and new employees. In view of the continuing integration of various technical subjects and that of technology with social and commercial specialisations, employees are obliged to extend their knowledge in order to keep up with developments.

The study of work among mechanical engineers at the MTS level examined expectations for the future of both employers and employees (De Vries and Heere, 1990). It is expected that work at the senior secondary vocational education (MBO) level will become increasingly specialised. In the future, an MTS mechanical engineer will specialise increasingly in a company-specific sector, e.g. a mechanic specialising in work on a particular machine. Employees and employers alike see this as the antithesis of what companies in fact wish to achieve, namely that their workforce should be capable of deployment in a wide range of jobs. Because of the increasing complexity of machines and other equipment, employees will need an increasing amount of time, further training and experience in order to become familiar with the work required of them. This development must, however, be distinguished from the fact that the actual operation of CNC machines is becoming ever more simple: the work of the machine operator will be less complex in the future.

If companies wish to react adequately to the increasingly rapid changes taking place in technology, markets and the labour market, new standards will have to be set for the organisation of work within the company, the qualifications of those they employ and the methods of skill management and development.

The degree to which the introduction of FPA will influence qualification requirements is not easy to assess at present. The Centre for Innovation in Training for Trade and Industry (CIBB) (1991) has recommended that – in view of the limited application of FPA presently, and the expected continuation of this trend in the future – it would not be advisable to place too much emphasis on FPA curriculum development in public-sector vocational education. It could, however, be dealt with on a small scale at the post-senior secondary vocational education level in the form of contract teaching.

The change in thinking from a rigid method of production to flexible production automation has brought to light new aspects for consideration by public-sector vocational education, including:
- organisational insights;
- the socio-organisational aspects of organisations;
- the relationship between the various jobs in a company;
- more emphasis on work planning;
- social skills;
- the ability to operate independently;
- flexible deployment.

3. Developments in Education

Changes in the curriculum

In order to achieve a better alignment of education and employment, measures are being taken to design modular programmes, to provide dual training (work placements/apprenticeship places in addition to theory), to prepare students for their first job by teaching basic knowledge and skills and to introduce new subjects in which students may specialise. These instruments are being employed at various levels in public-sector education. In addition, the establishment of regional centres has played a major role in dealing with the question of how technological changes can be introduced into the education system.

This section will discuss the instruments referred to above as they relate to CNC machining, with a distinction being made between three levels: senior technical school (MTS), the apprenticeship system and regional centres. First, the consequences of technological developments in the metal industry for the MTS programme in mechanical engineering will be discussed. The apprenticeship system and developments with regard to regional centres will then be examined. Finally, a separate section will be devoted to developments in senior secondary vocational education (MBO), the apprenticeship system and regional centres with regard to Flexible Production Automation.

The MTS mechanical engineering programme

In the 1980s it gradually became recognised that in view of the rapidity with which technological advances were taking place, the continuous updating of curricula and tailoring them to meet the demand from the labour market for certain types of training was not going to be possible. As mentioned in Section 2, the work of MTS mechanical engineers will become more specialised in the near future, focusing on a particular branch or product (De Vries and Heere, 1990). On the other hand, it is also true that companies are seeking employees who can be deployed in a broad range of jobs. According to Pieters and Mulder (1988) the response by education to the demand from industry cannot be simply to prepare personnel for specific jobs. Refresher courses in product-specific or company-specific subjects will be part of the normal work situation. In order to provide some idea of the extent of the problem at the MTS level, we will indicate firstly the types of jobs MTS mechanical engineers are finding and look at the difficulties they experience in adjusting to the work situation.

Jobs and adjustment difficulties of MTS mechanical engineers

MTS students who have successfully completed the mechanical engineering programme are to be found in a wide variety of jobs. Thijsen and Mulder (1987) found that 58 per cent found work on the production side after gaining their diploma. Six per cent found work as CNC machinists in production departments; only 1 per cent worked in jobs where non-machining CNC techniques were employed. Several years later De Vries and Heere (1990) found that the total number of those with an MTS diploma who were employed in CNC jobs was 10 per cent. Those who had followed the new programme in Production Technology more often found work in production departments (including CNC production workers) than those who had followed the general programme in mechanical engineering.

With regard to the education-work interface, Thijsen and Mulder found that in the view of these students there were few discrepancies between the knowledge and skills they had learned and those required of them, but that the difficulties concern attitude. They reported that too little emphasis was placed during their training on adaptability, problem-solving ability, ability to work under pressure, communication skills, a realistic assessment of personal ability, versatility, quality awareness and a critical approach. The study by De Vries and Heere, which surveyed mechanical engineers who obtained a diploma between 1980 and 1985, found that virtually all of them had experienced one or more problems on first starting work. On the other hand, most of those questioned did not consider these initial difficulties to be serious problems but rather viewed them as a challenge. The employers took note of these problems, which also included knowledge of and skill in practical activities, and provided supplementary training.

New employees initially experienced difficulties in working with modern machines, owing to lack of experience. Other initial problems concerned knowledge of mathematics and command of language. For the specific group of metal workers doing machining work, the following problem areas were reported: techniques for clamping the workpiece, operating CNC machines and machining synthetics. For the other occupational groups distinguished, only the work planners had problems with CNC, and these related to programming. De Vries and Heere recommended improvements in attainment targets but also in curricula and teaching (e.g. allocating more teaching time to certain subjects and covering subject matter better). The recommendations concern: the relationship between theoretical subjects; the relationship between theory and practical lessons; linking both theory and practical lessons to the work situation; use of Dutch; business studies; materials science; and mathematics. Generally speaking, they advocate a more practical approach.

Basic knowledge and skills in senior secondary technical education (MTO)

The national plan for innovation in the Mechanical Engineering departments of MTO institutions (February 1984) states that the fundamental concepts and basic skills which must be learned should relate to:

a) the way in which drawings are prepared and work planning carried out if products are to be manufactured by computer controlled machines;

b) working with external programming locations, where programs for numerically controlled (NC) and computer numerically controlled (CNC) machines are made off-line;

c) the operation of NC and CNC production machines, both in direct communication and using programs made at external programming locations;

d) pre-production steps, such as providing materials and tools and familiarity with automatic material transport and automatic tool exchange;

e) measuring using modern digital measuring systems, both with conventional and CNC machines and as a final check on products (measuring department).

The University of Twente carried out a study to determine which basic automation skills in the mechanical engineering sector students should have mastered by the end of their programme (Nijhof and Mulder, 1986). This study, entitled "Basic skills in vocational education", was carried out as part of the Information Technology Promotion Plan (INSP).

The basic skills in production techniques for the General Mechanical Engineering programme include (Nijhof and Mulder, 1986, p. 231):

a) conventional machining and non-machining technology (materials, tools, processing conditions, tolerances, the metalworking process, measurement and control systems);

b) principles of control for NC and CNC equipment (turning, milling, drilling, punching, spark erosion, deformation, etc.);

c) the operation of NC and CNC turning and milling machines (the machining process, operating the clamping device and determination of depth of cut);

d) transforming a work drawing into a workpiece program in an NC or CNC programming language;

e) pre-setting machine tools;

f) input of data about the workpiece program with the aid of a computer (including the input of tool corrections);

g) modifying a workpiece program on an NC or CNC machine;

h) operating digital measuring equipment for the quality control of workpieces;

i) taking account of safety procedures during production processes using automated systems.

The new programme in production technology

The list of objectives derived from the study on Basic skills in vocational education (Nijhof and Mulder, 1986) served as the starting point for a follow-up study on curriculum development for the new programme in Production Technology. The senior secondary technical education (MTO) mechanical engineering departments have offered the new programme in Production Technology in addition to General Mechanical Engineering since the early 1980s. In 1988, six schools were offering the programme [Development Plan for the Technology Sector, Association of Senior Technical Schools (VMTS), 1988]. The course in production technology provides training for jobs in production technology only. The main subjects for the programme include: basic information technology, control technology, NC and CNC machines, robotics and computer aided design (CAD) systems. Students electing to take this as a diploma programme are expected to possess a higher degree of skill in the application of production technology than students taking the older programme in General Mechanical Engineering (see above). The aim of the latter is to train students to design machine parts and steel components; the Production Technology programme concentrates on the implementation of programmed workshop technology with the aid of CNC turning and milling machines, mastery of the entire production process, of which programming, machining and quality control are major components, and the ability to use the control technology of the machine. Students who have gained a diploma in General Mechanical Engineering must be able to perform the following jobs: mechanical engineering draughtsman, constructor, group leader in the technical drawing office, work planner, calculator, maintenance mechanic, technical clerical assistant and technical commercial assistant. The jobs open to a successful student of Production Technology are: operator of computer controlled machine tools, workshop programmer, quality controller, skilled technical worker and work planner for programmable machine tools.

At the end of the 1980s, some elements of the Production Technology programme were extended to the General Mechanical Engineering programme. CNC machining, but also other subjects such as CAD systems, which several years earlier had been seen by the initiators of the new programme as specific to Production Technology, are now considered valuable for all MTS students of mechanical engineering. This being the case, offering Production Technology as a separate subject would seem to be unnecessary. De Vries and Heere (1990, p. 58) therefore question the need for a programme in production technology as such in their study carried out with a view to the development of attainment targets (see below).

Modular programmes and attainment targets/credit units

Throughout secondary education endeavours are being made to develop and introduce a modular structure, based on the policy memorandum entitled "Modular teaching in secondary education". In senior secondary vocational education (MBO) the introduction of a modular structure is part of the MBO Sector Formation and Innovation (SVM) operation. The modules will be based on attainment targets, which are being developed by the Technical Education-Metal Industry Consultative Forum (BOTO-M) (see Section 1). The first generation of attainment targets was based on existing examination syllabuses and training curricula. An MTO diploma in Mechanical Engineering at present comprises seven certificates or credits, distributed over eight semesters [Departmental Plan for Mechanical Engineering, National Institute for Curriculum Development (SLO)/ Association of Senior Technical Schools (VMTS), 1987]. The basic syllabus is divided into four credit units. Certificate 5 is awarded for the period of work placement, which may be spread over the third and fourth years of the programme. The other two certificates cover more specialised subject matter at various levels; the subjects "machining technology", "workplace machining techniques" and "practical lessons in machining" are included in both.

The second-generation attainment targets are based on training profiles. De Vries and Heere (1990) carried out a study on behalf of the Technical Education-Metal Industry Consultative Forum (BOTO-M) of the work of MTS-trained mechanical engineers in order to obtain up-to-date information for the modification of attainment targets and options (see Section 2). The study concluded that the senior technical school (MTS) programme in Mechanical Engineering should be general for as long as possible to ensure that MTS-trained personnel can be deployed flexibly in industry. Even before the advent of CNC machines their broad general training ensured that these employees could move up to managerial positions. This pattern should continue in the future. In order to give all MTS-trained personnel the opportunity to progress to higher positions, the training should provide a basis for jobs in work planning, project management, quality control, commercial and administrative support and managerial positions.

The BOTO-M study produced a number of interesting points with regard to attainment targets. For the occupational group of metalwork machinists (see Section 2) the importance of a good knowledge of equipment is emphasised, since they will require knowledge and skill in this area more than the other groups. The requisite knowledge and skills in the field of numerical control techniques is also considered more important for machinists than for other groups. Materials science does not require in-depth teaching for any of the occupational groups. For the groups being trained for initial employment, which includes machinists, the subject of mechanical engineering (construction theory, calculation of machine tool parts, applied mechanics and steel constructions) is important. Industrial mechanisation (hydraulics/pneumatics and electrotechnology) and technical drawing are important for all groups, including the machining group. Business administration subjects are important mainly to those interested in progressing to higher positions. Since in principle all MTS-trained employees have the opportunity to do this, these subjects form an important part of the programme.

In 1981, the Association of Senior Technical Schools (VMTS) proposed three vocational training variants for technical education: the existing long senior secondary technical programmes (MTO); senior secondary craft education, a new variant designed to produce highly skilled craftsmen; and short senior secondary vocational programmes (KMBO). In the legislation governing the MBO Sector Formation and Innovation (SVM) operation, a theoretical training variant was added, which was designed for those transferring to higher vocational education.

In November 1988 the Association of Senior Technical Schools published a technology sector development plan which proposed four training variants for senior secondary technical education, namely a long programme, an intermediate programme, a short programme and a theoretical variant (for those going on to higher vocational education). Schools have been able to experiment with the intermediate MBO programme since 1 August 1991. Proposals have also been made for a four-year dual variant for senior secondary vocational education (MBO), under which apprenticeship training and MBO would be combined with the intermediate programme. The programme would comprise a two-year period for the theoretical basis and school-based practical work, followed by a two-year period containing a school-based element and an industrial training component.

Developments in the structure of apprenticeship training in the metalworking sector

The Metal Industry Training Organisation (SOM) began introducing modular elementary training programmes based on occupational profiles in 1988; in August 1991 several modular programmes were introduced at the advanced level as well.

Based on the research project, "Occupational analysis and future study", the Centre for Innovation in Training for Trade and Industry (CIBB) (Metal Industry Training Organisation, SOM, 1987) has distinguished 20 training profiles divided into four occupational groups. An outline of these profiles for the machining group is given below.

Training profiles for machining

1. turning: a narrow job range which only scored highly on one activity cluster, that for turning itself;

2. milling: also a narrow profile with the accent on milling itself;

3. milling: this profile differs from the previous one in that a higher level of difficulty is involved;

4. machining: this profile contains a combination of turning and milling;

5. machining: this profile differs from the previous one in that it involves a greater number of activities relating to grinding and a higher level of difficulty;

6. CNC machining: this profile contains a combination of all the activities in the previous profiles plus the activities associated with CNC machining.

In addition, the bench fitter/toolmaker group distinguished in the CIBB study is also relevant to CNC machining. Two training profiles in machining and toolmaking fall within this group: these are all-round profiles, each of which includes machining and fitting, and toolmaking. The two profiles differ in level of difficulty.

The SOM divided its training programmes into three occupational groups on the basis of the CIBB study: machining, construction and assembly/maintenance. The application of new technologies occurs in all occupational groups, e.g. CNC turning (see Figure D3).

The training programmes in machining have a linear, branched structure. After learning the basic skills students move on to machining techniques such as turning. The subsequent path followed depends on the degree of skill (accuracy, complexity) required in a particular field.

Figure D3. **New technologies in occupational groups**

	GENERAL OCCUPATIONAL GROUPS			OTHER
	Machining	Construction	Assembly/ Maintenance	
New Technologies	CNC CAM	CNC Robot CAM	Robot PLC CAM	CAD

Source: SOM (1991, p. 16).

Flexible Production Automation (FPA)

The Association of Senior Technical Schools (VMTS), representing senior secondary vocational education (MBO), and the Metal Industry Training Organisation, representing part-time vocational education, have developed co-ordinated plans for the introduction of Flexible Production Automation (FPA) in secondary vocational education. Both MBO authorities and those responsible for apprenticeship training have proposed setting up a workshop where on-the-job training can take place and where theoretical learning and practical work would go hand in hand. To promote hands-on experience, all the jobs encountered in industry and their interactions would be simulated, the emphasis being placed on control systems and the related information processing needed for the operation of production and assembly systems. Senior secondary technical schools would like to see a maximum of 80 hours of FPA training irrespective of which programme a student takes. Since emphasis is placed on business administration and automation, specific knowledge related to CNC machining must be acquired in the subjects in which the student is specialising. Through job rotation the student would become acquainted with all the different jobs simulated in the workshop.

The plans prepared by the VMTS assume a minimum configuration with a partially automated pre-production phase, a production/assembly workshop and a partially automated assembly line. This configuration could be expanded to a fully automated environment. The basic configuration would have 10 computers linked in a network (1 minicomputer and 9 PC/ATs). Five computers would be used for pre-production work, five for courseware and one by the teacher. Peripheral equipment would include an A3 plotter and a printer; a number of video discs would also be required for the courseware. The following software is envisaged:

For pre-production activities:
- an integrated production control package;
- a CAD software package for product design;
- a software package for planning;
- a spreadsheet program for calculation purposes;
- optimisation software for the logistics side.

The work planning could be totally manual in the beginning and automated at a later stage in conjunction with the introduction of computer-controlled machine tools and/or other equipment.

One of the first steps in the FPA project initiated as part of the Introduction of New Technologies Project (PRINT) was the fleshing out of the concept of FPA by a group of experts, and setting out the changes to be made in senior secondary vocational education (short and long programmes), junior secondary vocational education and day-release training for apprentices. This was followed by the preparation of a technology profile to be used as a basis for an educational framework and the development of teaching materials. The technology profile was drawn up in 1991 along with a number of recommendations for the introduction of FPA technology in vocational education. In view of the predominantly conventional nature of the recognised FPA jobs, the conclusion was reached that it would be undesirable to change current vocational training programmes radically in order to accommodate FPA technology.

The structural development process of FPA (the creation of frameworks and technology profiles) outlined above came to a stop with the change-over from the PRINT project to Project Management for the Effective Promotion of Technology in Education (PRESTO). As mentioned earlier, schools may acquire machines and courseware for an FPA unit on their own initiative, through PRESTO, on the basis of a Technological Innovation Programme.

At present, one of the few options available to schools wishing to introduce FPA is the FPA simulation model developed by Festo Didactic. This is a fully automated production unit for gear and pulley transmission systems. The hardware consists of three independently functioning parts: a machining unit, a robot and an assembly line. The parts are arranged in relation to each other in such a way that when equipped with an integrated control system they can form a production unit.

Patterns and shifts in participation

Full-time day programmes in senior secondary vocational education (MBO) and the apprenticeship system experienced turbulent growth in the early 1980s. The introduction of short senior secondary vocational programmes (KMBO) in 1987 and efforts to double the number of apprentices after 1985 reinforced this trend. Since the early 1990s, attendance in both full-time education and the apprenticeship system have declined due to the downward demographic trend.

In all there are 64 senior technical schools (MTS) in the Netherlands with a mechanical engineering department. In 1987/1988, 17 924 students followed the programme in mechanical engineering and in 1987 2 828 students were awarded an MTS diploma in general mechanical engineering (De Vries and Heere, 1990).

4. Responsiveness: Conclusions

With regard to optimising the responsiveness of vocational education to technological developments, not only is the interaction between the labour market and education relevant, but the processes taking place within vocational education also play a role. This section will deal primarily with the latter aspect. The actors involved in these processes are the representatives of public-sector vocational education, the trade unions and employers' organisations, commercial and non-commercial establishments and the government. Taking a number of topical themes as a basis, this section will examine briefly the nature and extent of the responsiveness of vocational education to technological advances.

Reactions to technological developments in industry

In the early 1980s Dutch industry was lagging behind other countries in the application of product and production innovation. The backwardness in industry was paralleled in vocational education which was criticised as being too little market-oriented and not responsive to the needs of companies; technical education was judged as lacking practical orientation and providing poor levels of technical knowledge and skills.

However, by the beginning of the 1990s, the gap had been virtually closed. Progress is discernible for example in the introduction of hi-tech equipment in vocational education, such as the setting up of CNC instruction machines in senior secondary technical institutions, within the apprenticeship system and in junior secondary technical education. The practical orientation of programmes will increase in the coming years with the implementation of dual training routes. Moreover, recent research has shown that those leaving senior technical school (MTS) now have little difficulty in adapting to their first job (Thijsen, 1988; De Vries and Heere, 1990).

Another development indicative of endeavours to make up lost ground is the extent of activity in vocational education in relation to Flexible Production Automation (FPA). It may even be asked whether some areas of education are not reacting too swiftly to new developments: it is very difficult at present to predict what the role of FPA will be in Dutch industry, and this in turn means that it is by no means clear what weight should be attached to it in vocational education. A central issue in the debate in the coming years will be just how great the time lag may be between the introduction of new technologies in industry and their implementation in education. New technologies are usually introduced in stages, and it will have to be made clear at what point the various elements should be included in

213

the curricula of institutions providing vocational education. A useful tool for this purpose is the classification used by Bakkenist, Spits and Co.: leading edge technologies, industrial technologies, technologies capable of introduction in the curricula, and technologies already in the curriculum (in Krins, 1991).

Although there are clear signs that education is making up the ground it had lost, not all of the problems relating to the alignment of education and employment have all been solved. Current problems relate to the rapidity with which technological advances have spread in recent years. CNC technology has now become established in the vocational education curriculum, at least as far as the technical operation of computer-controlled machines is concerned. Because of the rapidity of change, however, the individual teacher has really not had the opportunity to study and digest the many questions on course content and teaching method arising from the introduction of new technologies in vocational education. There are also very few textbooks on CNC techniques to assist the teacher.

The sector organisations, the education support structure and educational research have elaborated new concepts, such as basic skills and transfer, in relation to new technologies, but the results of this have not yet taken root in the schools. In the meantime new technical concepts are arising in connection with Flexible Production Automation (FPA), and schools are under pressure to deal with these as well. All these aspects need to be given consideration, for instance, in in-service training for teachers.

Top-down or bottom-up

From the 1980s onwards, a number of curriculum projects concerned with the introduction of new technologies, such as CNC and FPA, were initiated: INSP (Information Technology Promotion Plan), PRINT (Introduction of New Technologies project) and PRESTO (Project Management for the Effective Promotion of Technology in Education). The innovation strategy underpinning these projects shows a shift from a top-down to a bottom-up approach. The dissatisfaction with INSP and PRINT was mainly due to the limited introduction of the results of development work (e.g. courseware) in the daily practice of those schools not involved in the development activities. For this reason, unlike the procedure in the latter two projects, in the PRESTO project initiative was placed with the schools. Although expectations are high, there are some doubts about the efficacy of the PRESTO approach, concerning the value added of innovations introduced in an individual school, in terms of their transferability to other schools. Also, the decentralised approach adopted by PRESTO, may be detrimental to centralised development work, for instance the preparation of an educational framework for FPA.

Co-operation between education and industry, and within the education system

The government appointed several committees to improve co-ordination at the national level between education and industry. The Wagner Committee (1984) believed that more far-reaching co-operation between vocational education and industry was essential to the improvement of the quality of vocational education and training, and that it should include the in-service training of teachers as well as the curricula content. The committee recommended that emphasis be placed on intensifying regional co-operation between education and industry and on organising curriculum development at the sectoral/branch level of industry. The Rauwenhoff Committee (1990) also recommended ways for improving the links and interaction between education and industry and outlined the conditions necessary for this. One of the key points in this committee's report was the concept of a dual system of vocational training.

The metal industry responded by changing the content and organisation of education and training. The co-ordination agreements reached between education and the metal industry, reflect national developments in this field:
- co-operation arrangements between education and industry;
- modification of curricula, using occupational and training profiles;
- initiation of innovation projects;
- expansion of training provision by means of contract teaching.

The merger of three national organisations to form the Metal Industry Training Organisation (SOM) at the beginning of the 1980s, and the collaboration between the SOM, the Association of Senior Technical Schools (VMTS) and the Technical Education-Metal Industry Consultative Forum (BOTO-M) (e.g. with regard to FPA) were significant developments that improved co-operation.

Emphasis on the regional level and autonomy of schools

The regional centres have a key role to play in transferring developments in new technologies to the schools. These centres provide a place of meeting, experimentation, and specialisation for industry and education. Through joint consultation, they aim to:
- meet the skill needs of their target groups;
- allow experimentation with new subject matter which can be introduced at a later stage in the education system (once a technology is no longer "new" but "generally employed in industry");
- provide refresher courses for employees and teachers on the use of new, advanced equipment;
- provide specialised courses for employees who are just starting their career and for those who wish to climb the career ladder.

This does not mean that vocational education schools cannot act independently to teach CNC techniques and FPA. In accordance with government policy, the basis for learning CNC techniques should be laid at junior secondary vocational level. The setting up of "technical information technology" rooms is one consequence of this. Senior technical schools (MTS) will introduce CNC techniques as standard subjects in their curriculum and will be provided with basic equipment in order to do so. The role of the regional centres in the instruction of MTS students in the field of new technologies may be undermined as a consequence. The tendency may be further reinforced by the introduction of block grant funding, which might mean that schools themselves will have to pay for the instruction given to their students in regional centres.

Bibliography

ALDERS, B., CHRISTIS, J. and BILDERBEEK, R. (1988), *Technologische ontwikkeling en werkgelegenheidsstructuur. De wisselwerking tussen programmeerbare automatisering en de kwalificatie en werving van werknemers* (Technological development and employment structure. The interaction between programmable automation and the qualifications and recruitment of employees), Netherlands Organisation for Applied Scientific Research (TNO), Netherlands Institute for Working Conditions (NIA), Apeldoorn, Amsterdam.

Association of Senior Technical Schools (VMTS) (1988), *Ontwikkelingsplan sector techniek* (Development Plan for the Technology Sector), De Bilt.

BAARS, W. (ed.) (1989), *MBO-almanak 90* (Senior Secondary Vocational Education Almanac, 1990), Samson, Alphen aan den Rijn.

BAKKENIST, SPITS and Co. (1984), *Nieuwe technologieën: veranderingen in bedrijf en onderwijs* (New technologies: changes in industry and education), Committee on Development Problems in Companies (COB)/Socio-Economic Council (SER), The Hague.

BRAVERMAN, H. (1974), *Labor and monopoly capital*, New York.

BRUIN, B. (1991), *Van PRINT naar PRESTO* (From PRINT to PRESTO), COS, 3,2, pp. 16-17.

COMMITTEE ON THE EVALUATION OF THE INFORMATION TECHNOLOGY PROMOTION PLAN (INSP) (1988), *Een eerste aanzet. Verslag van een sobere toekomstgerichte evaluatie van het INSP-programma* (First steps. Report on a sober, future-oriented evaluation of the INSP Programme), Ministry of Education and Science, Zoetermeer.

COMMITTEE ON THE EVALUATION OF THE INFORMATION TECHNOLOGY PROMOTION PLAN (INSP) (1988), *Evaluatie van het INSP-programma in het veld automatisering* (Evaluation of the INSP Programme in the field of automation), Ministry of Education and Science, Zoetermeer.

COPPENS, L., BOORSMA, P.B. and KOELMAN, J.B.J. (1989), *Externe bekostiging in het beroepsonderwijs en het wetenschappelijk onderwijs: eindrapport* (External funding in vocational and university education: final report), Centre for Higher Education Policy Studies (CSHOB), Enschede.

FRIETMAN, J.E.M. (1990), *De kwaliteit van de praktijkcomponent in het leerlingwezen* (The quality of the practical component in apprenticeship training), Institute for Applied Sociology (ITS), Nijmegen.

FRUYTIER, B. (eds.) (1988), *CNC-machinebedieners, Productie- organisatie en Flexibele automatisering* (CNC machine operators, production organisation and flexible automation), Committee on Development Problems in Companies (COB), Socio-Economic Council (SER), The Hague.

GEURTS, J. (1991), "Regionale bureaus onderwijs in voorbereiding" (Regional education offices in preparation), *Volwasseneneducatie* (Adult Education) 1, pp. 3-8.

216

HARING, H.A. and de MARE, R. (1991), *Beroepsopleidingen en pleidingsbehoefte flexibele produktie automatisering* (Vocational training and FPA training needs), Metal Industry Training Organisation (SOM), Woerden.

HAVE, K. and FRUYTIER, B. (1987), "De invoering van flexibele bewerkingsmachines" (The introduction of flexible machine tools), *Tijdschrift voor arbeidsvraagstukken* (Journal for Labour Issues), 3, 1, pp. 27-37.

HEERE, F., GILS, G. van and FLAPPER, E. (1988), *Scholen en bedrijven, werken ze samen?* (Schools and industry, are they cooperating?), Committee on Development Problems in Companies (COB), Socio-Economic Council (SER), The Hague.

JONG, P. de (1991), *Opleiden binnen het leerlingwezen in FPA* (FPA training in the apprenticeship system), SOM, Woerden.

KAYZEL, R. (1986), "Automatisering en vakmanschap" (Automation and skilled work), *Tijdschrift voor arbeidsvraagsukken* (Journal for Labour Issues), 2, 1, pp. 60-71.

KERN, H. and SCHUMANN, M. (1970), *Industriearbeit und Arbeiterbewusstsein* (Industrial work and worker awareness), I and II.

KRINS, D.P.M. (1991a), "Technologisch concept" (A technological concept), in Pauwels, P.A.W. and Weide, P.A.G., *Technologieprofielen flexibele productie automatisering* (FPA technology profiles), National Institute for Curriculum Development (SLO), Centre for Innovation in Training for Trade and Industry (CIBB), 's-Hertogenbosch.

KRINS, D.P.M. (1991b), *Introduktie van Flexibele produktie-automatisering in het beroepsonderwijs v.o.* (The introduction of FPA in secondary vocational education), Gouda.

MINISTRY OF EDUCATION AND SCIENCE (1984), "Op weg naar een gezamenlijke verantwoordelijkheid" (Towards joint responsibility), *Final report of the Open Talks on the proposals of the Wagner Committee on vocational education*, The Hague.

MINISTRY OF EDUCATION AND SCIENCE (1990), "Report of the Advisory Committee on New Technology and Education", *Coltof Report*, Zoetermeer.

MINISTRY OF EDUCATION AND SCIENCE (1990), "Regionale centra. De evolutie van een idee" (Regional centres. The evolution of an idea), *Opstap*, series 6, Zoetermeer.

MINISTRY OF EDUCATION AND SCIENCE (1990), "PRINT rapportage 1989" (Report on the Introduction of New Technologies Project 1989), *Opstap*, series 10, Zoetermeer.

MINISTRY OF EDUCATION AND SCIENCE (1990), "Activiteiten PRINT 1990" (PRINT activities, 1990), *Opstap*, series 15, Zoetermeer.

MINISTRY OF EDUCATION AND SCIENCE (1990), "Verslag van de staat van het onderwijs in Nederland over 1989" (Report on the state of education in the Netherlands in 1989), Zoetermeer.

NaBoNT (1990), *Halverwege. Interimrapport over het project NaBoNT* (Halfway. Interim report on the Refresher Training in New Technologies NaBoNT project), Projectburo NaBoNT, Twijnstra Gudde.

NATIONAL PLAN FOR INNOVATION IN THE MECHANICAL ENGINEERING DEPARTMENT IN MTO (1984), Working Party on Innovation in the Mechanical Engineering Department in senior secondary technical education (MTO).

NIEUWENHUIS, A.F.M. (1990), *Complexe leerplaatsen in school en bedrijf* (Complex training places in school and industry), Northern Institute for Educational Research (RION), Groningen.

NIJHOF, W.J. (1991), "Het ontwerpen van basisvaardigheden voor het beroepsonderwijs" (Devising basic skills for vocational education), in Dijkstra, S., Krammer, H.P.M., Pieters, J.M., *De onderwijskundig ontwerper* (The Educational Designer), Swets and Zeitlinger, Amsterdam.

NIJHOF, W.J. and MULDER, M. (eds.) (1986), *Basisvaardigheden in het beroepsonderwijs* (Basic skills in vocational education), Institute for Educational Research/Technical Education, The Hague.

PAUWELS, P.A.W. and WEIDE, P.A.G. (1991), *Technologie-profielen flexibele produktie automatisering* (FPA technology profiles) 's-Hertogenbosch: National Institute for Curriculum Development (SLO), Centre for Innovation in Training for Trade and Industry (CIBB).

PIETERS, J.M. and MULDER, M. (1988), "Nieuwe Technologieën in het beroepsonderwijs" (New Technologies in Vocational Education), in Pieters, J.M. and Mulder, M. (eds.), *Produktie-automatisering. Een onderzoek naar curriculum en instructie in het Middelbaar Technisch Onderwijs* (A study of curriculum and teaching in senior secondary technical education), University of Twente, Enschede.

PND (1989), *Studiedagen en docentenstages voor docenten uit het voortgezet onderwijs* (One-day courses and placements for teachers in secondary education), Practical In-Service Training Centre for Teachers (PND), Assen.

POUTSMA, E. and ZWAARD, A. (1987), "Automatisering en arbeidsinhoud. Effecten van CNC-apparatuur in kleine, industriële bedrijven" (Automation and job content. Effects of CNC equipment in small industrial companies), *Tijdschrift voor Arbeidsvraagstukken* (Journal for Labour Issues), 3, 1, pp. 16-26.

REIJMERINK, C.H.L. (1988a), "Regionale voorzieningen in de Werktuigbouwkunde" (Regional facilities for Mechanical Engineering), in Pieters, J.M. and Mulder, M. (eds.), *Produktie-automatisering. Een Onderzoek naar curriculum en instructie in het Middelbaar Technisch Onderwijs* (Production automation. A study of curriculum and teaching in senior secondary technical education), University of Twente, Enschede.

REIJMERINK, C.H.L. (1988b), "Apparatuur in het MTO" (Equipment in senior secondary technical education), in Pieters, J.M. and Mulder, M. (eds.), *Produktie-automatisering. Een onderzoek naar curriculum en instructie in het Middelbaar Technisch Onderwijs* (Production automation. A study of curriculum and teaching in senior secondary technical education), University of Twente, Enschede.

ROOS, Y. de (1991), "Project nieuwe technologieën beroepsonderwijs start met hoge verwachtingen" (New technologies project in vocational education starts with high hopes), *Werking*, 2 May 1991, No. 8, pp. 35-37.

SCHULER, Y.D. (1989), *Contractactiviteiten in het beroepsonderwijs: een studie naar de betrokkenheid van scholen voor (kort) middelbaar beroepsonderwijs en beroepsbegeleidend onderwijs bij de opzet en uitvoering van contractonderwijs* (Contract activities in vocational education: a study of the role of schools providing – short – senior secondary vocational courses and theoretical training for apprentices in the planning and implementation of contract teaching), ABC, De Lier.

SLO/VMTS (1987), *Afdelingsplan Werktuigbouwkunde. Participerend leren en moduleren in het MBO* (Departmental Plan for Mechanical Engineering. Participatory learning and modular teaching in senior secondary vocational education), National Institute for Curriculum Development (SLO), Association of Senior Technical Schools (VMTS), Enschede. De Bilt.

SOM/PCBB (1987), *Beroepenanalyse en toekomstonderzoek stichting opleidingen metaal* (Occupational analysis and future study, Metal Industry Training Organisation), Metal Industry Training Organisation (SOM), Educational Advisory Centre for Training for Trade and Industry (PCBB), SOM, Woerden.

SOM (1988), "Eindverslag moduleringsproject" (Final report on the modular teaching project), SOM, Woerden.

SOM (1988), *Met modulen aan het werk. Informatie over de invoering van gemoduleerde opleidingen van de SOM* (Working with modules. Information on the introduction of SOM modular training courses), SOM, Woerden.

SVM COORDINATION GROUP (1988), "Ontwikkelingsplan leerlingwezen" (Development plan for the apprenticeship system), *SVM-informatie* (SVM Information), No. 17, pp. 12-20

SVM COORDINATION GROUP (1990*a*), "Van Opstap naar Instap. Een innovatief arrangement voor de invoering van nieuwe technologieën in het beroepsonderwijs" (An innovative arrangement for the introduction of new technologies in vocational education), *SVM-informatie*, No. 42, pp. 3-10.

SVM COORDINATION GROUP (1990*b*), "Regeringsreactie op het advies van de Commissie Rauwenhoff" (The government's response to the recommendations of the Rauwenhoff Committee), *SVM-informatie*, No. 42, pp. 17-19.

SVM COORDINATION GROUP (1991*a*), "RBO-rapportage" (Report on the Regional Education Offices), *SVM-informatie*, No. 45, pp. 3-21.

SVM COORDINATION GROUP (1991*b*), "Rauwenhoff. Uitgebreide commissievergadering over Rauwenhoff" (The Rauwenhoff Report. Augmented parliamentary committee meeting on the Rauwenhoff Report), *SVM-informatie*, No. 47, pp. 12-15.

SVM COORDINATION GROUP (1991*a*), "Beleid Nieuwe Technologieën (PRINT) moet worden herzien" (New technologies policy – PRINT – must be reviewed), *SVM-informatie*, No. 39, pp. 23/24.

SVM COORDINATION GROUP (1991*b*), "PRESTO. Nieuwe technologieën in de klas" (Project Management for the Effective Promotion of Technology in Education – PRESTO – New technologies in the classroom), *SVM-informatie*, PRESTO annex No. 48, June 1991, pp. 22-26.

THIJSEN, J.A. (1988*a*), "Middelbaar Technisch Onderwijs: aansluitingsproblemen op de arbeidsmarkt" (Senior secondary technical education – MTO: the mismatch between education and employment), in Pieters, J.M. and Mulder, M. (eds.), *Produktie-automatisering. Een onderzoek naar curriculum en instructie in het Middelbaar Technisch Onderwijs* (Production automation. A study of curriculum and teaching in senior secondary technical education), University of Twente, Enschede.

THIJSEN, J.A. (1988*b*), "Trends in produktie-automatisering" (Trends in production automation), in Pieters, J.M. and Mulder, M. (eds.), *Produktie-automatisering. Een onderzoek naar curriculum en instructie in het Middelbaar Technisch Onderwijs* (Production automation. A study of curriculum and teaching in senior secondary technical education), University of Twente, Enschede.

THIJSEN, J.A. and MULDER, M. (1987), *Aansluiting MTS-werktuigbouw en arbeidsmarkt* (MTS Mechanical Engineering: the alignment of education and employment), University of Twente, Enschede.

van TERWISGA, H.B. and SLUIJS, E. Van (1990), *Opleiden voor de toekomst. Onderdeel van bedrijfsbeleid* (Training for the Future. Part of company policy), *Stichting toekomstbeeld der Techniek* (Technology for the Future Foundation) Samsom, Alphen aan den Rijn.

van TIENEN, J.H.M. (1991), "Nederlandse marktsituatie vraagt om flexibele produktie automatisering" (The Dutch market situation calls for flexible production automation), *Unie. Tijdschrift voor Beroepsonderwijs* (Union. Journal for Vocational Education), 16, 4, April 1991, pp. 17-20.

van den BERG, E. and REIJMERINK, C.H.L. (1989), *Moduleren in het m.t.o.* (Modular teaching in senior secondary technical education), University of Twente, Centre for Applied Research in Education (OCTO), Enschede.

van den ENT, D. (1990), *FPA in het MTO* (FPA in senior secondary technical education), Association of Senior Technical Schools (VMTS), De Bilt.

VERZANTVOORT, M. (1991), "Projecten LBO geven hechte basis voor vervolgopleidingen" (Projects in junior secondary vocational education provide firm basis for further education), *Uitleg*, 14, June 1991.

VRIES, I.E.M. de (1990), "De beroepspraktijk van de MTS-er werktuigbouw: Groepsprofielen" (The work of MTS-trained mechanical engineers: group profiles), *Research voor Beleid* (Research for Policy), Leiden.

VRIES, I.E.M. de and HEERE, F. (1990), "MTS-werktuigbouw: Beroepspraktijk en aansluiting" (The MTS mechanical engineering course: alignment with the workplace), *Research voor Beleid*, Leiden.

VRIES, I.E.M. de., WEENING, H., and HEERE, F. (1989), "MTS-ers werktuigbouw: Gevraagd in vele functies in een breed beroepenveld" (MTS-trained mechanical engineers: in demand in a wide variety of jobs in a broad occupational field), *Research voor Beleid*, Leiden.

OECD PUBLICATIONS, 2 rue André-Pascal, 75775 PARIS CEDEX 16
PRINTED IN FRANCE
(91 94 06 1) ISBN 92-64-14298-3 - No. 47591 1994